T0123505

Elderly Lives
Matter Too

Elderly Lives Matter Too

JOHN C. WALSHE

ELDERLY LIVES MATTER TOO

iUniverse books may be ordered through booksellers or by contacting:

iUniverse
1663 Liberty Drive
Bloomington, IN 47403
www.iuniverse.com
844-349-9409

ISBN: 978-1-6632-3078-2 (sc)
ISBN: 978-1-6632-3077-5 (hc)
ISBN: 978-1-6632-3079-9 (e)

Library of Congress Control Number: 2021921536

Print information available on the last page.

iUniverse rev. date: 02/07/2022

CONTENTS

CHAPTER 1

Introduction

For the purpose of this book we will consider elderly as those that are at least 65 years of age although as we all know that there are many who are old before their time. In the United States there are 55 million elderly people and 274 million would like to be elderly someday but not too soon.

Please consider that as I write this story I'm inspired and guided by a quote from the Holy Bible in Mathew chapter 10 verses 19 and 20 which says "But when they deliver you up, do not worry about how or what you should speak. For it will be given to you in the hour what you should speak. For it is not you, but the Spirit of your father who speaks in you." My fragile memory best tells that I started to be reborn eight years ago in a Federal Prison in Texas from a demented state of mind to be a messenger and a tool of the Lord Almighty for the good of mankind especially the elderly and mentally ill. My rebirth has been in process that continues until the present day.

One of the Main points of this book is to question should we incarcerate the elderly especially who suffer from a mental illness? If we incarcerate the elderly, how should they be treated? Our prisons are full of elderly people who have suffered a mental breakdown and are presently suffering from a mental illness. Also, can we treat a 70-year-old as we do a 20-year-old while incarcerated? The obvious answer to that question is no but yet we do treat them the same. I wish to demonstrate that incarceration time for the elderly is much worse than it is for the young or middle age and even worse yet for the mentally ill. This should be taken into consideration when prosecuting and sentencing the elderly or mentally ill. Can you treat a mentally ill person the same as a person who is not suffering from a mental illness? I would like to believe that most Americans would answer the previous two questions with a big "No". Yes, I will agree there are a minority who are still so dangerous to their fellow man even at a late age that they have to be incarcerated but again I believe it is a small minority. How should we treat elderly who have mental breakdowns as so many will? In the United States if a person has a mental breakdown, they are three times as likely to wind up in a prison than an appropriate hospital or mental institution. Should our prisons be filled with the mentally ill as they now are? The older we get the more susceptible we are to a mental breakdown as the incidence of dementia substantiates. As an example, consider how vulnerable the elderly are to Alzheimer's disease the largest form of dementia as we age. The incidence of Alzheimer's disease is seventeen percent for the age group of sixty-five to seventy-four years and forty-seven percent for 75 to 84 years. It almost triples in just a decade. Before we prosecute, do we make the proper effort to diagnose to find out why the elderly and people as a whole commit crimes? In my case why does a man in his so-called golden years become a criminal after living a productive, law abiding and good life? Did I just repress my criminal instincts and desires for six and a half decades or did I repress my feelings from traumatic events which could lead to mental illness?

If the answer is yes, should we just punish as being imprisoned does and should they also be abused? Should we bash an elderly man's head off a wall who just a year before suffered a massive heart attack at the hands of a prison guard which resulted in heart function of a mere twelve percent and not one but two triple "A" aorta aneurysms? This document illustrates the atrocities that can happen when we don't recognize and appreciate the limitations of the mentally ill and elderly. We recognize limitations in children, but humankind returns to childlike states with age. With children their immunity to diseases increases with the elderly their immunities decrease.

This book also tells the story of how an elderly man went from being a very shy and abused little boy to a so-called self-made multi-millionaire to lying in his own human waste on a prison floor in solitary confinement. It describes his tortuous treatment while incarcerated at eight penal institutions from age 67 to 73 years of age, an elderly man's golden years, when most men are contemplating retirement or actually retiring. It describes how this man endured and recovered from over fourteen assaults and inhumane treatment at the hands of deputy sheriffs, prison guards and inmates which resulted inpatient stays at four general hospitals and numerous clinics. That was if he was fortunate enough to receive proper medical care in most cases he didn't. It describes his attitudes and motivation to rise again to a near normal state to be able to write this story after having suffered three heart attacks, heart surgery, two strokes and two very dangerous aorta aneurysms much of which were caused or initiated by the inhumane treatment. To recover from the terrible abuses of incarceration he also had to overcome the complications of four major psychiatric disorders and five major circulatory disorders. He endured the preceding while enduring the pain and agony of his large intestine hanging out of him twelve inches so inhumanely like a large banana for five years. While enduring the assaults and abuse some surgeons were very reluctant to operate on him because his heart was too weak but not too weak to be abused. The guards and deputies may have knocked him down but in spite of such he bounced back to rise again even at a late age.

Let's say that this man was properly tried, which is very controversial, and convicted mainly of the crimes of nonpayment of business taxes and securities fraud. The following questions remain, was he adequately diagnose when his mental health disorders took years to develop and some are attributed to is military career? Should he have been tried when he lost the memories of his life from age 47 to 72 years? He couldn't even remember his youngest son's birth or upbring that he participated in. If he was guilty as charged how should a man of his physical and psychological profile been treated by the penal system? Why does a man who was convicted of white-collar crime ultimately wind up in the maximum-security section of a level V maximum security prison? Again, what is most interesting and very inspiring how did he recover and endure to return to almost a normal state. Let me state that while incarcerated at one period his heart function was a mere twelve percent almost complete congestive heart failure. This was after he was placed in a choke hold by a guard while having an angina attack. Even 2,500 years ago the well-known Athenian philosopher Plato questioned if we should prosecute and incarcerate the elderly.

As you read this writing, please keep in mind that the elderly are the initiators of our lives, and we wouldn't be here without them. Do we treat them accordingly? Our treatment of the elderly is basically based on our attitudes towards them which is based on our basic beliefs about them. What are those beliefs as manifested by our societies' actions? Do we see the elderly as just used up old humans who are no longer much use to society? Do we see them as just a burden that we have to care for? As stated none of us would be alive today without the elderly. Many of us use the elderly mainly our parents as an excuse for many of our problems and dissatisfaction with ourselves. We are quick to talk about the generation gap, but we fail to realize that without the elderly there would be no generations. Our Creator about 3,300 years ago expressed how we should treat our parents. At that time before birth control almost every adult was a parent. Our Creator through Moses gave us the "Ten Commandments". The spiritual laws which preceded all the laws of mankind, and their basis is the "Ten Commandments". Let me specifically refer to the fifth commandment which states to "honor your father and mother". That commandment does not have conditions attached to it such as only if your father and mother are perfect and free of any indiscretions. We blame our parents and our upbring for so many of our issues and disorders. Let me state that the world no matter what some religions claim is still waiting for the perfect person to be born. At the same time the world is still waiting for the perfect parent to be developed. Even if society could develop the perfect parent could society also guarantee that parent would not falter and make mistakes? Let us also realize that no matter how bad you may perceive your parents to be or have been they could have aborted you! So, no matter what you may think otherwise besides your Creator, you also owe your parents the gift of life and the elderly who preceded them. By the way, your parents at your conception did not dictate or control your genetics by natural law they simply passed them on. It is very interesting that most of the pictures, paintings, drawings, etc. of our Father in heaven and our Creator are that of a bearded Elderly Man.

Of the eleven most developed countries in the world America ranks last in their treatment of the elderly. The United States ranks at the top of the list among developed countries in income per person, gross domestic product and in so many other ways except for its treatment of the elderly. In many cities today the average rent is higher than the average social security payment. Historically and even in American we have judged societies by how they treat their children and the elderly. It appears that Americans have a lot to learn about how to treat the elderly. We don't like to think about the elderly no more than we like to think about and accept ourselves getting old. Consider the ways we try to camouflage our aging. Americans spend more than sixteen billion dollars a year on plastics surgery. It is a huge industry in this country and the world.

Let me ask again do we think of the elderly as weak and of less use to us as they age? Let me say what the elderly lack in physical strength they make up for in the wisdom of the years. Is water under the bridge soon forgotten just like all the good that that elderly did, and some fortunate ones are still doing? I don't believe that in the United States that we recognize the contribution that the elderly have made to emergence of our standard of living, to our increased life span and the civility of our existence. Since the year 1900 our life span has increased more than thirty years. That wasn't an accident or due to evolution. We don't respect the elderly's knowledge and the so-called wisdom of the years. I say that because we don't seek it enough. We don't respect the sacrifices the elderly made to make our lives better. Think about some of the greatest lessons in life are contained in the elderly's histories and especially what I term "should haves". They say that history is 20/20 and that is because history is fact. Look at your own thinking some of your greatest lessons in life come from examining what you have done and now realizing what you "should have" done. We can learn in many ways and I believe the most learning occurs from doing and then looking back and saying to yourself if I had that to do over again "I would have or should have". We tend to learn the most from our mistakes and failures. The elderly memories until they get too old and their memories fail are full of very intelligent and brilliant "should haves".

The elderly brains as a whole are as full of knowledge. Their brains are some of the best and greatest libraries. We rush to the internet and books for knowledge, but we know that experience is the greatest teacher. Who has more knowledge than the elderly? We read the biographies of the dead instead of listening to those who are still alive. I sometimes wonder what my life could have been and what I could have achieved if I knew then what I know now. The elderly may not have the latest knowledge, but I believe that they have some of the best knowledge.

Always keep in mind that as we blame the elderly for our issues, we are teaching the next generation how to treat us. As we treat the elderly so will we be treated as we age. Americans have to concede that the Asian cultures have more wisdom than we do when it comes to treatment of the elderly. When I visited China and Japan as a grey haired elderly American man, I came home with a backache from the population bowing down to me and myself reciprocating. Historians have found that some of the most ancient civilizations worshipped their ancestors.

We live in a negative world because of our primal bias towards the negative to insure our survival. Sometimes our world can be dangerous therefore I believe that every day that you are above ground as an accomplishment or a success. The more difficult the day the greater the success. The elderly are naturally more accomplished and successful than the young because they have lived longer. Most have overcome some significant obstacles and disorders in order to survive which makes them no matter their status or plane in life very successful people. Let's give credit where credit is due. Let's celebrate the elderly and cherish them by our actions and attitudes towards them.

Ask yourself as you age as all of us hope to and may have a mental breakdown, which is more and more likely, as we age how do you want to be treated? Do you want as I was treated which is described in this book? It is not just about me it is about the elderly. It is about the elderly and the elderly who suffer and will suffer from a mental breakdown. It is or more likely that vulnerability to mental health disorders will increase as our life span increases. Today that vulnerability is manifested in the different forms of dementia. The brain is like any other human organ it deteriorates with age and stress. Life can become more frightening and stressful as we age. Most of us whether we openly admit it or not have a fear of what will happen to us physically and economically as we age. The young can look forward to growth the elderly have to fear, dependency, deterioration, and death.

This document also illustrates that you can put an elderly man through a living hell and he can with God's blessing and guidance still emerge in somewhat normal state. The story illustrates that you shouldn't underestimate the power of the elderly to be reborn and rejuvenate with the proper attitude, beliefs, purpose and meaning to their lives. This story also illustrates that we shouldn't condone what was done to him or others like him because if you do it one, you can do it to a minority and then a majority like the African

Americans with segregation or the Jewish people in the Holocaust. It starts with one and when it is condoned it is done to more. Let us keep in mind that all of us would like to be elderly some day and that day has a tendency to come about sooner than we may like. Life is too short.

This story took almost thirty-four months to write this story because after I left prison in August of 2018 my cognizance was still deficient for almost thirty months and so was my memory. The pile of notes that I left prison with was almost two feet high. The first edition of this story had to be edited eleven times. It was very taxing and difficult to write this story because I had to relive all the assaults and abuses in my mind in order to write about them. At times my memories caused my blood pressure to go through the roof which is very dangerous for a man who suffered two strokes, three heart attacks and harbors two dangerous triple A aorta aneurysms. It is well known that high blood pressure can cause fatal heart attacks or strokes especially for a person who has a history of them. I also suffer from post-traumatic stress disorder from my military service which was exacerbated due to my incarceration. Many times it became perilous to my physical and mental health for me to recall what happened to me. It took almost three years until this final writing and editing to get my panic attacks under control. To say that it was painful to write this book is an understatement. It was also very painful for my loved ones to read it. I thank God for the wisdom to cause me to take notes when my memory failed me. I ask for your patience and understanding to forgive my repetition and restatements because I still suffer from a memory deficiency in not remembering in some cases what I already expressed in different ways. Some repetition was done for emphasis. Because of the abuse that I endured it has taken almost three years to recover from the abuse and I continue to recover. I'm still very sensitive to any type of violence and loud noise. When I'm exposed to violence even if it doesn't involve me, I still become a victim of it. I suppose that my sensitivity to violence even if it is fictional will continue for an unspecified time in spite of my efforts to the contrary.

Here is another reason of why I wrote this book. Consider this if you would like a shocking example of how Americans view the elderly. New York is our fourth largest state in population and the third largest in gross domestic product. New York barely ranks just behind Texas and Texas ranks second GDP. If New York was a country, it would rank ahead of Russia and Canada in gross domestic product. During the pandemic Governor of New York State sent at minimum of 6,300 very vulnerable elderly people from hospitals into unprepared nursing homes where they languished and died. Federal and state officials stood by let him do it. Just like three officers stood by while George Floyd died. Now they estimate that the number of those New York elderly victims who were sent from hospitals to nursing homes is at least 14,000 deaths. We knew how vulnerable the elderly are to disease especially Covid nineteen. We have known for years how the elderly are susceptible to diseases! We give lip service to how we treat the elderly in the United States but in actually we treat them as a population that is all used up and that is no longer of use to us. Our actions define who we are as compared to our words. Only the worst third world countries would treat the elderly as bad as New York State did. What was done in New York could be considered genocide. It is a manifestation of how we think of the elderly in this country. Former Governor Andrew Cuomo sent unfortunate elderly to their death under the pretense of freeing up hospital beds to accommodate Covid nineteen patients. New York had the option of placing newly infected patients to the hospital ship the USND Comfort or the Javits Center which was set up as a makeshift hospital as answer the overcrowded hospital conditions. New York didn't bother to use those facilities. Instead of using those alternate facilities, Governor Cuomo chose a group of people who were not strong enough to speak for themselves. You can understand one man making a mistake or being misguided but a whole state and a whole country? The country stood by without loud protest and allowed the elderly to be placed in such vulnerable conditions.

Moving people no matter their age while they are sick is traumatic for them. Imagine lying in a hospital bed suffering from Covid nineteen complications and having to be moved. Suffering from Covid nineteen is traumatic enough but being moved into an entirely new atmosphere adds to the trauma. That stress can exacerbate symptoms. I wonder how many people who suffered from covid nineteen in hospitals would like to have been moved no matter their age. It was traumatic enough for the elderly to be taken from their homes among loved ones to be hospitalized. Many of these elderly people were too weak to speak for themselves and were dependent on an honorable society to speak for them and protect them from harm. Those who could have spoken up and didn't are as guilty as Governor Cuomo. Those who stand by and witness abuse and do nothing about it are also perpetrators of the abuse.

In Michigan they claimed that they didn't have time to determine how many elderlies died in nursing homes from the pandemic. We don't even have time to count the dead? We found time to count the dead during our wars. Those elderly who perished in those nursing homes were in a war for their lives. How insignificant can the elderly lives be to us and how cheap can elderly lives be in Michigan? In Sterling Prison where I was incarcerated for over three years, they put elderly patients with Covid nineteen in solitary confinement to languish and die in solitude instead of setting up a temporary clinic.

Consider how the country erupted and is erupting with how we treat our African American population. Consider how many people spoke up with what happened to those elderly people in New York. How dare any American Government say we don't have time to account for the dead. These are all manifestations how elderly lives matter least in the so-called pecking order of age groups. We didn't hear of such outrageous behavior in the other developed countries of the world, nor we did hear it in the underdeveloped countries of the world. We know that human lives matter in the United States because of how the country reacted to the death of

George Floyd in Minneapolis which was one man. It was an example of how we view African Americans is the U.S. One wrongful death is too many how about fourteen thousand? There were protest about what happened to Palestinians in Gaza where 211 people lost their lives. That was in a foreign country what about our own country. Some Americans insisted that President Biden step in to put a stop to the killings. In New York almost 14,000 elderly lives were sacrificed, and little was done or said about it. We didn't hear of anyone asking President Trump to step in to put a stop to what was happening to the elderly in New York nursing homes. If someone said something to President Trump the news media didn't bother to report it? Why should the news media report it the victims were just elderly? The country stood by without loud protest and allowed the elderly to be placed in such vulnerable conditions. Do I need to write more about it? Please let me to ask you to ask yourselves if what happened to the unfortunate elderly in nursing homes in New York would have happened to the young or middle age?

Sooner or later, we will all be elderly. Sooner and even later comes faster than we would like to think it does. People with titles and authority over others should keep in mind as our titles fade away so does the significance of our lives to the masses. Please allow me to close this chapter with a verse from the bible new living translation Peter 1:24 "People are like grass; their beauty is like a flower in the field. The grass withers and the flower fades away".

What I write is supported by official records from the courts, jails, prisons and security tapes if they chose not to destroy them. It can also be supported and proved by my seven hundred page plus medical record for the seven and a half years of incarceration and witness statements. Please allow me to finish this chapter with one more quote from the Holly Bible published by Gideons, Mathew 25:40 "Assuredly I say to you, inasmuch as you did it to one of the least of these My brethren, you did it to Me."

CHAPTER 2

My Background

My name is John C. Walshe. I'm a 76-year-old man who was born in Huntington, New York, my father was an Irish immigrant whose parents were deported from Ireland to Canada because they were revolutionaries as were our country's founders. My mother's parents were born in Poland. My mother's father was conscripted into the Russian Army. At that time that part of Europe was controlled by Russia. I was raised in a town about fifty miles east of New York City on Long Island by the name of Kings Park. It is a town about 17,200 people. When I was growing up there the largest employer was Kings Park State Hospital, a mental hospital which housed about ten thousand five hundred patients. Like many other mental hospitals, it is now closed. That is one of the reasons today the mentally ill especially the elderly are three times as likely to wind up in prison than an appropriate institution. When I was growing up I never thought that I would have a need to be in a mental hospital but I was wrong. I became a victim to those mental hospital closures.

I'm considered by the by the U.S. Veterans Administration to be eighty percent disabled due to my military service. Yes, I'm a veteran who served our country in many ways. I was raised to be a Catholic priest, but I felt the need to serve my country, so I volunteered to serve my country during the

Vietnam War by joining the U.S. Air Force. I was a successful businessman for forty-two years and became a multi-millionaire by risking mine and my family's financial future. The companies I developed created over two hundred sixty good jobs for the benefit of our society.

I have been married twice for eighteen years and fifteen years. I am currently single. I'm also the father of five honorable citizens of which two were adopted once they were lovingly given up for adoption at birth. Three of my children are wonderful parents as manifested in seven lovely grandchildren. Two aren't loving parents yet. I was humanitarian mostly in support of disadvantaged children's causes until I was overcome by a life devastating disorders known as and pseudo dementia and dissociative amnesia. I also suffered from a posttraumatic stress disorder and acute anxiety which made my incarceration more torturous than the norm. Pseudo dementia known as severe major depression and mimics almost all the symptoms of dementia. For twenty- seven years I was diagnosed and treated as a bi-polar which as it turned out I didn't have. I overcame the complications of those disorders for years but later in life they overcame me with life devastating effects.

During the during seven of my elderly years from 67 years of age to 73 years of age. I was incarcerated at eight institutions, four general hospitals and numerous clinics. I was placed in the solitary confinement or what is called the "Hole" eleven times despite Federal Court Rulings and Colorado Department of Corrections guidelines to the contrary. I state to the contrary because I'm considered "At Risk". I will further define "At Risk" in my writing. Most recently I was a prisoner at a maximum-security prison in Sterling, Colorado for a white-collar crime termed securities fraud. I don't remember but basically, I either neglected or forgot to give an investor in a new company I started information about how I lost the company I owned and operated for twenty-six years. I was housed in the most dangerous units of the prison with some of the most dangerous men alive. I used to humor myself, which you have to do to survive the torchers of prison life, by saying that I was getting a PhD in endurance, confinement and penology.

At the same time, besides having to endure the complications of four major psychiatric disorders, I also suffered from five major circulatory diseases. They being hypertension, hypercholesterolemia, cardiovascular disease, type II diabetes and kidney disease. All of those circulatory systems diseases affect the functioning of the brain since the brain uses twenty-five percent of the body's blood supply even though the brain only represents two percent of the body's weight. As we can imagine the brain does require a clean and pure blood supply.

Cardiovascular disease is narrowing of the blood vessels which will restrict blood flow to and from the heart and brain. Kidney disease interferes with the kidney's ability to filter waste products from the blood. Type II diabetes is considered death to the brain because it affects the brain's supply of glucose, the brain's fuel. Two thirds of diabetics will develop dementia. Hypertension damages the walls of the veins and arteries. It was common while I was incarcerated for my untreated hypertension disorder for my systolic blood pressure to reach readings of two hundred plus. No wonder I developed two triple A aorta aneurysms and suffered two strokes. Hypertension causes resistance to proper blood flow to the heart and leads to heart attacks. High cholesterol creates damaging plaque in the blood vessels and the brain, one of the main causes of heart disease and dementia. Needless to say those diseases need to be attended to with the proper care in order that their complications don't worsen in their negative effects.

I believe that so much of my success in life was achieved to prove that I was capable to achieve success after being repressed in my childhood by verbal and sexual abuse. The verbal abuse made me feel inadequate in my ability to succeed. The sexual abuse made me feel dirty, guilty, shameful and unworthy of any respect. In so many people the shameful feelings can lead to illicit drug and alcoholism. I recall always feeling very grateful to anyone who would accept me. I thank God that I never used alcohol and illicit drugs. What is interesting is that I rarely experienced feelings of inferiority while incarcerated because there were so many prisoners with much worse backgrounds than I. Also, it was because each day I had to overcome some incredible challenges to survive and that made me proud of myself. You don't question your manhood having survived and endured the tortures of the maximum-security section of a maximum-security prison where you are constantly under the threat of being harmed not just by inmates but prison staff. With your guts protruding out of your groin like a large banana you learn to tolerate pain or you don' survive.

One of my mother's brothers would sexually abuse me. I would have to perform sexual acts on him. I never told anyone about it because I was embarrassed. I allowed the sexual abuse by not speaking up about it so I could feel accepted by men which I needed as a little boy especially from my father which was not forthcoming. I would judge that my father just tolerated me as compared to my sisters and brother. Sometimes he referred to me as a fathead and a moron. In my opinion it was difficult for my father to accept others when he didn't accept himself. I'm sure that my father had his issues from his own rearing. I had to bear some of the consequences of the abuse even in my old age, but I have learned to overcome them and make them motivators instead of demotivators. It is like the scars on my head, temple and forehead. The scars are always there but everyone has their share of scars. Because of the sexual abuse as a child, I have always strived to be the perfect gentleman around ladies by holding them in the highest regard. The human body was to be respected not abused in any way. I finally confessed the sexual abuse to my younger brother when we were on a health care mission together in Nigeria.

My father was an alcoholic and used to beat me under the pretense of teaching me how to box. As an adolescent I would to get into physical confrontations with my father when he used to berate my mother. I felt very guilty about those confrontations even though I was defending my mother. I've always detested violence because of the physical confrontations with my father. I loved him and I didn't want to hurt him overall he was a good man and did his best with me in spite of his limitations. Those feelings inferiority continued until this day. In his later years when he sobered up my father did everything that he could to make up for his misdeeds. I have very loving feelings for both of my parents. When I watch or observe violence, I become a victim to it.

As a very young boy I used to counsel my father in the evenings about his alcoholism, but it fell on deaf ears. The only time that I could talk to him was when he was drunk because other times, he was too moody and irate to tolerate my lectures. I have fought my whole life to overcome the ravages of verbal abuse. Until this day I strive to win the approval of others, but it served me well in my sales and business career. I always felt inferior to others, so I learned how to put on a good act. Again, let me state that approval by others was forthcoming in prison because prisoners would admire my endurance from all the abuse at my late age especially by the guards. They also admired my determination to overcome the negative aspects of my diseases. Many of them told me how my actions inspired them.

I understand from notes that I took from discussions with my mother that right after my birth that I was returned to the hospital several times with an unknown disorder of which the professional staff did not think that I'd recover; they told my parents that I was near death and would probably die. Obviously, I did recover. I'm not aware of what effect that had on me. I do remember that after that because of my tenuous health I was not allowed to play with other children other than my two older sisters who pretty much kept to themselves. I entered school several times and then was withdrawn. I understand from my parents that I was late in developing intellectually. I liked riding my bike, but I was only allowed to ride it in our yard and not on the street. It made me feel inferior to other children. It made me feel like an odd ball and unacceptable.

I did not meet my father's expectations of a son or mine when it came to sports or academic achievement. I barely got by in my schoolwork. Because I could not meet my father's expectations when he attempted to teach me sporting games, I never participated in any team sports. Also having job after school and on weekends was more important to me. It made me feel worthwhile. There are some sports which I hate because my father would not talk to me when he was watching them on the TV. He would use the excuse that I'm reading the newspaper or watching the ball game on TV. It is a constant struggle to overcome an inferiority complex developed in your childhood.

I started working outside of the home at the age of twelve taking care of our family's yard and other people's yard. At the age of fourteen when allowed by New York State Child Labor Law, I started working in a stationary store and later on in a local drug store after school every day and on weekends. I believe my ambition caused me to be more accepted by my parents. Again, it taught me that I had to earn other people's love and acceptance or that I had to buy it monetarily through my work and deeds. There was no other way for me even until very late in my life. I yearned to be accepted and loved just for myself and not for what I could do for others. But I learned that you love yourself by being of service to others.

My life as a young boy was made up of loneliness and underachievement in academics and sports. But, on the positive side it motivated me in my adult life to prove that I was somebody who could achieve. I had to prove the doubters wrong, and I did. Again, let me state in most of my adult life I thought that I had to achieve any love and acceptance through my work, doing things for others and in essence I bought love. I don't feel sorry for myself. Instead, I'm proud of myself for achieving in spite of my childhood handicaps and I may not have achieved as much without them. I believe that most of us have had their share of childhood issues.

I was raised to be a Catholic priest to please my mother and grandmothers. I have always loved doing God's work by helping others. I've always been a giver and a caretaker. I felt the need to serve my country, so I volunteered to serve my country in a time of war by joining the U.S. Air Force even though I am afraid of height. I learned to deal with fear by challenging it. At that time many of my contemporaries we're starting to tear up and burn their draft cards. Some of my loved ones and friends were saying Johnny don't go but I went and did my duty right after the frightening event my cousin, a marine corps captain, lost both his legs in Vietnam.

According to my performance reports I served very honorably for four years. I received my basic training in San Antonio, Texas, and my training as a medic in Montgomery, Alabama. I got my first taste of prejudice when a black buddy and I were refused service at a lunch counter in downtown Montgomery. I had volunteered to serve in Vietnam even though I heard that the enemy considered the death of a medic equivalent to the death of twelve soldiers. Vietnam was considered the war of amputees. The enemy didn't want to kill you they wanted to severely injure through the loss of a limb to the horror of your fellow soldiers. I was afraid to go to Vietnam but in spite of my fear I volunteered to go just like joining the Air Force even though I was afraid of height. The Air Force decided I that could better serve at my final duty post at the hospital located at the Strategic Air Command Headquarters south of Omaha, Nebraska. As stated, I served in medical administrations in the hospital commander and administrator's office. My performance ratings were outstanding.

On evenings and weekends, I attended classes at the University of Nebraska, Omaha campus, so I could be commissioned as an officer. I would also tutor other senior airman and officers who were working to gain a bachelor's degree to enhance their post military resumes before they retired from the military. I had originally decided to be a career airman. By the end of my tour of duty in at SAC, three and a half years I had accumulated three and half years of college credits. In 1966 I met my first wife Suzanne, so I also worked part time as a bartender and waiter to pay for her engagement ring. I lived on about three hours of sleep a day. I achieved the rank of sergeant. I was offered an opportunity to be commissioned as a lieutenant and attend the University of Missouri to study for a master's degree in hospital administration. I was admired by the upper echelon for my ambition and my excellent performance of my duties and at the same time attending college what is the equivalent of full-time basis. I had no desire for illicit drugs of alcohol because addiction ran in the male side of my family, and I was afraid that I could become easily addicted. I avoided all types of addictive behaviors such as gambling except that I smoked cigarettes because as a young teenager I thought it was macho or manly as was portrayed in the media in the sixties and seventies.

Because I married Suzy a year before my first tour of duty and ended and she became pregnant with our first child Rene' I decided to leave the Air Force when my tour of duty ended. Rene' was born by caesarean section because Suzy was diabetic. Rene' reached nine pounds in seven months which is common for a baby of a diabetic mother. If the pregnancy had gone full term Rene' would have been stillborn. When she was born and taken to the nursery, I went to see her. The doctor asked me if I was Roman Catholic, I said that I was the doctor told me to get a priest to baptize her because at that time children of a diabetic mother could die in the first three days of birth. When the priest arrived at the hospital nursery, he asked me what I wanted to call the baby. I didn't know. I went to see Suzy in the recovery area so I asked her and she told me to name her Belinda Rene' but when I arrived back at the nursery I changed to Rene' Suzanne. I spelt it, the male version of René, which means born again in French, because her birth was tenuous, instead of the female version Renee. I forgot to tell Suzy that I changed the name of the baby so when Suzy got Rene's birth certificate, she called me to find out what I did, but she wasn't annoyed at me. Well Rene' lived and became a very beautiful and tall woman of six feet tall. She is a wonderful professional, wife and a very devoted mother. I'm very proud of Rene'. Her two sons are developing into very fine men. She worked for me in the business for twenty-two years which wasn't easy working for her father who had declining mental health. I'm a very proud father and grandfather. My children are great parents as manifested in my seven grandchildren.

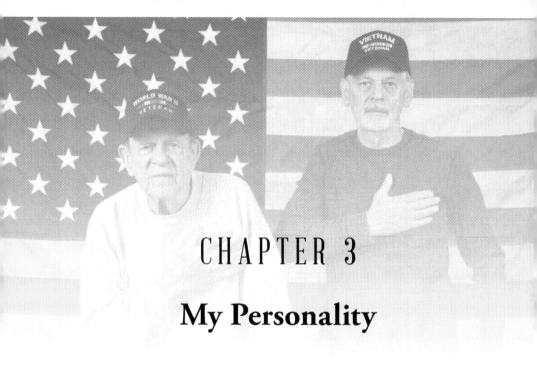

CHAPTER 3

My Personality

I'm a workaholic. A type "A" personality. I always have to be productive accomplishing something. I live by my watch or the clock. I also watch my actions like a hawk and I'm super critical of myself. I have to resist the tendency towards perfection. I tend to be too demanding of myself. I'm very intense and what they term uptight. I tend to be overly aware of dysfunction in myself and react by being overly critical of myself which I believe led to my mental health disorders. I don't readily forgive myself even when things are not my fault or out of my control. I'm very neat and orderly. I tend to be a good manager of myself. I practice when I'm sane good self-discipline. I'm very kind, generous, compassionate, empathetic, gentle and loving man. I'm not as motivated by money but strive to create greatness in myself and in my work. I'm very good at motivating myself and take pride in myself in being able to motivate others. I strive to be very respectful to others. I value people greatly and love to add to their lives even in the smallest ways. I like to make people smile and lift their spirits by seeing the good in them. It is very difficult for me to say no to any honorable request. I try to be a gentleman with the opposite sex and value them as you would a wife and especially as mothers. I hate any type of sexual perversion especially with children. I love children and watching them play. They are the epitome of human energy they run instead of walking whenever they can. I believe in honoring the human body as one of God's creations. To denigrate a human being in any way is absolutely wrong and there is never an excuse for it. I dislike profanity and vulgarity and I believe that when an individual uses it, they denigrate themselves, those that hear it and what is being said. I'm very sensitive to rudeness and rejection by others.

My personal hygiene is excellent. Even though I have been very rich I lived by moderate means. While incarcerated I learned to live on nothing and I'm glad that I did learn that. It didn't bother me very much to be stripped of all worldly possessions. As stated, I don't use alcohol, illicit drugs, smoke or gamble. I strive to be an excellent father, grandfather and companion for the lady in my life. I am religious and very spiritual in my thinking. I believe in Christianity and all religions. I respect the righteousness and goodness that they behold. I'm a very moral person and hold myself to a high moral standard.

I'm liberal in most of my thinking and practices especially with the unfortunate. I believe that God expects us to share our riches with others. As our worldly riches increase so does the responsibility to share them with the less fortunate. Riches don't accrue to mankind fairly and equally. I used to cringe when I heard how prisoners resorted to illicit drugs to deal with the pain of their deficient and dysfunctional rearing. I have always strived for the approval of others but not so much in my later life. I try not to judge especially after losing my mind or look down at others no matter their plane or stage in life. I believe very much in honesty, integrity and strive to have purity in my thoughts. I believe they are key to successful, happy, and contented life. I consider myself to be a very good man. I don't believe in taking advantage of others in any way. I'm very accountable to God and God's judgement of me. I'm very nonviolent and cringe when I witness violence as I did continually while incarcerated. I don't own or use any type of weapons especially guns. I don't believe in their use, and I do believe in gun control especially when you consider the amount of mental illness and, also the prolific use of alcohol and many types of mind-altering drugs. Many assaults are spontaneous in nature. I don't like to hunt or kill anything except for self-preservation and nourishment.

My prejudices are against illicit drugs, excess consumption of alcohol, sexual deviancy especially with children. Too many of my fellow prisoners experienced sexual abuse as children. I love children no matter what age even those in adulthood. I believe that we mature in our own time and circumstances.

CHAPTER 4

My Business Career

In the fall of 1968 I joined Xerox Corporation as a sales representative selling to and serving the wonderful people in Southwest Iowa. I feared rejection but I overcame my fear to provide for my family very well in a sales career. I believe that you have to challenge your fears and not just accept them. Xerox was noted for their excellent sales training programs. I also finished my bachelor's degree at the University of Nebraska and graduated in January of 1969. I continued my education by attending night and weekend classes to attain a year of credits in business administration so I could gain entrance to the master's degree program in business administration. Xerox reassigned me to urban sales so I had the pleasure of calling on great businesspeople in Omaha. I was later promoted exclusively to major account sales where I called on some excellent major corporations and organizations such as the State of Nebraska, the University of Nebraska, Union Pacific Railroad, Creighton University, etc.

In June of 1970 an internal medicine doctor named Jack Lewis who practiced with his father in Omaha contacted us. He treated Suzy and myself for our diseases. Jack said that a baby upon his birth was being placed for adoption and to see if we wanted him. Suzy and I were delighted to say yes and so three days after his birth Christopher was picked up at the hospital by our lawyer where Suzy worked and delivered him to our apartment. That had to be a first in that a lawyer delivered a baby. When I got home from work Suzy said to me, look what we have and there was Chris laying cuddled up in a fetal position so adorably in a playpen. Chris is a very fine man.

What is very interesting is when Christopher was three days old and needed a home Suzy and I gave him one. Almost a half a century later when I was leaving prison and needed a home Chris, and his lovely wife Jody gave me one. It just goes to show you that when you put out good it ultimately returns to you. Wait until you hear the story how a man from Nigeria saved my life and why he did so. The goodness that you do sooner or later always arises and returns to you.

At Xerox Corporation I was promoted again to sales manager for major account sales, so I had salespeople in the states of Iowa, Nebraska, South Dakota and North Dakota. I began traveling overnight most of the time working with to coach those salespeople. I had started working a master's degree in business administration, but I had to stop because I was traveling so much of the time. We had also adopted our third child, Carol Ann; so I didn't want to leave Suzy with the entire burden of rearing all the children.

I used to trade stocks and commodities to make extra money, so after my seven-year career at Xerox Corporation I became a stock and commodities broker for a company in Omaha for two years. I found that I preferred in person outside sales much more than selling to people over the phone. Plus, at that time the markets were very unstable, and I didn't like the possibility of people losing money based on my recommendations. It was much less stressful for me to sell a product that I could stand behind one hundred percent; so I returned to copier and printer sales.

In 1977, I went to work for a copier company called Savin Corporation which sold Ricoh copiers and printers. It was based out Valhalla, New York, and was later acquired by Ricoh Corporation. I moved to Seattle and travelled the Northwestern U.S. teaching and helping Savin dealers and their salespeople how to sell to government organizations. At the time Ricoh was the world's largest manufacturer of copiers in units sold. I was later promoted to give sales training seminars throughout the U.S. on how to sell to large government institutions. I also wrote books on how to do the same. Each Monday morning, I left Seattle and traveled to a major city and even to some remote ones in the U.S. to teach. I even found myself on Kodiak Island. I would write books and support materials in hotel rooms at night and on airplanes. Needless to say it was taxing on my mental and physical health and my family to be working such long hours and traveling so much.

In my limited spare time, I liked to renovate houses starting with the ones that we lived in and other houses. I was able to build up a lot of equity in the houses because of the quality of my renovations and the market appreciation.

CHAPTER 5

The Washington State Company

For five years I called on independent office equipment dealers throughout the United States teaching their salespeople how to successfully sell governments, institutions and large corporations. Some were very successful some were not as successful. I came to realize that there wasn't anything separating me from them for I had been successful in sales, sales management and sales training for over fourteen years. I realized that there was nothing very unique about the successful dealers except their desire to be very successful and their persistence that they approached the business and the market.

I realize that I had the ability to be a very successful office equipment dealer. I knew from studying business and in particular marketing that you didn't have to be original, but you could be a very good copy especially a better copy to be successful. Consider the different names in the fast-food industry especially the hamburger chains how unique are they from each other? They just market what they claim to be a better hamburger and how they serve it but it is still a hamburger.

Through consultation with successful dealers that wouldn't be a competitor I developed a very detailed business plan outlining projected revenues and expenses. I knew whatever knowledge that I didn't possess such technical service and in depth accounting I could hire. The business plan indicated that I would need about $200,000.00 in capital to start the business and operate it. I knew that I could probably borrow part of it from a bank, but I would need an equity partner for part of it. I found that partner in Portland, Oregon. I decided in 1982 to start my own copier sales and service business in Seattle market with a partner from Portland, OR. I was able to borrow money and use the real estate assets as collateral to come up with almost $90,000.00 as my share of the equity to start the business. The economy was so bad that I had to borrow money at loan shark rates of twenty percent even though I had the collateral and an excellent credit rating. When I started that business, I was the sole economic provider to a family of five people. I understood that even in the best economic environments the chances of success of new business start-ups are about five percent. My stress level was very high because I leveraged all my assets and was heavily in debt to start the business. The pressure to succeed was very high because the financial health and stability of my wife and children were at risk. I was risking my family's financial health, so I had to succeed. Failure was not an option.

I was raised to do God like work by becoming a priest and hear was a chance to do just that as an entrepreneur instead of a priest. In starting a company, I could create good wholesome jobs. It was like when I was in sales, I knew that every time that I sold something twenty-one people went to work which gave my efforts very honorable purpose. In many third world countries you see young children with their bones protruding out instead of the bellies because daddy is unemployed and can't find a job. He can't find a job in a poor economy because there are none. You then see creating good jobs as doing God's work just like my sales work. The more honorable the purpose and Godly the purpose the greater the motivation. As a result, the greater chance of beating the odds against success and becoming very successful as we did.

I owned half the stock in the company and my partner in Portland,

Oregon owned the other half. I was in control of the operations in the Washington company except when it came outside financing. We also established a leasing company where we kept and financed all of the customers' leases for the equipment. I believe that the key to making the company such a quick success in such a negative economic environment in addition to be highly motivated was that I was fortunate enough to recruit the best people and properly motivating them. As I mentioned the philosophy of the company is that the company existed not just to make money but to create good jobs consisting of excellent pay and benefits. Also, we were going to be and were the very best at customer service. I believe in and we practiced that very high employee morale is key to high productivity, compliance and therefore success.

The Washington company was so successful that just two years later my partner made me an offer to buy my share of the company for over eleven times my original investment. At the point, our revenues were about four million a year or about eight million in today's dollar values. Because I was so heavily in debt by financing my economic future to start the company, I accepted my partner's offer. I also bought out his share of another startup company in Denver Colorado and relocated to Denver in 1984.

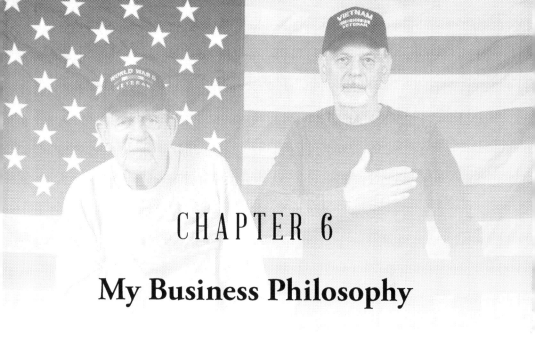

CHAPTER 6

My Business Philosophy

The employee should be treated and were treated in my companies as a customer. We should always keep in mind that the average employee spends at a minimum of two thirds of their waking hours preparing for work, commuting to work, at work and commuting home from work. The better the employee is treated the better your chance of success. You can't run a successful business or organization by yourself and the more you try to go it alone the higher your frustration and stress level. Always keep in mind that you are too close to the forest to see the trees and employees have insights that you don't have. They are the ones with the most direct customer contact. The employees witness and see things that you don't. High employee turnover leads to poor productivity and high training cost. Many employers fail to consider that it takes time and effort to get the so-called lay of the land and learn all the idiosyncrasies of the organization. It is part of, if I may phrase, the so-called start-up cost of the employee besides that of the organization.

In today's society we are afraid to trust our fellow humans and our employees. There is so much negative news which we are inclined to hear about fraud and deception. We fail to put criminology into proper perspective. Criminology and mental illness are not synonymous. America is the home of the world's largest population of prisoners. It has more people incarcerated than China which has over four times the population. There are roughly 2.3 million people incarcerated in the U.S. in a country of 326 million people. That means that approximately out of 140 people just one is criminalistic in nature. Now, when you consider that many of prisoners are incarcerated for mental health reasons because as stated in our great country people with psychiatric disorders are three times more likely to wind up in a prison than a mental health hospital. That could easily amount to at least fifty percent of the incarcerated population if not more as the staff of penal institutions would substantiate. I could go on and on but it means that maybe one out every 280 people truly want to intentionally harm us in a criminalistic way. That is about .0035 percent. We spend fortunes in trying to protect ourselves and our organizations from less than one half of one percent of the population.

The negative news causes us to become overly cautious when it comes to our fellow humans and so we treat them accordingly. Yes, the employee will naturally want more but an employee properly motivated and in good state of mind will give more. Most are not ignorant enough to bite the hand that feeds them. An employer is able to give more to them when they are not paying out a fortune in security systems, lost productivity and procedures to guard itself. I saw in prison that inmates who were treated badly were less compliant; therefore, it took more effort and therefore cost to control them. The same was true with the staff when morale was low so was compliance and productivity suffered.

Employers instead of spending so much money on protecting themselves from a very small minority of employees are better off spending that money on salaries and benefits to motivate their employees. Education solves a lot of problems. Again, we are not about to bite the hand that feeds us and not about the hand that feeds us well which applies to customers and employees. You can't exist successfully by overly protecting ourselves from our fellow man when we will live in a society and world where we are so dependent on our fellow humans. Even if you are very reclusive and live in the most remote parts of this country sooner or later you will need the assistance of other human beings. Whether we like it or not and no matter how independent we think we are in societies and the world is very interdependent. Yes, some people will take advantage of you but don't allow the actions of a small minority dictate how you treat the known majority. You have to take some employee theft as a cost of doing business.

In the final end every penny you spend on recruiting the best will attract the best and produce the best results coupled with the best training and coaching. Most people want to do a very good job but many simply don't know how and that is where training and motivation come in. Money spent on training is well spent not only for the short term but the long term. Many employees see it as a benefit. I started in sales for Xerox Corporation and saw their sales training program as an excellent benefit to enhance my career. Besides making me more productive it made me more employable.

At my companies the customer was never considered as wrong no matter what even if the customer was trying to take advantage of us. If the customer was trying to take advantage of us, we just saw that as an advertising expense to create good will. That way everybody knew how to act and how to treat a customer. Our honorable philosophy towards the customer also enhanced employee morale. In twenty-six years of operation, we never sued a customer and we had 12,000 of them. Our customer service was the best in the industry. When the customer called for service, our response was the fastest. When the technician serviced the machine problem, he or she then checked the whole machine to insure that something else didn't go wrong as soon the service technician left or too soon after. The technicians had the best training, parts and tools. The customer appreciated us getting to their location very fast to minimize downtime which interrupted their workflow, but they didn't want to see us too often.

CHAPTER 7

Colorado Company

In 1984 after I sold my share of the Washington I bought a startup company in Denver Colorado. I moved to the Denver area to take over its operation. Even though the following represents one third of my life and over half my adult life because of dissociative amnesia that caused the loss of the memories of the latter 25 years of my life, I have very little memory of those years from age 47 to 72 years. Most of what I write comes from the memories of my daughter Rene' who worked for my company for twenty-two years and my son Christopher who worked me for seventeen years. The company grew to a company of $28 million in revenue which would be about $40 million in today's dollar values. Overall the company had over 260 employees and nine offices. Five of the offices were in Colorado and four offices were in Washington State.

The company was also one of the larger benefactors to the Colorado Christian Home for Disadvantaged Children located in Denver. I sat on the board of the home, because I believed so much in disadvantaged children's causes. During this period of time, I helped found and was on the board of directors of Tech National Bank in Denver.

The Loss Of The Colorado Company

I estimate that from when I took over the operations company from a start-up company it grew successfully for seventeen years until my divorce in 2001 from Rebecca. I was a very devoted family man. Rebecca and I married in 1986 after my divorce from my first wife Suzanne also in 1986. Rebecca and I divorced in mid-2001. We had two children. John who we call Johnny and still do was born in 1989. Alexander who we call Alex was born in 1992. I don't know when dissociative amnesia started to take its devastating toll on my memory, and it wiped out the memories from Alexander's birth when I was 47 years old forward until age 72. It wiped 99% of my memories for twenty-five years. I can't even remember what hospital Alex was born in and I was present at his birth. I remember Johnny being born three years earlier because when I was presented with him at Boulder Community Hospital, I was so happy and proud that I took him and showed him to everyone that I could at the hospital. The hospital staff had to look for me to bring Johnny back to the nursery.

I understand that Rebecca's and my confrontations were very emotionally difficult for me. I don't recall very much if anything at all about our relationship. Some mental health professionals and family members claim that Rebecca and our dysfunctional relationship escalated my mental health disorders and were the cause of dissociative amnesia.

I believe that because of the dysfunction in my marriage that I became more reclusive and private at a time when I needed a lot of help. As I look back and hear how I was, the suicide attempt in 2001 at the time of my divorce should have been a big red flag of my mental dysfunction. I wasn't self-conscious enough to perceive that I had some huge mental health issues. My loved ones didn't recognize how sick I was since people falling into dementia act normal most of the time and that symptoms come and go. That is why sixty percent don't seek treatment until the disease has taken too much of a hold on the person's life. Consequently, I did not seek professional help for my mental health disorders as I had before which exacerbated them.

After my attempted suicide I continued to own and operate the company for the next six and a half years. I believe that for a while the company stagnated and then started to decline because of my mental health. At some point I started to make a lot of ill-advised decisions which hurt so many great employees, customers and the company as a whole. When I started to regain my cognizance after being incarcerated for almost four years, I felt so guilty and ashamed that on a daily basis I would pray to God to take my life. I just couldn't believe or comprehend how I could make such bad decisions. To me in my case guilt is one of the most difficult parts of recovering from the disease. Many of those bad decisions affected so many people negatively. People who had placed their confidence in me and were so loyal to me were hurt. I had just run out of steam and kept on falling deeper and deeper into depression until I finally totally shut down to the point where I lost touch with reality and fell into a state of dementia.

Devastation is such an inadequate word to describe what I felt when I started to recover my cognitive ability and what I still feel. I ask myself why didn't I didn't realize or recognize my deficient state or what could I have done? How did I go from being a multi-millionaire to waking up on a prison cell floor in solitary confinement lying in my own human waste? I tried my best in my life to live it by a high moral standard.

I can only imagine which I hate to do what happened to my business, the great employees, and customers. When I think about how it affected my children, grandchildren, siblings and my mother to say the least it is depressing. I ask myself: how can I ever make up for or even accept the wrongs? I wanted so much to blame someone for my demise, but I couldn't. I still say to myself if it was brain cancer people would understand but not with dementia. The only way I can accept my conduct is by seeing it as something I wasn't in control of, but I was in control. It was like a natural disaster such as a flood or a blizzard that does so much damage. Now I realize that if I am going to stay on the road to recovery, I have put the past behind me and move on with my life. If I don't let go of the past it will devastate me again.

When prisoners would ask me what I did to become successful, I say from my heart and mind that it takes honesty and integrity. They would say you are crazy. At the same time, I would ask myself how much I unknowingly or desperately violated that principle. Please allow me to say again that I'm so very sorry to anyone who was hurt by my conduct as a result of my mental disorders. I know that I can't change the past and the only thing that I can do is to help bring mental health to the forefront of social recognition so that more can be done about it.

When I was still employed at the company in 2007 and the beginning of 2008, we got behind on payroll tax submissions because of cash flow. I presume that was due to operating losses. I also presume that I didn't want to reduce staff due by laying off employees. My notes tell me that I met with an officer of IRS about the problem and discussed it. I told her of the audit we had done of service commissions due from our main supplier. We were late on tax deposits of approximately $600,000.00 and there was $1,200,000.00 due in receivables. I understand that I developed a repayment plan for the payroll tax deposits. We had also got behind on 401K submissions for some employees, but these were caught up and paid. I was still accused of stealing from the 401K plan.

My payments to my ex-wife Rebecca were also delinquent. I presumed that because of my relationship with Rebecca was very hostile that she and her divorce lawyers would take legal action against me. I declared personal bankruptcy so I could reorganize my personal debts in particular to Rebecca and save the company from Rebecca's foreclosure. My post-divorce payments to Rebecca for alimony amounted to $12,000.00 per month and $28,000.00 in rent. The total amount was $40,000.00 per month which would be approximately $61,000.00 in today's dollar values plus there were other benefits such as automobiles and legal expenses.

The reason why the court awarded such a large post-divorce payment was that the company had been very successful before my mental breakdown. I wasn't cognizant enough to challenge the courts award. I was in a very passive and stupefied mental state.

In spite of my personal bankruptcy Rebecca through her attorneys foreclosed on the company and fired me; my daughter Rene' who acted as general manager, the controller, the auditors and my son Christopher quit in protest. Rene' had been with the company for twenty years and Christopher had been there for seventeen years. Rebecca through her attorneys had terminated or alienated all the people who could run the company successfully. I was powerless financially and mentally to stop Rebecca. I'm not blaming Rebecca Walshe for the deterioration of the company prior to Rebecca's takeover the operations of the company. I am blaming her for the demise and liquidation of the company by indiscriminately and capriciously terminating the key employees who could have insured the company's continued existence.

I understand that Rebecca would not answer my telephone calls or respond to my messages. I also understand that on three occasions I attempted to visit the company to ensure that things were properly on to be turned away by the Denver Police and told not to return with threats of legal action. I was powerless to do anything because of Ms. Walshe's actions. She could have sold the assets of the company including the customer base which was worth a lot to competitors since there was a continual flow of revenues from contracted maintenance and supply agreements. In my opinion when Rebecca took over the company it became her responsibility to ensure that the overdue tax deposits and other obligations were paid since it was a corporate debt and not my personal debt. In my opinion Ms. Walshe could have sold the company or its asset and satisfied all obligations. Why she did not I do not know. I still have not had any communication with Rebecca since prior to her assuming control of the company. I understand that the government shut the company down a few months after she took control of it. I wrote to her from prison concerning the children without a reply.

When Rebecca Walshe terminated me in essence, I was destitute because all of my liquid type of assets were in the company. There was nothing in personal checking or savings accounts. I was sixty-three years old and in my adult life I was never guilty of any incident or accusation of dishonesty, deceit or greedy behaviors. I challenge anyone to find just a hand full of people that I ever refused an accommodation or a favor prior to my mental breakdown. Consider my humanistic endeavors especially towards disadvantaged children. I was always a very kind, loving, generous and honest man. I believe that we do have to account for and pay for the sins that we commit in life. In my case, it has been through incredible feelings of guilt, not just incarceration and the incredible abuse I endured while incarcerated. In my opinion if I had recognized how my mental health had deteriorated and was more attentive to it, I could have avoided all the problems both personal and professional.

CHAPTER 8

Insanity And the Justice System

Colorado law defines insanity as a condition of mind caused by mental disease or defect that prevented the person from forming culpable mental state that is an essential element of a crime charged. The law provides for proper treatment of the mentally ill in the justice system but crowded court dockets and the desire for expediency to clear the dockets can counteract the intent of the lawmakers. Instead of crowded dockets you wind up with crowded jails and prisons where mental health disorders are exacerbated. When the individual is ultimately released back into society they relapse back into crime because the original cause the problem was never properly addressed, and it grew in size. This is manifested in such high rate of recidivism of well over fifty percent. Ultimately society pays the price for not properly diagnosing and treating mental health disorders in the beginning of the legal process. You might say they postpone incurring the cost, but they ultimately incur a much bigger cost with a lot more victims. Ultimately society didn't save the cost by closing so many mental institutions one way or another they incurred a higher cost. One example is alcoholism and illicit drug use especially among veterans. Mental health disorders can and do create a lot more innocent victims than just those who are inflicted with the disease or disorder as an example consider the unbelievable number of mass shootings. How can we begin to describe the amount of overwhelming grief the loved ones of the victims have to endure? The incidence of mass shootings is growing at a very frightening rate. That is why mental health disorders have to be brought to the forefront in society just like we have with cancer. Society has to stop stigmatizing mental health disorders so they can be readily recognized and treated. The negative effects of mental health disorders can't be adequately controlled when individuals are afraid to admit that their existence because they will be shunned by society because of stigmatization. Mental health disorders are not an indication of character flaws no more than the common cold.

In my case a judge refused to let the jury hear my diseases because the case was the oldest on his docket. He was more concerned with his calendar than truth and justice. He just said that I looked all right to him and so he wanted his court calendar to look the same. Another judge when I wrote to her about my dilemma about the possibility of being abused in the jail, she ignored my letter. I had a history of being assaulted at least six times in that jail and suffered two heart attacks there. She did at least admit in court receiving it but a few days later my concern was manifested when I was knocked unconscious. My jaw is still out of alignment from that assault. Two days later after the assault I was diagnosed with two strokes and one of them from the most recent assault.

Another judge continually chastised my attorney because he didn't properly prepare for the case. The judge just chose to ignore what is termed ineffectiveness of the counsel by a court appointed attorney. It made me wonder and question if the trial should have been stopped or continued? Six months later I was manifesting the symptoms of Alzheimer's disease and the prison was contemplating transferring me to a mental institution. At the time I was in such a passive state to care. We appoint or elect judges to ensure justice and truth are being served. Is it fair to the accused when judges are unable to judge their own behaviors or what goes on in their courtrooms and admit mistakes? Like any profession we don't expect judges to be perfect just fair. We should be able to expect them readily admit mistakes like anyone else in any other profession. I believe that mistakes are not readily admitted because the justice system is so taxed and backed up with cases.

You might say to yourself that this guy must be crazy if he readily admits that he went insane. Society locks people like me up. People like me in the condition I was in should be properly diagnosed, treated and institutionalize in the proper institutions if necessary so they have the best chance of recovering in a timely manner. Recovery shouldn't just be left to willpower and chance as it was with me. I readily admit that I had significant mental disorders and went insane, but I am becoming sane again. I'm regaining my sanity in spite of incredible odds against it in a penal environment which is more likely to exacerbate a mental health disorder or disease. I'm regaining my sanity because I was willing to admit I had very damaging disorders and I had to do something about them. I asked myself how did I go from being a self-made multimillionaire to lying on a prison floor in an animalistic state?

Let me state again there shouldn't be any negative stigma attached to mental health disorders, no more than any form of cancer. This year about one third of Americans will suffer from some type of mental health disorder. More than fifty percent of Americans will suffer from a mental health disorder sometime in their lifetime. I consider psychiatric diseases cancer of the mind and should be brought to the forefront so they can be treated as cancer is treated. There are more people inflicted with mental health disorders than with cancer. Under the right conditions and circumstances the diseases are treatable and people do recover to live normal lives again as I have. I believe that most are chemically based. Why else do the majority of them react positively to medications? The brain's communications system, neurotransmitters are made of chemicals. The one thing we know for sure the sooner the problem is recognized, and responsibility is taken for it the sooner healing and recovery can begin. The problem with some mental health disorders is that a person loses their self-consciousness like in the case of dementia. It is up to their loved ones to convince them that they need professional help in the most loving way as possible without denigrating them. This is where stigma can become a real curse. It keeps people from seeking help early enough to keep from exacerbating the condition as prison does. Stigmatization keeps people in a state of denial which serves to exacerbate mental health disorders. As stated before, that is one of the reasons why sixty percent of the people that are inflicted with dementia don't seek professional help soon enough.

We shouldn't lock these people up in what I term "Meat Lockers" and forget about them because like any problem not properly attended to it will only grow in size especially in prison. Again, let me state we see this all too often in our society as manifested in murders, mass murders, suicides, illicit drug use, the opioid crisis, obesity, etc., etc. I believe that it is a terrible shame that the suicide rate is so high among Vietnam Era Veterans those that served us honorably in an unpopular and possibly an unjustified war. It is like when they are no longer of any use to society as they once were, we forget about them. Not once during my incarceration or prosecution did I sense that any consideration was given to my Vietnam Era voluntary and honorable service to our country. It wasn't even brought up at my trials or sentencing hearings. It not only pertains to me but others. I knew one Hispanic Vietnam Veteran in prison whose skin was turning black and peeling off like a layer of an onion from exposure to agent orange. When he asked for dermatological care, he was refused and told that it was just old age. That wasn't what he was promised when he took the oath to faithfully serve our country. It is like when we say we should have never been in that war we forget those who were willing to risk their lives to fight in that war. I met many Vietnam, Iraqi and Afghanistan war veterans in prison whose service was soon forgotten especially as they aged. I wasn't treated as an honorably served veteran but as an item on a judge's court calendar. May I say My Life Matters Too! Why else were my guts allowed to hang out of me like a large banana for five long and very painful years? What about the good that I did after serving my country in a time of war? It is time that we are quick to properly diagnose as we are to prosecute.

CHAPTER 9

Psychiatric Diseases in General

Psychiatric diseases are very difficult to diagnose because no two people experience them exactly the same. Generally, there is a lack of knowledge especially public knowledge about the workings of the brain as compared to the other vital organs such as the heart. That is unfortunate because the brain is the true heart of the matter. The brain because it is enclosed in a cranium, it is very difficult to observe its workings plus in the brain things happen in micro-seconds. A neuron is so tiny that 20,000 of them can fit on the head of a pin and each neuron has 15,000 connections. By the time a person reaches 60 years of age they suffer from a noticeable decline in cognitive ability. The hippocampus which is the home of short term and intermediate memories shrinks by as much as twenty-to-twenty five percent. Your memory starts to decline at 50 years of age. In dementia the hippocampus is usually the first area of the brain to decline. There has been much talk about this during the last presidential election. Why are we so afraid to admit that the brain declines just like any other human organ? The answer is that it is very unpopular to do so because of stigmatization.

We hear of a person's so-called ability to think on their feet; that ability declines noticeably with age. In my case it took and still takes much longer to assimilate what is being presented and to come to conclusions compared to my younger years. Depending on how complicated the material it can take hours and days to come to conclusions. It is more difficult for me to see the whole a picture and for at least three years I couldn't perceive any part of the picture. When people would ask me, don't you understand? I didn't. It leads me to question my competency to defend myself at the time of the accusations were made when it took me so much longer to assimilate, understand or come to conclusions. When I look back at my Federal Trial, I exhibited every symptom of dementia because one of my diseases mimics dementia. I showed all its symptoms except for obesity and lack of education. I'm prone to dementia in fifteen ways and demonstrated over twenty symptoms of it. I can't help but question why didn't my defense counsel, prosecutors or mental health professionals at Aurora Mental Health where I was supposedly evaluated see it? As stated before, at that time I couldn't even remember my youngest son's birth or upbringing, but I was present for both. Alexander at the time was 19 years of age. I still have no memory of the same. At the least common sense would cause you to ask why does a man resort to criminalistic behavior after more than six decades of life?

Again, please let me state despite the inhumane abuse and mental health shortcomings through God's Grace I'm coming back to life. I kissed death four times and endured more than fourteen inhumane assaults, but I'm functioning again. Please allow me to state again out of gratitude that I endured and survived all the hostile acts and assaults because of my faith in God. It demonstrates the power of belief.

In this book I'm attempting to describe to the best of my ability what happened during the last decade of my life and somewhat before. I will attempt to describe in spite of my mental disorders how I went from being a multi-millionaire to lying in my own human waste on a prison floor in solitary confinement hollering in pain. I will do my best to recall the facts in spite of the fact as stated before that I suffer and have suffered from four major psychiatric conditions; two of which even the ancient Greeks associated with death. May I state again that I also suffered from five major circulatory conditions which affect the functioning of the brain. Two of the psychiatric conditions dissociative amnesia and pseudo dementia caused me to lose a great portion of my memory which represent more than half of my adult life. Consequently, a lot of the information came from friends, precious children, siblings and other loved ones such as my first wife Suzanne. It also comes from my fellow inmates and records such as legal and medical.

Dissociative Amnesia

Dissociative amnesia is a mental illness which affects as much as one percent of the population and affects women 2.6 times more than men; it causes people to have a mental breakdown of normal brain functions such as consciousness, awareness, and perception because of memory loss. People become very confused even about their identity. It is also called psychogenic amnesia. Some of its symptoms mimic those of dementia and Alzheimer's disease which may be one of the reasons they thought that I suffered from Alzheimer's disease in the Federal prison when I arrived there at 67 years of age. Alzheimer's usually strikes its victims starting around the age of 65 years. It causes a person not to be able to function normally, professionally, and personally. Dissociative amnesia caused me to lose the memories of the later twenty-five years of my life basically from the age of 47 until the age of 72 years.

It left such a void in my life. The things that you would like to remember and live over and over again in your mind you can't. I understand that it is caused by overwhelming stress. It is thought that a certain portion of a person's life is so painful that the person blocks out any memory of it. I'm not aware what those events were in my life. The stress can also cause paranoia and delusional behavior. It is like I don't want to know what happened to me out of self-protection or survival. The memory or memories still exist but they are so deeply buried. It may be possible to recover and recall the memories at a future date when I'm mentally stronger. They say that the difference between hindsight and foresight is facts but no memory, no facts. Some of the memories may be lost forever because of two strokes. As stated, I couldn't and still can't remember my youngest son's birth or upbringing which I participated in. Think about it; how do you tell a child that you can't remember his birth or my other children's and grandchildren's upbringing? How bad can your memory get? It is a real tragedy. When you lose your memory, you lose your life and all the precious moments of your life. It is like they never happened. It is like you never lived during those moments in time. It is like you were asleep for years.

I like to think that even though I lost the memory of loved ones I didn't lose the loving feelings. I tell my loved ones that. I can't remember any of my children's graduations, weddings or my grandchildren's births to say the least. One day when I was talking to my oldest sister on the phone in prison, she told me that she has been married for over fifty years. I can remember attending her wedding in New York before leaving home for the Air Force in 1964 but I can't remember any of my children's weddings, graduations, or my grandchildren's births. I can't remember my own two weddings or any of my graduations which I worked so hard to accomplish. My oldest son tells me I was his best man at his wedding, and I don't remember his wedding. You would think that I would remember such an honor. I have been told well at least you won't remember the bad events. That is true but if you experienced something bad at least there is usually a valuable lesson attached to it. I lost the benefit of the so-called "Wisdom Of The Years".

You don't appreciate your memories like loved ones until they are gone. Amnesia and dementia destroy your internal picture album. It is like my life was robbed from me. I wondered and still at times wonder where did my life go? At times I feel so cheated because much of my life was deleted. Let me ask again where did my life go? What do your memories represent if not your life? Think about the times when you are or were able to think back and enjoy some of the happiest moments in your life. What if you can't remember them? It is like losing the jewels of your life or a fortune in savings account. What is a legacy made up of?

Also, when you lose your memory, you lose the benefit of your previous life decisions, so the quality of your decisions is diminished. Socrates said an unexamined life isn't worth living but what if you can't remember more than half of your adult life? When it came to defending myself against accusations and crimes I couldn't. How can you tell you tell your attorney what happened when you can't remember what happened? I couldn't remember that facts to bolster my defense. The same is true for psychiatric professionals who are trying to evaluate you. Consequently, much of my life for a decade was a living hell as manifested that I fell victim to so many major diseases. It is like I died which I came so close to several times during my incarceration. You would like to leave a very positive legacy, but my mental health diseases robbed me of that privilege.

It confuses people that I remember and understand some things but not others. My only retort is that I understand and remember what God wants me to remember to do God's work. To mental health professionals I remember things that are very significant and distinctive but that isn't always the case. I understand that it is easier to remember things and events if they are emotional or traumatic in nature. That wasn't' always true in my case when you consider my not remembering my youngest son's birth or upbringing. I was able to remember most assaults by guards but not assaults by inmates. It is like I couldn't remember things that were expected or routine in nature such as inmate abuse in prison. I'm glad that I had the sense to take so many notes.

I feel very grateful because starting about the age of 71½ I started to be able to establish new memories. That has increased with each month especially that I'm not subject to the stressors of prison life. It is an indication of how stressful prison life is. You don't truly recognize how stressful being incarcerated is while you are incarcerated. Again, let me state that I understand that my memory loss is mostly psychologically versus biologically based due to my strokes and with time and prompting those memories may surface again. I would love to at least remember my children as they were growing up. I watch little children play and wish that I could remember my children doing the same.

Examples of Major Events of which I Have No Memory

- My Federal Trial
- My six months Incarceration at a Federal halfway house
- My post Federal Trial six months of incarceration at the Denver County Jail
- My first in inpatient stay at Denver Health Hospital
- My incarceration at a Federal Prison in Oklahoma City
- My inpatient stay in an Oklahoma City Hospital
- My graduation from the University of Nebraska
- My high school graduation
- My first seventeen months in Federal Prison
- My first eight months at the Adams County Jail
- Spotty memory of the years 1975 to 1992
- Hardly any memory of my twenty-six years as an entrepreneur
- No memory of my four inpatient mental hospital stays.

I can go on and on with the list. If I can't remember the very significant then how was I to remember the less significant? I'm more likely to remember the old over twenty-five years than the new which is called the "amnestic syndrome."

Disassociation

When I disassociate which is common for me to endure overwhelming stress and severe pain I space out and mentally go somewhere else. It is akin to my mind floating out of my body and especially my brain so I can endure the abuse and pain.

I appear to see and hear but I don't. Nothing that the other person is saying or doing has any meaning to me. I'm aware but I'm just not conscious of other people's words or actions. I wasn't even conscious of being knocked unconscious and experiencing concussions. Penal officials interpret disassociation or aphasia as me being obstinate or disobedient. You will read what tragically happened to the lady in Loveland, Colorado at the hands of the police. It affects the egos of some law enforcement personnel. How dare this old prisoner disobey my orders or not recognize my authority? So, in many cases I was thrown into solitary confinement and abused. The same is true for many of the inmates especially members of gangs. I found out from being severely beaten that the worst thing you can do is to ignore a fellow prisoner which is common with disassociation. As stated, there were several instances when my life was threatened. People hate being ignored especially prisoners who have been abandoned. There are plenty of those in maximum security. When you disassociate you are nothing but a human in a vegetative state. You are not really human but a vegetable.

Pseudo Dementia or Severe Major Depression

When I was extradited to the Adams County Jail a psychiatrist a Dr. David Fohrman diagnosed me with pseudo dementia. It has symptoms which mimic Alzheimer's disease which is the largest form of dementia. As stated before, I understand that it is actually severe major depression. I fell into such a deep state of depression that I lost touch with reality. That is another reason why at the Federal Prison they thought I had Alzheimer's disease. I consider pseudo dementia a temporary form of dementia because that is what it was like for me.

Many psychiatrists, psychologists and neuroscientists claim that a person suffering from severe major depression is powerless to help themselves. Most of the mental health professionals that I encountered in penal system didn't know what pseudo dementia was. It puts you into a state where it is difficult or impossible to be in a real state of awareness and especially of consciousness. It is difficult to be aware of reality, significance of events and to focus on priorities and realize what they are. Many people are driven to suicide as I was because you're thinking becomes so distorted. As stated, I attempted suicide and I also contemplated it many times all due to depression. Depression is a chemically based condition. Serotonin is a neurotransmitter which promotes a feeling of well-being and happiness. Depression can diminish the positive effects of serotonin and low levels of serotonin cause depression. Major depression can lead to dementia and along with stress can shut the brain and body down. It can also diminish the workings of the body's vital organs such as the heart and kidneys as it did with me. The cardiology staff at the Platt Valley Medical Center after they did a nuclear or stress test on my heart said that I will be prone to a form of dementia for the rest of my life. Dementia was one of the causes of my mother's death, so it is in my genes.

Pseudo dementia caused me to lose my cognitive ability and my memory for many years; how many I don't know because of the other diseases affecting my memory. Over the years I have been diagnosed and treated for several psychiatric disorders where they can share common symptoms. Pseudo dementia is the only one that fit my condition when considering my symptoms of the main disease that caused my personal and professional downfall. By my nature and psychiatrically I'm very sensitive to any pressure or stress in my life which makes me very prone to pseudo dementia. Starting businesses and my divorces took an excessive toll on me. During my second marriage I was diagnosed as being bi-polar. I have very few and only spotty memories of my second marriage. I believe that I went through extreme mental trauma because of the dysfunction in the relationship. I tried to and I believe that I was a very dutiful and devoted husband and father. With pseudo dementia you are there but you are not there in your thinking and consciousness. Trauma is defined as a psychological injury caused by an event or injury. I tried and was very careful not to repeat the same mistakes as I did in my first marriage. The reasons that I believe that my second marriage took an enormous toll on my mental health was the fact that I had three inpatient mental hospital stays and the divorce led me to suicide. I didn't react positively to the drugs prescribed for bi-polar disease. As I look back, I was much more deeply depressed than manic. I believe that the manic episodes were attributed to my acute anxiety disorder and PTSD. As inferred the diseases are so very interrelated that they are difficult to separate and diagnose. Because they are so interrelated, they can be disastrous as they were in my case.

My suicide attempt was very illogical, unreasonable and irrational since I had so much to live for after my second divorce. It was a very selfish act and a sure sign of a demented state. How does a man go from being a multi-millionaire with no illicit drug or alcohol use to destitute if not for severe major depression or dementia? When I had a heart attack, I wasn't even cognizant of it. Some mental health professionals claim that Alzheimer's disease the largest form of dementia can only be totally and accurately diagnosed in an autopsy. Dementia affects a person's ability to make sensible and sound decisions. Without a question it affected my judgement. I thank God that my instincts and habits kept me from committing violent acts. Now as it turned out I was unknowingly suffering from Post-Traumatic Stress Disorder, PTSD, going back to my military career. PTSD along with my other disorders made being incarcerated even more tortuous.

My Risk Factors for Dementia or Pseudo Dementia

- Age 70 plus years of age
- Was a smoker for 40 years until age 55
- Three Heart attacks
- Two Strokes

- Heart Surgery
- Heart Palpitations
- High Cholesterol
- Large weight loss one third of body weight
- Loss of Sense of Smell
- Hearing Loss
- Four inpatient mental health hospital stays.
- Substantial Memory Loss
- Dramatic Decrease in Cognitive Ability
- Suicide Attempt
- Loss of Muscle Mass
- Loss of Emotional Ability
- Grand Mal Seizures

Major Diseases That Contribute To My Demented State

- Hypertension
- High cholesterol
- Cardiovascular disease
- Type II diabetes mellitus
- Acute anxiety
- Major depression
- Dissociative amnesia
- Kidney disease
- PTSD
- Panic Attacks
- Angina Pectoris Attacks

Contributing Factors to my Demented State

- Infant Diseases
- Child Abuse

- Childhood Sexual Abuse
- Fatal Automobile Accident
- Exposure to Nerve Gas
- The Stress of Starting five New Businesses
- Two Divorces
- Loss of a Business
- Loss of All Worldly Possessions
- Becoming Destitute

We hear how powerful the brain and the mind are, but we don't hear how delicate the brain is. At least I didn't realize how delicate the brain was until my mental health diseases took their devastating tolls of my life. The only ones that fully appreciate the devastation of diseases like dementia are those who live with or are close to loved ones who are afflicted with it. That is because its victims don't recognize that they have it. The true victims are the loved ones and associates. As stated earlier, as I look back on my life in my opinion pseudo dementia had the most devastating effect on my life personally and professionally.

Memory impairment is pandemic for people fifty years plus. It is one of the biggest problems people have in midlife on. It is important that the demented state be dealt with as early as possible, but I didn't deal with it because it wasn't diagnosed as it is with sixty percent of its victims. There are four FDA approved medications which can help retard memory loss. Even though I was a veteran I was not administered any of them in any penal institution where my memory loss was very obvious. At the Federal prison I couldn't even remember where the bathroom or dining hall was.

In my case I found physical and mental exercise to be very important to emerge from the demented state. I can't overemphasize how important it was to me and for me to exercise. On many occasions at the Adams County Jail, Denver County Jail or the Colorado Department of Corrections I was restricted from physical exercise because of being placed in the "Hole," lockdowns. Plus, I was in severe pain and immobile from my hernias. For almost two years I had to deal with the threat of two aorta aneurysms rupturing if I exerted myself too much. The more I was restricted to a cell without a break the more demented I got. One of the biggest problems for the brain is cardiovascular disease which I suffer from because as stated previously the brain is so dependent on good and pure blood flow. I didn't receive any appropriate care or consideration in housing placement for my cardiovascular disease which fostered three heart attacks and prolonged my demented state. You don't place an inmate with a history of stroke and heart attacks in maximum security with very violent offenders. As stated, I was housed in the most perilous sections of the jails and prisons. For almost three years I fell into an animalistic and vegetative state where I couldn't as stated even find the men's room, my prison cell or even the dining hall. In prison or jail they don't treat your disorders in best cases they just tolerate you.

While incarcerated as the records state I received hardly any psychiatric care even though I suffered from four psychiatric disorders just like with my heart disease. In most cases they don't have the ability and where they have the expertise, they don't have the time. Most mental health professionals told me that knew very little about dementia and its different forms especially pseudo dementia.

As I look back over the last two decades, I was in a retarded state. In my case it attacked my mind which is considered the software and the brain which is considered the hardware. At the Federal prison I even unknowingly deposited my human waste wherever I felt like it such as an untrained animal. It is a disgusting fact of my mental retardation. I couldn't nourish myself properly, so I lost one third of my body weight. I had to be placed on food supplements because of my physical deterioration.

When my mind shut down my body followed. I had to be catheterized to urinate and I wore urinary collection bags. It is my belief that I developed hernias and hemorrhoids from having to strain so much to be able to have bowel movements. I developed physical disorders such as type II diabetes, major dehydration, hypertension, high cholesterol, kidney disease and my cardiovascular disease worsened. I fell into a very frightening vegetative and animalistic state. My research tells me that if I'm not careful I have a five hundred percent chance of falling back into that demented state if I don't manage my stress level. That is a real challenge in the penal system. History can repeat itself with pseudo dementia. As some researchers say eighty percent of all physical disorders start in the mind.

Dementia comes at you and inflicts you like a thief in the night. It devastates your life. It robs you as it did me of a civil existence and everything that you worked so hard to build. I couldn't I even remember my dear children's lives? To say it is a tragedy is an understatement. It robbed me of so much of the good things I did in my life because I have no memories of them. Because of it now I'm stigmatized as a criminal and because of mental health disorders.

At the beginning stages of dementia, most of the time you continue to act normal while dementia does its silent damage. It does its damage silently because it strikes the elderly whose lifestyles are so dominated by traditions, customs, procedures, instincts and our old friends, if you established the right ones, habits. It is like you are not in control anymore; it seems like everything is automatic. You don't think about it instinctively you just do it and hopefully you do it right and properly.

When it comes to things that require thought especially deep thought that is when the damage becomes obvious to others, but they aren't sure. They are used to the normal or old you. The out of the ordinary decisions are the ones that are so illogical, unreasonable and downright ridiculous. You don't realize that you made a bad decision and how bad it is. People are afraid to criticize you. You don't see the end to realize that you screwed up because you're not even cognizant of the present. You don't realize all the ramifications of your decisions before and after you make them. You just want to get whatever it is over with. You don't have the ability to project into the future when you are struggling to be cognizant of the present and especially the past.

As inferred before one of the symptoms of pseudo dementia and dementia is the loss of so much of your consciousness and awareness of the significance of events in your life. People think that the words consciousness and awareness mean the same thing but in a psychological world and sense they don't. They have two different meanings and are triggered in different ways. They are located in different levels of the mind. You can be aware of something but not conscious of it. This confuses people. Awareness is an automatic act whereas consciousness is triggered by an internal decision to concentrate. You could say that consciousness is a higher level of awareness and perception. Consciousness attaches significance and a deeper meaning to a perception. You can walk around in a state of being aware of your surroundings as I did but not conscious of them which has to be generated by a decision by you. I was aware of my surroundings, but I was too overwhelmed and worn out to make the decision to be conscious of them. I needed help. I needed energy because I had none because the depression wears you down. It is and was in my case the brain's way of protecting itself from too much overwhelming stress. That was manifested when my brain fell into a vegetative and disassociative state for thirty-two months of my incarceration. When my brain had enough rest and time to recover that is when I suddenly started to emerge out of my vegetative, animalistic and disassociative state. What people thought was a miracle was just a state of incubation and recovery. In the Federal Prison my last two months there they referred to me as the "Miracle Man" when I emerged from that demented state.

That scenario along with disassociation caused me to be very misunderstood. I am very good on putting on a very positive appearance to the public. I developed and perfected that ability from being in outside sales where you have to put on a very positive appearance. My economic existence and survival and that of my family depended on it. Even when

I was praying for my death at the Adams County Jail, I was receiving compliments for being so cheerful and positive in my manner. I put on that act for so long that it became second nature to me. I performed without being conscious and sometimes even aware of it. Positive habits and being aware but not conscious led to so much confusion about my mental health. It also led to so much abuse while I was incarcerated. It makes proper screening, evaluation and diagnosis of paramount importance in order to avoid atrocious assaults and abuse that I have endured. Age and deviant behavior from the norm should trigger that something is wrong. Victims of Alzheimer's and dementia towards the end of their lives can even turn violent. As stated, the diseases and their related ones are ghost-like in nature. There are few warning signs that you are being inflicted with diseases like dementia or that you have them. It may be obvious to others but not to you. It isn't painful to fall into a state of dementia because as stated you aren't conscious.

What you feel emerging from a demented state is devastating psychologically where suicide becomes a very real and appealing option. The extent of the guilt feelings is just so overwhelming. The worst thing you can do is wonder what you were like in that demented state and what you could have done. Your imagination becomes a real danger to you if you have a conscience and don't control your thinking. You retreat into your own little world. In the demented state you just allow the world to come crashing in on you without giving it a second thought. You just want your life to end. It is so easy for someone to take advantage of you especially in jail and prison because of your retarded state. You don't dare to judge others because you don't remember what you might have done in a demented stated.

Even the most traumatic events in your life that should have an effect on anyone such as death of a very dear loved one means nothing to you. When they told me that I could go to prison I couldn't have cared less. They might as well have told me I was going to Disneyland. When they told me that I was going to prison I didn't care. While in prison when my very dear mother, who I loved very much and was very devoted to me, when they told me that she died I couldn't, nor did I even want to cry. There was no mourning or grief. You just become unbelievably passive. You easily turn the other cheek. In the Holy Bible Mathew 5:39 he quotes Jesus "If someone strikes you on the right cheek, turn to him the other also", I sure unconsciously practiced that quote in my demented state. As with amnesia you lose very precious memories. This is especially true for the very positive events such as my children's graduations, weddings and my grandchildren's births meant absolutely nothing to me. Any person would cherish those types of memories. Not me! It makes me wonder how I appeared or was perceived by others when significant events were happening in their lives. I must have come off as a "cold fish" without the ability to be fully conscious, aware, and perceptive of the significance of events in people's lives especially my loved ones. They must have thought that I didn't care. I certainly couldn't have been as they say, "Mr. Personality." I was emotionally dead.

Even the name or term pseudo dementia is a curse. To the average lay person, the term pseudo means false, so when my public defenders and the judge heard pseudo dementia, they automatically figured that there was nothing wrong with my memory or mental health. In spite of my pleadings, they continued to think that I was alright. Who is going believe the accused? There were very few scientific papers published for the lay person about the pseudo dementia prior to my trials. Instead of researching further for my benefit and to discover the truth as a trial and legal professionals should do, they continued to think the same way which deprived me of justice. All they had to do was to call the Texas prison or read the medical records from the Texas prison and they would have realized that there was something wrong with me. The appeals attorney, Mr. Borquez, referred to my psychiatric condition in the appeal but his writings were ignored by the appeals court. When you start to recover from pseudo dementia it validates people opinion that there was nothing wrong with you. But what causes a man to go from being a self-made multi-millionaire to lying on a prison floor and alienating most of his former associates along with many of his family members?

When I started to be cognizant the only reason that I didn't commit suicide was to keep from hurting my loved ones more than they were already hurt. The more that my cognitive ability, consciousness and awareness improved the more guilt increased. The more guilt I felt the more I attracted negativity into my life. Thoughts and behaviors do attract the same like a magnet. Dementia used to be referred to as senility and is mostly associated with old age. Let me state again for emphasis it causes a deranged state of mind. It affected my ability to reason, rationalize, being logical and have sensible and sound thinking. The disease also affected memory like amnesia did. The oldest person is no more than childlike without a memory and conscious ability as I was for thirty-two months of my incarceration. I wasn't even aware that my memory was failing. It was so difficult for my loved ones to watch me deteriorate especially when I had been so successful for decades. There was no outward reason such as alcohol or illicit drugs. My loved ones became the real the victims! I don't recall if I even cared about them. I became narcissistic which is part of the disease. I just didn't care about anything, or did anything have the meaning that it should have had to me. I was no longer proactive and would just very passively observe my life fall apart and deteriorate. I lost everything including my mind! When that happens you definitely have lost it all. It was like what were normal life's challenges became mountainous and too overwhelming for me to deal with. I just wanted to get whatever it was over with no matter what the cost in any terms. It is like I was on a crazy drug trip although I never did drugs. It is like I lost all ability to feel in an emotional and even a physical sense. As stated, I fell into a vegetative and unresponsive state to endure. It was like my mind went into a state of hibernation or deep sleep but on a positive side that brought me back to life. When I couldn't deal with any more stress my mind would rest and rejuvenate itself. I was a walking dead person seeing the world and events from the opposite end of a telescope. I could no longer see the whole picture or even part of it. Being narrow minded is an understatement. When it came to my first two trials I just sat in court and let the prosecutors condemn me without any retort on my part.

I lost a good part of my personality. In the past where I drew people to me because I cared about them, I was driving them away. I became the epitome of narcissism and selfishness. I took advantage of a lot of people including my loved ones. There is no physical or even emotional pain or guilt associated with a demented state as a warning signal. When I started to recover from the demented state again about eight months after I got to the Adams County Jail, I appreciated pain because of its warning signals. I also hated myself and the state that I was in. I used to ask myself why didn't I know what was happening to me? How did it happen? How could I have avoided it? The best answer that I could come up with was overwhelming stress and the lack of ability to deal with stress by myself especially without God in my life. I became very irritable, intolerant and inpatient with myself and others. I would drive others away. I just wanted to punish myself for the bad and negligent person that I became. I still have some of those feelings especially guilt when I become frustrated or overly stressed. I couldn't accept myself and the wrong I had done and the people that I hurt. At times I regretted my recovery from the demented state and having to face and deal with reality. At the time I didn't know for sure I could only imagine all those I had hurt and the wrong I had done.

When I was released from prison and had to hear the actual facts of my selfish wrongdoings, once again I wanted again to end my life. I could only think when I would hear of the incidents, I couldn't have done that but ultimately I had to face and accept the fact that I did do those wrongs. It seemed that there was no end to the amount of guilt that I felt and would have to deal with even today. I used to wonder what negative opinions others had of me, especially my loved ones. How could anyone love or even accept someone like me and the ugly person that I was and what I had done? You can't expect others to understand your disease when you can't understand it. Society as a whole doesn't understand it. As stated, most of the mental health professionals that I encountered in the penal system were mostly ignorant about pseudo dementia. Most never heard of it. At one time when I was a motivator of people, I became a demotivator. That is so hard to accept for a person who most of his life suffered from a self-image or self-esteem problem. I would think about my suicide attempt at age 56 and regret that it was only an attempt and that I didn't succeed in killing myself, but it wasn't meant to be. I couldn't and wouldn't forgive myself therefore I couldn't expect anyone else to forgive me which only made things worse.

My best guess is that my retardation in some areas of my brain started about seven years of age mostly from verbal, sexual abuse and being so restricted in normal childhood activities. I dealt with bad events by just trying to eliminate them from my mind but what I didn't realize I was suppressing them instead of dealing with them. That led to depression. I was just never good enough and yearned for acceptance and recognition. As stated earlier in my early teenage years I learned that I could buy recognition and acceptance by earning money and doing good deeds for others. It is hard to rationalize without a memory.

Again, let me state I don't want anyone to feel sorry for me or to pity me. What I would like is just for them to understand me and know that the wrong that I did during that demented state wasn't the real me or who I wanted to be. I will try to understand if they can't forgive me the wrong that I did and the hurt that I caused. I find it very difficult to forgive myself especially for not being mentally present for my children, loved ones and associates. But now I realize that I have to forgive myself if I'm going to live a successful life again. I'm starting to tell myself that I have been punished enough no matter how others may judge me. Forgiveness has to start from within me.

Please allow me to close this section by stating to the loved ones of people who are inflicted with dementia. When your loved one's behavior becomes unacceptable or ugly as mind did it is the disease and not them. They may become abusive towards you and others. Towards the end they can even become violent. It is the time for unconditional love and understanding on your part. Again, it is the disease and not your loved one!

CHAPTER 10
My Mental Health Background

The psychiatric professionals claim that one very traumatic event or emotional shock can cause brain damage and brain dysfunction. An injury to the brain can have exponential consequences on the brain and its functioning. It is known as the butterfly effect. We hear how amazingly powerful the brain is, but we rarely hear is how fragile the brain is. It is a jello like mass of only about two pounds not what you would consider very sturdy or strong. During my incarceration I was knocked unconscious at least four times that I can remember. That had to have a very negative effect on my brain. When you think about it the brain is so fragile that is why our Creator encased it in a skull. It is the most important and vital organ in the body. The human brain only differs from an ape's brain by one percent, so it is easy to see how easy it is to cause brain damage, dysfunction, or distortion. Our brains differ from an animal's brain in that we have a frontal lobe and any damage to it can have a dramatic and devastating effect on our lives. As will be stated during an assault at the Adams County Jail I received damage to the frontal lobe of my brain when I was thrown against the concrete wall and my head was pushed into the concrete floor. You will also read there were several other assaults which can affect the brain.

It is my belief that mental health disorders don't have their basis in character flaws or personal weaknesses. When it comes to mental health diseases even though they are so prevalent in society you may as well be labeled as a leper than to have that stigma. In my case I suffer from four major ones which increases the size of the stigma. When you add to that of being a prisoner or an ex-prisoner it just adds to that stigma exponentially. You are also shunned by society because of a suicide attempt. Society ignores the fact that in spite of my mental health disorders I overcame their negative side effects and went on to be successful in many ways. The justice system overlooks the good that I did in my life. I have to admit that I am also very critical of myself as was the justice system.

It is a proven fact that parts of the brain's functioning such as memory starts to decline at age 50 if not sooner. Please excuse my redundancy but I estimate and try to recall from discussions with friends and loved ones that my mental decline started at age seven or eight when I was continually and tragically raped. The decline escalated while in military service in my early 20s, and it escalated at my first divorce at age 38 because of guilt. I blamed myself for that divorce since it was caused by me having an extramarital affair. My decline escalated at my second divorce and a suicide attempt at age 56 which was a large manifestation of the deterioration of my mental health. It escalated again when I lost my company and was destitute at age 62. It took over a quarter of a century to build that company. I fell into a vegetative and animalistic state at age 66 when I was incarcerated and remained that way until age 69 when I finally started to regain some level of normal cognizance level of which I still am still recovering. I think that I'm back to a normal level of cognizance, but I thought that three years ago when I was released from prison. As I look back especially through my writings, I have to admit that I wasn't normal.

I understand from my notes and from my mother during training either basic or technical to be a medic in the U.S. Air Force I was inadvertently sprayed with nerve gas. I also understand that can lead to demented behavior or actual dementia in later life. There is no mention of it in my military records, but I sure manifested all the signs of it. Some long-term effects of nerve gas don't show up until later in life which is termed "Silent Toxicity." After my exposure to nerve gas, I suffered from memory loss and PTSD symptoms. It made me more vulnerable to health disorders especially mental health disorders.

While serving in the Air Force at the age of 21 years I was involved in an automobile accident. The accident occurred because another airman ran out in front of a vehicle and my car struck him. I was driving to the hospital where I worked. The authorities determined that the man committed suicide. But I still felt that I did something wrong even though I didn't. As I said I'm very critical of myself. The accident was thoroughly investigated because the airman and I both had security clearances to enter the headquarters building of the Strategic Air Command Headquarters Building where the war room is located. It is where they can initiate an attack especially nuclear attack.

Because of the traumatic effect that the accident had on me, killing another human being, I was hospitalized and received psychotherapy. At the time I was diagnosed with acute anxiety. It was very traumatic for me because I'm a nonviolent and gentle person. I was also diagnosed with PTSD which is considered an anxiety condition. After the accident I became depressed and very reclusive in my behavior. I believe that at this time the deterioration of my cognitive ability and memory started to increase again from my childhood trauma. I found it very difficult to concentrate on my studies at the University of Nebraska which I attended in the evenings and weekends. I believe I was an average student, but I had to struggle to be just average because of my deficient memory and difficulty in concentrating.

After a year I reverted to the typical John Walshe conduct and attitude of I can handle it. I just suppressed my feelings which is dangerous, and I moved on with my life as I did as a child. I just automatically block out the memories of my negative experiences especially if they are very painful experiences so I can get on with my life and not feel sorry for myself. I don't know if I ever adequately dealt with the sexual abuse as a child. Memories of it hounded me when I was put in solitary confinement in prison. I don't react well too much stress and will disassociate.

After attending psychotherapy in the Air Force at the age of 21, I sought psychotherapy at the age of 39 during my second marriage. I sought professional help but that was mostly for mood swings through two psychiatrists, a Dr. Oppegard and a Dr. Oliver and a psychologist, a Dr. Richmond. I didn't hesitate to find a solution to what others had seen in me as manifested in my conduct of mood swings. I voluntarily submitted to three inpatient mental hospital stays for bi-polar disease at Boulder Community Hospital, Centennial Peaks Hospital in Louisville, Colorado, and at the world-renowned Menninger Clinic in Kansas. I was disappointed in those inpatient stays and prescribed medications because I didn't demonstrate any improvement in my moods and mood swings. I also had an involuntary stay at the mental health hospital in Greeley, Colorado, because of my suicide attempt. I was very attentive and not timid about my mental health diseases while I was cognizant of them. As stated earlier for twenty-seven years I was treated for bi-polar disease through medication, weekly therapy and inpatient stays from which as stated I never sensed much improvement. Now, the mental health professionals attached to the Veterans Administration tell me that I'm not bi-polar. I endured a lot of hurt and pain over the years from being misdiagnosed which is very common with bi-polar disease. It was no one's fault it is just the nature of bipolar disease being so hard to accurately diagnose. The Veteran's Administration has diagnosed me with acute anxiety, major depression, panic attacks, disassociative disorder and post-traumatic stress syndrome. Most of those disorders has its origins in my military service and other traumatic events in my history. I believe without a question my mental health disorders were exacerbated during my incarceration.

I was a very devoted family man that when the dysfunction in my personal life escalated so did my mental health disorders especially depression. At the time of my divorce from Rebecca I went to bed with a bottle of pills and wine to commit suicide. I understand that I called my sister in New York to say goodbye and she notified the proper authorities. I barely remember waking up in a mental health hospital in Greeley, CO, and seeing my brother standing by me. That is all I can remember about my attempted suicide. I wasn't cognizant of it. I don't believe or recall that the suicide attempt was planned. I believe that is was spontaneous as so many are. I don't know where I got the pills since I never used alcohol or drugs. There was alcohol in the house for guest use. That attempt should have been a very big warning for me to get into therapy. I didn't have a lot of confidence in psychotherapy or medications since I didn't sense any improvement in my mood and mood swings when I was misdiagnosed with bi-polar disease for so many years. That was seventy percent of my adult life.

I believe that the demented symptoms were due to severe major depression or as termed pseudo dementia. I attribute my increase in anxiety to my incarceration for 7½ years of incarceration at eight different institutions. I definitely attribute my increased panic attacks, angina pectoris attacks, grand mal seizures and escalated PTSD to my incarceration. Mental and physical aging don't necessarily coincide. Dementia is not necessarily synonymous with aging and occurs over a long period of time. I define it as the brain aging just like other organs of the body. I also believe that the brain is made up of many mini brains and dysfunction in one area doesn't reflect on other so-called mini brains. Even though I couldn't remember I could creatively write. I took piles of notes as to what was happening to me because of my deficient memory. As an example, I believe my cognitive ability is returning to normal, but I still don't have any sense of smell and neither do I have any memories of 25 years of age 47 to 72 years. But I have been able to form and establish new memories which I couldn't for a third of my lifetime. I am so grateful that I can establish new memories. It is hard to explain what it is like to be a mental invalid without the ability to remember or be cognizant. As stated before, it is like being a vegetable. You are in no man's land no wonder the ancient Greeks associated it with death. You might as well be dead when you are not cognizant of your surroundings.

It didn't occur on me as it should have that my divorce in 2001 had taken such a toll on me that I attempted suicide. Psychologists claim that you have a 1,200 percent chance of something very negative happening to you because of a divorce. It took a tremendous toll on my being. I was down and out but I got up and tried starting over again to be a productive citizen, father, and grandfather once more.

Because of the abuse I endured in prison I have panic attacks where I have to keep from striking myself. I believe that panic attacks are based on unresolved guilt where I want to punish myself for the wrong that I may have done. I will address that in a later chapter. I believe the guilt judgments and feelings built up over the years. I lacked good self-esteem because I was too critical of myself. I'm now after being out of prison for more three years starting to get my panic attacks under control. It took a lot of self-examination and psychotherapy which I'm now able to do to exert better self-control. I couldn't establish enough self-control or volition ability in a very negative, hostile and high anxiety environment. That is just part of being incarcerated in the maximum-security unit of a maximum-security prison where you are subject to abuse. It just compounded my anxiety disorder. At the time I wasn't cognizant of how stressful that was. Now I believe that uncontrolled stress is a real murderer. Living in a maximum-security unit it takes a tremendous toll on your being.

CHAPTER 11

Federal Court Rulings "At Risk"

By Federal Court rulings because of my age, psychological and physical profile I'm considered "At Risk." It means that because of my fragile state I'm very vulnerable to harm and hurt resulting in pain and suffering well beyond the norm. The law is clear and persuasive according to good humanitarian values that to cause pain, suffering and distress or hostile feelings in a person who is considered "At Risk" is synonymous with physically assaulting them.

An assault is an attack which can be physical, verbal, emotional, spiritual, neurological or simply sensory in nature if it causes some type of pain or great discomfort in a person. This is especially true for the elderly because they experience painful feelings more intensely than the young or middle age. Actions and stimulus to a painful, hurtful and damaging level in the elderly occurs much faster and frequently than younger people. Assaults against people "At Risk" are considered "Hate Crimes." Again, please let me state that it can be sensory in its nature and does not have to be just physical or verbal in nature and still cause great pain distress and suffering. Consider how a person feels when they lose a beloved to death particularly a child or a very close lover. It has driven many people to suicide.

As inferred an elderly person's neurological, circulatory and other systems experience sensory overload faster than the young's. It can easily cause or intensify diseases such as dementia, dissociative amnesia, major depression and acute anxiety as I am a manifestation of. You are then more sensitive to sensory overload. Presently because of my heart attacks, strokes and abuse I am very prone to panic, and angina pectoris attacks. I realized the validity of this on a daily basis through pain and suffering in the prison environment where my PTSD was escalated.

We readily recognize our human limitations of age in the world of professional sports, but we don't readily recognize our psychological limitations due to age. We are starting to with the increased prevalence of dementia and its primary form Alzheimer's disease increasing as the populace ages. We now realize that diseases such as the different forms of dementia are not necessarily synonymous with old age. They are like heart attacks in that they can afflict the young.

Please keep in mind as you read this document that the courts have ruled that prison officials can also be found to be deliberately indifferent if they fail to protect prisoners who are obvious victims or have been identified as "At Risk". This is true if a prisoner is identified as "At Risk" if they are a placed in danger from others who are known to be aggressive and violent.

While incarcerated I was literally a defenseless old man, yet I was terribly and inhumanely abused by law enforcement and some by inmates beyond comprehension. Instead of my weaknesses being recognized as being brought on by age and being respected as enduring societies have done through the ages, I had to endure the tortures of fourteen violent assaults, several life threats, at least ten very hostile acts. I also had to endure numerous threats of beatings in a very hostile environment filled with animosity and violence.

Most of my fellow inmates had histories of violence and were very prone to it. I lived in a state of fear which escalated into terror. It resulted in me suffering three heart attacks, two strokes, I had heart surgery, and developed two triple A aorta aneurysms. My heart is so weak that a defibrillator was implanted in my chest. But due to my strong faith and beliefs I am functioning at a normal state.

I define for this writing a hostile act as being traumatic in nature in its effect physically or psychologically but not necessarily violent in nature. Words and acts can have as much effect as punches, physical strikes, etc. An example of a hostile act that I endured is when I had a seizure instead of being properly diagnosed and receiving if necessary medical care I was placed in solitary confinement. At times when my cellmates would call for medical care for me when I was having a seizure they were ignored.

For the penal system to cause pain and suffering in an inmate without penological justification is well beyond the judgement of the court and is definitely wrong. It is considered "Cruel and Unusual Punishment" and is in violation of an inmate's Eighth Amendment Rights of the U.S. Constitution. The penal system can only inflict reasonable and humane punishment which is limited with those who are considered "At Risk." Never mind the fact that I'm considered 80% disabled due to my military service to my country seventy percent of which is due to mental health disorders.

To say the least for a man of my age or any age with my mental and physical profile to be abused it is absolutely wrong. I was exposed to excessive risk especially for being considered by the law as "At risk." Today I can't even watch fictional violence in a movie or the news because I suffer from Post-Traumatic Stress Syndrome which its intensity was elevated in jail and prison. When I see a fight even if it is fictional, I'm a victim to it in my mind. Trying to recover from an attack in prison is extremely difficult because of the stressful atmosphere. You need adequate time and rest to recover, but that opportunity just doesn't exist in prison or jail. An attack mandates an automatic refractory period. Before you can fully or even partially recover from an attack you have another one. This is because the hostile, antagonistic and violent atmosphere makes you very susceptible or vulnerable to more of them. My diseases and disorders such acute anxiety or depression lowered my immunity and increased my vulnerability to attacks. Those who perpetrated the assaults and attacks and those who condoned them will have plenty of excuses.

While incarcerated for almost three years I fell into a vegetative state and suffered from major dehydration which drastically affects the brain's functioning since the brain is a jello type mass that is eighty percent water. Two of my diseases which cause memory loss and impaired judgment the ancients Greeks associated with death, but tragically no jury heard that I had any of them. Dissociative amnesia wasn't diagnosed until after my first two trials, but it robbed me of the memories of 25 years of my life or half of my adult life roughly from 47 years of age until 72 years of age. I believe that two strokes robbed me of a lot of the vital memories from childhood until age 47 years. Those diseases took years for me to develop as my psychiatric and personal history indicates. They didn't pop up overnight.

CHAPTER 12

Noise Pollution and Hyperacusis

Hyperacusis is defined as an intolerance for everyday noise that can cause significant distress. People such as myself who suffer from PTSD and those who are subject to the negative effects of prolong loud noise are very susceptible to panic attacks from the noise. The World Health Organization considers prolonged exposure to loud noise as one of the worst environmental stressors to humans. It causes hearing loss, insomnia, it increases heart rates and blood pressure which lead to heart attacks and strokes.

We hear a lot about the environment in jails and prison but not how noisy they are. Noise is most commonly defined as a sound that lacks agreeable quality and can be very unpleasant and damaging to the senses. The noise levels can be very painful especially for the elderly because their neurotransmitters are more sensitive to it. Let me state again it is a proven fact that excess noise can cause heart disease and exacerbate the contributing diseases such as high blood pressure. Without a question noise places a hardship on the brain and nervous system especially of the elderly. Let me please emphasize that loud noise has a very noxious effect on my life.

In jails and prisons the buildings are made up of concrete and steel so there are no acoustics to absorb or diminish the noise. They are like thunder domes. The noise is amplified as it reverberates off the ceilings, floors, walls and fixtures. The doors and their encasings are made up of steel and when they are opened or closed it makes a noise like a hammer hitting steel. The toilets that are in the cells are usually made of steel and are at least twice as noisy as conventional toilets. Because the toilets are located in such a small cell with no acoustics when they are flushed it is like a gunfire in the cell. The noise from a flushed toilet causes you to cringe to tolerate it. When you have to flush it tends to aggravate your cell mate which you don't want to do in a maximum-security unit if you value your life.

Some inmates would punish you by continually flushing the toilet which as stated makes the sound like a firecracker or gun going off continually in that small and confining unit the size of a bathroom. One flush would serve to startle you and multiple flushes would torment you. My limited vocabulary doesn't allow me to adequately describe how tortuous multiple flushes of the cell toilet can be on your nervous system. It's akin to being located on a battlefield with guns blasting away.

It seemed to me that the public address systems are much louder than conventional P.A. systems because of the prison environment. Each announcement is like a physical assault to my person because of my handicaps. Some guards yell when making announcements out loud to harass the inmates which it causes you to be startled especially when it is unexpected. As stated, some of the guards enjoy slamming the cell doors and the slots in them to get their kicks or just harass. In the elderly it is like being shocked with a live electrical cord. It can cause heart palpitations and tachycardia. My heart would pound so hard that it felt like it's going to explode out of my chest cavity. It is triggered by an automatic response that there is little that I could do to control it.

The noise levels of the pod, the day rooms and the cells mimic that of a heavy metal rock concert. At a rock concert may be enjoyable but the longer you are at one the more taxing it is on your nervous systems. Imagine being at that concert continually for sixteen hours a day after day, week after week, etc. etc., which is the waking hours in prison pod. I was so sensitive to noise after a brain injury that I could not spend any time in the dayroom. I would restrict myself to my cell.

The Russians and Bulgarians found in their research on learning after the Second World War they found that certain types of noises can have a negative effect on life. When they played symphony baroque type music to plants the plants grew faster. It also enhanced learning in people. When they played very loud rock type music to plants the plants died. Normal conversational tone is sixty decibels and seventy plus decibel levels have the tendency to arouse. Decibel levels of 140 plus will cause brain and hearing damage. Some societies have used loud noise as torture. Acceptable decibel levels apply to the average age person of what could be considered of normal mental health not a person with mental health disorders. This is especially true for the elderly and people who have circulatory system disorders which impede good blood flow which is critical for hearing.

The prisoners are allowed to play music as loud as they pleased. There is no attempt to control the music blasting out of the cells especially pounding type of music which is taxing on the nervous system. Sudden or continual noise can and does causes me to have panic and angina attacks. The guards refuse to do anything to control the noise. The guards complain that the inmates refuse to listen to them. The inmates see playing loud music as a freedom and their lives while incarcerated lack so many freedoms. If you dare to complain about the loud music, I can guarantee you that you won't complain again. If you complain the prisoners will taunt and torment you by getting physically close to you and hollering or making loud noises very close to your ears. Inmates are not known to be very compassionate and love any chance to ridicule you. The environment creates fear of ever-present nervous system or brain damage which as stated creates the number one cause of death too much stress. After spending the last three years overcoming my major health disorders caused by too much stress and the fact that I was able to overcome them, I never doubt the damage stress can do to the mind and body.

It has been proven that as a person at the age of forty their eyesight weakens the same is true for being capable of doing two things at once at age fifty plus years. This also applies for a person of fifty plus years being able to hear and decipher two or more voices at one time. To hear multiple voices depletes their ability to understand what is being said and too much exposure can arouse them. It causes chaos in the mind. Ask an elderly person and they will tell you that it is very tiring and taxing on their nervous system to hear multiple voices at one time such as discussions where people interrupt each other or arguments. There are plenty of arguments in prison. Listen to news media discussions when the participants interrupt each other, and you will get a sample of what I'm purporting.

A pod is made up of forty-eight two-man cells or about a hundred inmates. In my estimation the noise level exceeds the maximum allowable decibel level. It even has a very negative effect of the nervous systems of the guards for just an eight-hour shift. The guards tell me that it takes at least an hour to 1½ hours for their nervous systems to calm down after an eight-hour shift. They are young to middle-aged people. Prisoners become tumultuous from being confined in such a noisy environment. If they are confined too long once they are released from their cells, they are so prone to violence and a fight is likely to start. The prisoner become very boisterous confined in a cage like environment. Also, prisoners because of the environment are prone to anxiety attacks. When that happens, it diminishes their volition ability, will power or self-control beyond normal level and all hell will break loose. Again, let me state the anxiety attacks can be more frequent because there is no mandatory refractory or recovery period between them. Once you have one in prison you are very susceptible to have another.

Another reason an elderly person is less tolerant of the noise because of the hairs on the cochlea which is in the inner portion of the ear. Those hairs filter noise and play a critical role in hearing. The hairs deteriorate with age and are not replaced or rejuvenated. Over time or extended exposure, the hairs are worn down. This is true for the young or old from continual exposure to loud or irritating noise. The eardrum then remains very vulnerable to sounds too loud or that last too long such as very loud music. Those sounds weaken or kill the sensitive hair cells on the cochlea especially in the elderly.

Consequently because of the weakened cochlea the noise has a more taxing effect on the elderly's hearing and nervous system. Overexposure to the noise levels can cause panic and angina attacks in a person especially the elderly. When I have one of those attacks, I will spend the next three hours trying to get over the crushing pain and tightness in my chest. By the end of a sixteen-hour day of being exposed to the noise it feels like you are going to have a nervous breakdown. Your cellmate could have a psychiatric condition which so many do. They continue to holler and moan throughout the night. Many just toss again and again throughout the night which inhibits healing sleep which is so essential in a negative environment.

The brain needs to rejuvenate itself and it does that through rest, sleep, and meditation. It needs a quiet and sedate atmosphere. The noise level in the penal environment creates fear of ever-present nervous system and brain damage. It contributes to circulatory system diseases. Excessive stress from excessive noise leads to depression which leads to dementia and exacerbates it. Again, it also drastically increases your vulnerability to panic attacks and in my case angina pectoris attacks or both. Their intensity has made me more susceptible to heart attacks and strokes. It is frightening! You are always on edge which is dangerous. Please keep in mind that outside of prison we use noise to alarm us of danger. Even nature uses loud thunder to alarm us of the dangerous lightning from storms.

I used to try to avoid places and people where loud noises and people with very loud voices are likely to be present. I had to be constantly on alert whenever I was out of my cell and tried to avoid noisy places and people. It wasn't possible for me to spend any time in the dayroom to play games or socialize with the other inmates. Consequently, I had to be very reclusive which is not recommended for a person who is prone to depression. You don't want to use one of the pay phones in the dayrooms because of the background noise. You can't hear the party you are calling, and they are asking you what is all that noise.

Consider how absurd it is to live in fear of a loud especially sudden noise. I still try to avoid people and places where there are loud noises especially loud voices. Recently I had to leave a store because a person's voice was too loud. I'm sorry but I couldn't tolerate it. For the first couple of years after I left prison even if someone in my presence coughed or sneezed loudly, I would have to flee the scene because it would trigger a panic attack. People would become alarmed around me.

The fear/terror response can be so intense as to cause permanent brain chemistry imbalance and brain tissue damage like a stroke. The Courts have ruled a prisoner must be provided with shelter which does not cause his degeneration or threaten his mental and physical wellbeing. The Courts have ruled that excessive noise "inflicts pain without penological justification" and violates the Eighth Amendment to the U.S. Constitution.

The noise is more taxing and painful when you realize that there is no productive justification for it or if it can be controlled and isn't. Recently when I watched a documentary on National Geographic, Rick Raemisch the former Director of Corrections for the State of Colorado remarked that he was alarmed by how noisy prisons were when he subjected himself to be incarcerated to learn what it was like. Prisons are designed for the young and healthy not the elderly or mentally ill. I learned firsthand that prison staff are not trained to be sensitive to elderly or mental health issues. Even the average person outside or prison has little appreciation for stressors that effect the elderly. Listen to some commercials on TV where the actors yell to gain your attention and you will see what I mean. Instead of gaining your attention they become repulsive. To most prison staffs the elderly are just an annoyance that have to be tolerated.

Please allow me to close this section about noise with a couple of quotes from Mother Teresa of Calcutta, the Roman Catholic Nun who was awarded the Nobel Peace Prize: "We need to find God, and He cannot be found in noise and restlessness. God is the friend of Silence. See how nature – trees, flowers, grass – grows in silence; see the stars, the moon and the sun, how they move in silence." Keep in mind what the Russians found about plant growth with rock type music. If we want to touch people on a spiritual level keep this quote in mind: "We need silence to be able to touch Souls."

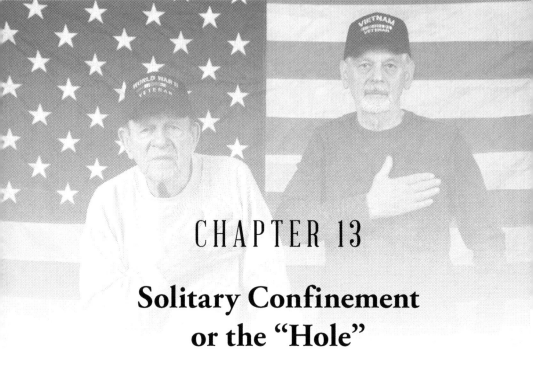

CHAPTER 13

Solitary Confinement or the "Hole"

W e send people to prison as punishment for crimes committed. No matter what anyone in the penal system claims otherwise especially in Colorado solitary confinement is a way to further punish those who are already being punished through incarceration and loss of contact with loved ones. You might term it as some psychiatric professionals do "double punishment". To say the least solitary confinement is a traumatic experience. According to Dr. Craig Haney a social psychologist at the University of California who is noted for his work among other things "prisoner isolation" solitary confinement is a "psychological toxic environment".

Colorado has held itself out as a role model for reforming the use of solitary confinement. In the Colorado Department of Corrections, the mentally ill are not to be confined to solitary confinement. It has been proven that solitary confinement exacerbates mental health disorders. In Colorado an inmate is not to be housed for over fifteen days in solitary confinement and while there they can be confined for twenty-three hours a day with a one- hour break. The United Nations Standard Minimum Rules for treatment of prisoners known as the Mandella Rules, named in honor of the former president of South Africa Nelson Mandella, states that keeping a prisoner in solitary confinement for over fifteen days is torturous. Nelson Mandella knew firsthand because he spent twenty-seven years in prison. In two Colorado prisons solitary confinement has been banned. It is to be used for prisoners who are dangerous to others or themselves. It is a very lonely and abusive existence especially for the mentally ill. As stated earlier I was diagnosed at Sterling Prison and the Regional Detention Center by a psychologist and confirmed by a neurologist with four major psychiatric disorders namely major depression, acute anxiety, disassociative amnesia and bi-polar disease.

At the Adams County Jail, I was diagnosed with pseudo dementia. In spite of that fact, I was housed in solitary confinement at the Department of Correction and the Adams County Jail eleven times. Later in this book I will describe the reasons I was placed in solitary confinement. At three Colorado prisons namely Sterling, Centennial and the Regional Detention Center I was housed in solitary confinement for over fifteen days. It has been found that the suicide rate in solitary confinement is fourteen times higher than confinement in the general population. I had been diagnosed with suicide ideation. While incarcerated in solitary confinement I was a man of 140 pounds 5'9" tall who had suffered from two heart attacks, two strokes, had heart surgery, a heart function of a mere twenty-six percent of normal. I also suffered from four other major circulatory system disorders. I didn't possess the physical strength to what you might consider much of a danger to my fellow man especially when my guts were hanging out of my groin like large banana. I wasn't what you would consider a "macho man". I was convicted of a white-collar crimes. As stated in other chapters of this book while in solitary confinement I was sprayed with chemicals right over where I had skin cancer, a guard ground his knuckle into my sternum where I had heart surgery, where an aorta is completely blocked and where that circulatory system function is dead. It is hard for me to describe how traumatic and terrorizing it is as a senile old man to be laying on the prison floor in solitary confinement suffering from an angina pectoris attack and have three guards attack you wearing helmets and bearing shields. As stated, one of those guards ground his or her knuckles into my chest, to say the least it is horrifying I hollered out from the excruciating pain. Until my dying days I will never forget it.

I spent my first three weeks at the Department of Corrections at the Regional Detention Center in solitary for a reason unknown to me at the time. Solitary confinement or the "Hole" as it is commonly called is actually a prison in a prison. The cell in which an inmate is confined is smaller than a normal household bathroom. It is well known that an abuser's number one tool is isolation. We exist in an interdependent world and our Creator did not mean for us to exist in isolation. There was no consideration given to my mental and physical condition. Some U.S. Courts have ruled that housing mentally ill prisoners under conditions of isolation is unconstitutional. There is ample support for the idea that placing mentally ill inmates in punitive segregation can constitute cruel and unusual punishment. At a very minimum inmates suffering from a mental illness must be screened by qualified mental health staff before they are placed in segregation. If they are segregated, they are entitled to adequate access to mental health care. My medical records will substantiate that this was never done in any of my eleven stays in the "Hole."

Segregation in particular constitutes cruel and unusual punishment for me because I'm over 70 years of age and I'm considered "At Risk". Let me state again I'm considered by Federal Court rulings to be considered "At Risk." Please allow me to state again I'm also considered to be eighty percent disabled by the U.S. Veterans Administration most of which is due to mental illnesses. Again, the courts have ruled that persons who are psychiatrically vulnerable to the effects of isolation must be excluded from it. It has been proven that prolonged idleness is very harmful for a person who suffers from dementia, acute anxiety or circulatory system diseases. The COVID nineteen Pandemic has demonstrated the very negative effects of isolation on the public. Anxiety, depression and suicide rates are increasing at dramatic rates even among children because of lack of human interaction. In my case nothing was as beneficial to control the negative symptoms of my diseases especially cardiovascular disease as just to be able to walk in the yard at least thirty minutes per day. I was denied that in segregation.

Please keep in mind that I wasn't prescribed, nor did I take any psychotropic drugs. The psychiatrists at the Veterans Administration had prescribed for me three psychotropic drugs but now I'm down to one. Walking served as my medication and my therapy since I didn't receive any psychotherapy. Because of the size of my hernias especially the inguinal hernia they inhibited from doing much exercise in my cells such as pushups or sit-ups. You can't exercise with your large intestine hanging out of you. Nothing was as beneficial to me as walking when I had an angina pectoris attack even though walking was painful for me. The Adams County Jail and the Colorado Department of Corrections officials chose to ignore those Federal Court rulings and placed me into what is termed the "Hole" at their discretion even though may I state again, crimes against my person are considered "Hate Crimes." They acted as if they were immune to having adhere to or obey Federal Court Rulings. They acted like they were above or the law or the law didn't apply to them or their actions. The guards' arrogance towards the law or even common sense was unbelievable. They acted in a way that was convenient to them instead of what was lawful.

At one time when I pleaded for medical care while in solitary because my intestine was strangulating, I was given two more weeks in the "Hole" after being there for 30 days. At that same time, I had to lay in my own urine for days because it was too painful for me to lift myself up to use the toilet. When I cried out in pain for medical care the guards told me that they couldn't take me to the medical clinic because I couldn't crawl to the cell door to be cuffed up. I remember trying to clutch the cell floor to endure the pain from inguinal hernia and feeling the dirt and grime on the floor. I said to myself John you can't get any lower in life than this. When a person lies in their own urine the urine turns to ammonia especially in the genital area and eats away at the skin especially for the elderly whose epidermis is much thinner than a younger man's outer skin layer. Once again let me state that the guard's solution to my pain and suffering was two more weeks in the "Hole".

For emphasis I will state over the course of approximately my last forty months of incarceration I was placed in solitary confinement eleven times. I will admit that the last time it was voluntary for my own protection when my life was threatened by a gang. Usually in solitary confinement an inmate is locked down in a cell for twenty-three hours a day. During my stays I was locked down twenty-four hours a day without a break. Again, let me state it has been proven that solitary confinement exacerbates the negative effects of psychiatric conditions and physical conditions especially cardiac disorders. Let me state again the seriousness of my heart disease that I now have a defibrillator and pacemaker implanted in my chest. It makes it very difficult for me to assimilate into the prison conditions. I can understand one or two indiscretions but eleven? They knew of my psychiatric disorders and heart disease at the Adams County Jail and the Colorado Department of Corrections. What were they trying to do? One Sunday night I was watching a National Geographic documentary called Solitary Confinement as stated they held out Colorado as a role model for having reformed the use of solitary confinement. What I described in this chapter happened after the so-termed reforms. I can only assume that they forgot to tell the penal staff about the reforms, or they are being hypocritical. What I state is an example of how society and our culture treat an elderly man and a disabled veteran in America. Being indiscriminately thrown in the "Hole" is a manifestation in our society elderly lives become very cheap when they are no longer of use like a worn-out machine. But I would like to believe that "elderly lives matter too" because they do! As stated, during the pandemic they were putting placing covid patients in the "Hole" to languish and die in isolation.

CHAPTER 14

Being Incarcerated

It has been proven that stress is the number one cause of death especially in the U.S. It has also been proven that environment in the prison is the most stressful of all the environments for the human being. This is because the prisoner has very little control over what happens to him and her in the prison or jail. It is a very hostile and dangerous place especially in the maximum-security unit of a maximum-security prison. Many prisoners especially those in maximum-security prisons and lodged in the maximum-security sections of those prisons have a history of violence and can be extremely violent. Gang members can gain recognition and rank in the gain by committing very violent acts. It seems that repercussions from prison staff doesn't mean as much to gang members as acceptance in the gang. While incarcerated you have no control of events, who you are housed with or where you are housed. The only control you have over your environment is how you will react to it and that is governed by your physical, mental and especially your spiritual health. In some cases, the more violent gang members are and willing to be violent for the gang the more status and rank they gain in the gang. Being housed in a very closed and small environment, 8'x10' and less than fifty square feet when you allow for the sinks, bunks, desks, toilets and other utilities, which must be shared by two people is painful. Imagine being housed in a room the size of a traditional home bathroom with another person especially a serial killer as much as twenty-four hours a day, day after day. You learn and practice good human relations skills or you die. Therefore, the prisoners become very anxious and are prone to yell and holler to fellow prisoners from cell to cell especially if they use drugs in order to communicate. When out of their cells they yell across open spaces instead of moving up to the person to talk in normal voice tones of sixty decibels. Prisoners are not known for good etiquette. It is like being at a professional sporting event for sixteen hours a day with all the hooting, hollering and yelling. It frightens me because the professionals tell me that I have a five-hundred percent chance of falling back into that demented state that I was in for almost three years if I'm exposed to a very stressful atmosphere. If you are in danger you must rely on the deputies and guards for assistance and their desire if any desire to help you. There is no privacy, and it is humiliating to urinate and defecate in front of another human. I was housed with rapists, murderers, serial killers, major drug dealers and users, etc. As stated, you are always on edge because you had to be aware of that some of these prisoners are capable of some savage and very brutal acts. You dare not do something to provoke or antagonize your cell mate in any way even inadvertently without being conscious of how your actions can cause them to become very hostile. I was assaulted by an inmate for very innocently shaking a small package of sugar for a cup of coffee which are common in cafes. The man got so mad that he threatened to kill me. He was incarcerated for murder. A cell mate threatened to kill me when I objected to him doing drugs in my presence. God help you if you were housed with an inmate who was going through drug withdrawals. If your cellmate became sick you could count on becoming so. Consider what is happening in jails and prisons because of the corona virus. It has the highest infection rate per capita of all environments. Sterling Prison was sued successfully by ACLU for treatment of the prisoners with the corona virus. As stated, many of the prisoners with virus were placed in solitary confinement until they died. How can you properly treat a prisoner with corona virus in solitary confinement? It is a manifestation how cheap your life is in prison. Let's admit it who cares about prisoners lodged in maximum security even their close relatives only their mothers seem to continue to care. Abandonment is so common in prison especially among the elderly ones.

Being incarcerated is more taxing and consequently painful for the elderly than the young or middle age. As stated, before I will define elderly as 65 years of age or more. Elderly brains and neurological systems very easily experience sensory overload and the longer that they are incarcerated the more sensitive they become too negative factors in the environment such as noise, animosity and hostility. In addition to what I wrote earlier about noise, excessive noise especially for the elderly interferes with the functions of the temporal lobe of the brain where the limbic system is located. The limbic system controls memory functions in particular the formation of new memories. It controls emotions, some behaviors and learning. The temporal lobe in the elderly usually has shrunken due to age from twenty to twenty-five percent which drastically affects your memory. Prison life escalates that deterioration. A year in prison for the average person is more like at least two or more years for the elderly because of their limitations due to age.

If you have dementia or are in the early stages of it, you become even more vulnerable to the negative effects of it in prison. It is natural that all of our vital human organs are negatively affected by age. It has been proven that the penal environment intensifies the symptoms of psychiatric disorders.

Some deputies and I will admit it was a minority saw their duty not only to contain and monitor but to punish. Morale among the guards is poor and this is expressed in animosity towards the inmates. Some of the guards would act like military drill instructors by getting right in your face and yelling at you. I suppose it enhances their masculinity. There is a reason that there is an age limit for basic training or boot camps in the military. As stated, some of the guards would slam the door or the slots in the doors as a means to punish the inmates. Hit a steel door with a hammer and that is what slamming cell doors sounds like in a concrete and steel cell. Other guards would like to punish by causing a lot of upheaval when searching the cells. Some didn't like having to search cells so they would make the inmates pay the price for it through these subtle types of abuse such as throwing your possessions on the floor that left no marks or scars on the inmate. Once I realize how deficient my memory was, I started taking numerous notes. Some of the guards resented my note taking and were suspicious of it, so after a cell search many of my notes and legal papers were missing. Some guards just enjoyed harassing inmates as if it was a sport or game because they knew the inmates' complaints would be ignored but it was a great way to satisfy their egos. At times I would observe some guards during lockdowns spitting on an inmate's food tray before passing it through the slot in the cell door. The low morale of the guards because of how they were treated by the system would cause them to take out their frustrations on the inmates. They believed that they were not treated right by the system, so they treated inmates the same. In their defense let me state they had to exist in fear of an assault by gang members. I witnessed some running away like rabbits in fear of their lives when there was an assault on a guard. Many guards used being a prison guard as a stepping-stone to a better position in law enforcement. Sterling Prison was considered by the prison guards as a hell hole. It is considered that worst prison in Colorado.

One of the most difficult things was being housed with inmates who were going through withdrawals from an addiction or from some type of psychiatric condition. You dare not irritate them in anyway even innocently. Illicit drugs are accessible in prison. As fellow inmates would say to me, we can get your whatever you want. You were continually on edge because the slightest thing could cause the inmate to erupt either verbally or physically. If they couldn't afford to buy their needed fix you were subject to their abuse. Some inmates would proposition you and if you objected to their sexual advances they would attack or assault you. I would get propositioned by the gay cellmates because they thought that may large intestine hanging out of my groin was my penis.

When you go to prison as an elderly man the inmates assume that you are a child molester. I used to get assaulted by the inmates continually until one of my cellmates had his wife check me out on the internet and found out that I was in prison for securities fraud. He told me that you have to show your intake papers to the other inmates so they will know why you're in prison so they will stop assaulting you. When I was house with a sex offenders and didn't protest it to the they would assume that I was a sex offender. My attitude and philosophy were that God places people in my life to administer to them and not reject them no matter what they were guilty of. Whenever I would change pods or cells the other inmates who didn't know me or my background would demand to see my intake papers. They would say we want to make sure you are not a weirdo. Some of these men were tattooed on every part of their bodies including the whites of their eyes. I used to say to myself who is the real weirdo here?

As to be expected prison is very difficult for those who are disabled in some way either mentally or physically. If you complained about a cellmate's abuse or assaults you were both considered at fault. If it got violent both of you were placed in solitary. No matter who initiated the attack.

When I was first incarcerated, I thought that my name was changed because all the inmates would refer to me as "Mother f-cker" or "C-ck sucker". Eventually I was nicknamed "Long John" because my guts hung out of me and which created a large bulge in my pant leg. The inmates couldn't say a phrase of a sentence without the term "Mother f-cker" in it. It was just part of the prison lingo. I never used that term myself. I said to myself there are certain parts of prison life that I don't have to assimilate to and didn't.

The currency in prison is postage stamps. Any service or favors that you paid for with the inmates were paid for with postal stamps such as haircuts or protection from assaults. You never used real money. Your family could deposit money on your account but that only used for commissary or canteen. I was one of the very fortunate because my family always saw that there was money on my account to pay for prison luxuries such as soda pop, coffee, candy, postage stamps, etc.

Prison is such an ugly place with its aged and dirty concrete walls, floors, and ceilings. The atmosphere needless to say is also very negative atmosphere. When I got to prison and realize how negative the atmosphere was, I resolved to myself never to let anything negative leave my lips or mouth. I said to myself John these people are exposed to so much negativity and you don't need to add to it. If what leaves you mouth isn't positive in nature, then let stay in there. I became determined to add whatever I could to the inmates and guards lives even if it was just a smile.

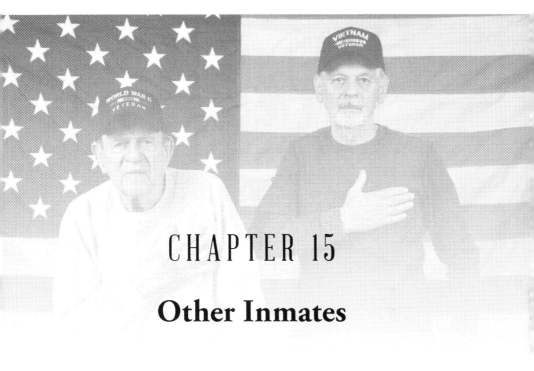

CHAPTER 15

Other Inmates

The first memory of being assaulted by an inmate was being housed with an inmate who was a murderer. He enjoyed verbally harassing me. When I complained about it to him, he just grabbed me by the throat and neck and threw me on the floor. Needless to say, knowing that this inmate was a murderer I didn't believe that I would survive his onslaught. Fortunately, after taking me to the cell floor, he just walked out of the cell and left me alone. I was able to leave the cell, so I asked the guards to be moved and fortunately the guards complied. On many occasions inmates threatened my life and, on several occasions, there was an attempt on my life. At first, I didn't fully recognize the seriousness of the threats and I didn't care because of my incognizant state.

Another time I was housed with a man who couldn't get along with his cellmates. He liked talking about little girls in profane and vulgar terms. When I asked him to stop, he pushed me up against the cell wall and punched me continually in the abdomen which terribly nauseated me because of my hernias. I asked to be moved to another cell. It seemed like my request was ignored until four days later I was ordered to be placed in the "Hole". On the way to the "Hole" I asked the female guard who was escorting me why I had to be placed in solitary and she said it was because I caused trouble by complaining about my cellmate. After I finished my stay in solitary confinement I was assigned to another cell and cellmate. From then on whenever the inmate who assaulted me would see me, he would threaten me. I learned the hard way early in the game not to complain and just use it as a lesson and part of prison life.

One morning I was walking through the dayroom, and I said good morning to a black man who was sitting at a table. I was just trying to be nice. He stood up and told me that he hated white men and if I ever talked to him again that he would kill me. From that point on I tried to keep my distance from that inmate. I couldn't believe how easy it was to provoke some inmates and to put my life in danger. All I did was to very pleasantly greet the man. That is an example of how dangerous it is to be incarcerated in the maximum-security section of a maximum-security prison. The place is just full of animosity and hatred. One time prisoner pulled me out of a top bunk and I landed on the floor. You had to keep in mind what is in some of the inmate's hearts if they even had one.

Let me state that I wanted nothing to do with drugs even by association when I objected to one of my cell mates doing drugs, he told me that if I ever objected to him doing drugs again, he would kill me. You had to take these people seriously because many of them were incarcerated for murder and some were serial killers. One of my cellmates stabbed a man fifty-one times. Another of my cell mates killed his three-month-old son. No matter how nice they may have seemed you didn't dare and provoke them. You were always on edge. They didn't make idle threats.

Some of the inmates would make knife like objects out plastic food trays, plastic spoon, toothbrushes or anything that you could make something sharp so they could use it to stab someone. Consequently, the razors and toothbrushes you were issued had flexible handles and grips on them. In the dining hall you were issued plastic spoons that you were not allowed to remove them from the dining hall. You were punished if they found spoons among your belongings during cell shake downs. The tenured inmates knew how to hide them just like other contraband. You frequently heard of inmates being stabbed. I had one blind roommate in a clinic that I was housed in while recovering from a heart attack who claimed that he was blind because he was stabbed in both eyes with a pencil.

If you were accused of being a snitch or informer, you were a dead man. Needless to say, you were constantly on watch for an assault. Some of the gang members used to come sit by me in the dining hall. They would tell me what used to do to their girlfriends and their girlfriend's children sexually because they knew it would revolt me. Consequently, I would leave without eating so they would have my food. They got a big kick out of arousing me. In the dining hall you didn't dare sit in the section that the gang members reserved for themselves. When the leader of the gang entered the hall, you would think it was their "Godfather". They all would say something in Spanish lingo in reverence to him.

CHAPTER 16

Inspiration

I was also inspired my some of the inmates. I had a cellmate who was almost 90 years old. When I saw him doing pull-ups in the yard no matter how much it pained him, I said to myself John, you can walk in spite of those hernias. I got to know another inmate who as a child fell on a screwdriver that he was carrying, and it punctured his forehead. That injury caused him to walk with his left foot perpendicular to his right foot. I said to myself if he can walk that way you can try running again even with your hernias. I did try running a few laps but had to stop when my hernias protruded further. I heard that if my hernias strangulated and ruptured it would cause my death. I walked no matter how much it pained me. I would just imagine that there I was walking downhill, and the pain was more tolerable. I used to say to myself John you can deal with anything that you put your mind to. I used to imagine pleasant things to tolerate the bad. Fantasizing was comforting.

As I observed the condition and treatment of many of my fellow inmates especially what they call lifers I used to say to myself: John, you have nothing to complain about. You could always step out of your cell and find someone who had it much worse and was in poorer condition than you. In my case most of the men I was housed with were "lifers" they were never going to leave prison except in a body bag. There was always a way to find inspiration in prison if you wanted it and needed it. There was always a way for me to lift yourself up. All you had to do was to step out of your cell and do something nice for a less fortunate inmate. There were plenty of less fortunate. I now say to myself if you want to be happy spend time in prison because you will learn to appreciate everything even to most basic things. You don't take much for granted in prison. You expect nothing so anything nice that comes your way no matter how insignificant you see it as a gift and that lifts your spirits.

Fortunately, enough for me my sisters in New York always made sure that there was plenty of money in my commissary account so I could buy things from the canteen and share them with other inmates especially those who were abandoned by their families. Needless to say, in maximum security there were plenty of lifers that were abandoned. They didn't even have the means to buy a can of soda or a cup of coffee. I remember one man who was restricted to a wheelchair and was suffering from dementia. I would buy him cans of pop and he thought that I was his guardian angel. I used to wonder why a man in his condition was housed in the maximum-security unit of the prison. The man wasn't cognizant enough to tell me his name. He would imagine that he was the son of the country singer star Hank Williams. It is interesting how your mind can find a way of comforting you when it is needed. When the pain and suffering became intolerable my mind would disassociate.

One of the things I liked to do to find inspiration in the Spring and early Summer was to look at the flowers and plants in a small garden along the walkway in the prison yard. As the plants and flowers matured, they looked so beautiful, and they amazed me. I used to say to myself that is so amazing. That beautiful creation was developed from just a small seed. Here was a miracle of God's creative ability. All that incredible knowledge to develop that plant was stored in a tiny seed. In humans we are developed in a similar way from a fertilized ovum. The greatest minds that ever lived were developed the same way. We can't see God, but we can see God's magnificence all around us. The information to build an automobile takes volumes. Here was all the knowledge to create a beautiful plant, flower or human, no volumes of instructions just a seed or an ovum. If you want to be inspired as I was think about God's magnificent creations and how that happened.

What is very interesting and surprising is that during my seven years of being incarcerated I experienced more understanding, care, love, and kindness than any man could hope for or expect from others especially very hardened criminals. I noticed that when I treated my fellow prisoners with respect a kindness and compassion the goodness within them would start to emerge. So how should we treat them? That is a subject that cannot be properly addressed in this writing because we are dealing with God's creations which society had a hand in distorting. But I know when you judge you must consider the whole person not just part of them or some incidences. I also know at my late age and years of incarceration at eight institutions that people who feel good about themselves do good things. Many inmates are suffering from mental health disorders. Unless death eliminates the disease or disorder most of the time those diseases and disorders will grow in size like a cancer of the mind. The diseases become more problematic especially in a penal environment.

Hiding the mentally ill in jails or prisons may satisfy some of the public's needs for protection and security but it creates a long-term problem. As with the victims of their crimes only empathy and compassion will ultimately solve the problem. The prisons are filled with people who emerged from their mother's wombs as cute little innocent infants. Let us not forget the principle that God does not make junk. Neither does God make illicit dangerous addictive drugs or force people to use them. The same is true for firearms. I don't know about you but I'm not about to tell God that with some people God did make junk. We have to ask what did society do wrong either directly or indirectly? Because of the maximum-security prison I was incarcerated at and the maximum- security unit of that prison I was housed in, I have associated with some of society's worst of the worst. You name the type of crime and these men have committed it but let me state again: what was so enlightening and amazing to me was the power of Godly love in dealing with these men of God's making and society's distortion. As an example, I learned that the prisoners who were guilty of sexual deviancy were sexually abused in childhood.

I'm not going to use inmate's names to avoid repercussions from guards or inmates. Please let me state that I'm very grateful to a lot of inmates who stuck up for me with the guards and inmates when they were abusing me. They did so without care for their own wellbeing. Several times I was saved from being raped when I was in that incognizant state and at the mercy of my fellow inmates. Several times they saved me from having the hell beat out of me. One of the things that used to bother me is whenever I walked the yard and saw an inmate in a wheelchair I would stop and try to cheer them up. Some of the guards would chastise me for doing so even though you could tell that inmate was in pain. Some of those inmates were near death and later I would hear that they did die.

CHAPTER 17

Inguinal Hernia

N ow, imagine this: we criticize North Korea for their terrible treatment of the American prisoner Otto Warmbier but for five years until April 17, 2018, I existed on a daily basis with my intestine hanging twelve inches out of my right groin like a large banana. It is called an inguinal hernia. I believe in my case was caused by having to strain too much to have bowel movements while in a demented state. At the same time my urinary function was shutting down. It appeared that as my mind shut down into demented state my body followed. The medical professionals and prison officials didn't seem to care because they refused to operate on it even though it was very painful. I can only assume that it wasn't in the budget to do so. On a daily basis the intestine protruded into my scrotum and stretched it. The intestine would press on the testicle and nauseate me. At times I would have to walk holding my scrotum in my hand to ease the pain and keep the scrotum from rubbing against the inner thigh. I must have looked like sexual pervert holding his genitals in public. Guards, medical personnel and prison officials would ask me what was wrong but none of them would do anything a about it. Any man will appreciate just how painful and nauseous is to have something pressing on or squeezing a testicle. The nausea can be and was intolerable. When the hernia would strangulate, I would have to bend over into a fetal position to tolerate the pain. At times I couldn't digest food without vomiting it back up. That pressure on the testicle also limits the production of the male hormone testosterone which did create a chemical imbalance in the brain which affects a person's behavior because neurotransmitters are made up of chemicals. I believe that it did affect my rationalization and volition ability. I was in continual pain which as any man could imagine was intolerable. Obviously, the pain became more intense when I walked or stood upright for prolonged periods of time. That inguinal hernia was so large that during my intake at Sterling Prison that when I was stripped naked Sergeant Tarver was so astounded when he viewed it that he called over four other guards to view it.

While I was at the Adams Jail, I was taken to the Platt Valley Medical Center for the surgeons to examine my hernias, in particular the inguinal hernia because it was so large. It seemed like the inguinal hernia used to strangulate or bend too far and cause blockages; especially when I was very stressed my abdomen and intestines would tighten up. The pain was excruciating. The surgeons at the Platt Valley Medical Center said that they were reluctant to operate to fix the hernia because my heart was too weak. They were afraid I would not survive surgery and being anesthetized. I had to just tolerate nausea, vomiting, excruciating pain, and lack of good nourishment by not being able to digest food. As stated at the Federal prison they refused to operate on it. I wish that the deputies at the Adams County Jail would have been as reluctant to abuse me as the incidents that I will describe in this document indicate. Imagine the surgeons are reluctant to operate on me because my heart function was too weak, but the deputies were not at all reluctant to harass and abuse me no matter what my physical state.

If that intestine strangulated and ruptured which was very likely I was dead man. When I walked the bulging scrotum would rub against my thigh and create large abrasions that were as large as a ripe red apple. As stated, I needed to walk at least thirty minutes no matter how painful it was to recover from my demented state that caused me to be incarcerated and for my cardiovascular disease. Walking was essential it served as my psychotropic medication and my therapy. Examine my medical record: there were no pain killers for the chronic and acute pain that I was subject to on a daily basis. I had to rely on very painful physical exercise for my therapy and recovery from my demented state. My inguinal hernia bulged so large in my pants that the guards even the female guards would make me strip naked to prove that I wasn't hiding contraband. When they saw the size of my hernia, they seemed shocked and horrified. The inmates would call me "Long John."

The hernia wasn't operated on until I couldn't intake any food for nine continuous days and my kidney function became very perilous. I was starving to death. I already was suffering from kidney disease. I believe it further damaged my kidneys which I endure the repercussions of to the present day. My kidney function got so bad that they thought I would have to be placed on dialysis. Prior to being operated on for the hernia I had to have blood transfusions of a special form of plasma. When the surgeon who had done numerous of these operations when he operated on me, he claimed that it was the largest hernia he had ever seen. The doctor at Sterling Prison classified it as immense. The doctor at Centennial Prison was so astounded by its size that she measured it for the record but couldn't operate on it. She thought that it would have to be spliced in order to get back into my groin and torso. The hospital surgeon in Canon City said they were unsure or very cautious about operating on me because of the triple "A" aorta aneurysms but they didn't have much of choice because of my failing health. If either of the aorta aneurysms ruptured, I was a dead man. I was in danger of bleeding to death. At the time I could no longer walk or even stand straight up. When the very experienced surgeon opened my abdomen, he shouted out in profane terms "Holy S-it" this is the largest hernia I've ever seen. The surgeon had to pull out almost twenty-one feet of intestine out of my abdominal cavity to get the extended intestine to go back into my groin so he wouldn't have to splice it.

After the operation some of the medical personnel and a doctor chastised me for letting the hernia go so long without having it operated on. They said to me "didn't you realize how dangerous that was?" They didn't know that penal system at the federal, state and county levels had refused for years to operate on the hernia. The day after my operation I was placed in the infirmary at Territorial Prison where I was wrapped in body chains directly over the incision which was extremely painful. I couldn't move without the body chains rubbing on the incision. Imagine rubbing a chain over a new large incision in your abdomen to sense how that would feel. It is torturous! It was like being stabbed over and over again and again. It was a miracle that it didn't cause a perilous infection.

To say that I suffered from chronic physical and acute pain from my large intestine hanging out of my right groin area like a large banana into my scrotum is an understatement. I would grit my teeth so hard to endure the pain that my teeth would break. Please keep in mind that teeth are made up of the strongest substance in the body. A tooth is stronger than any bone in the body. That demonstrates how hard I had to bite down to endure the pain. The physicians that categorized it as huge and have questioned why I was sent to prison in that condition? They most questioned why I remained incarcerated without it being operated on for over five very long years. As stated, it greatly limited my ability to walk or stand and sit for extended periods of time. I had to be able to lie down in a fetal position to relieve the pain. Please allow me to state again I was very vulnerable on a daily basis to my intestine strangulating and rupturing which can be and usually is deadly. When I tried to describe its size to a meeting of the guards with senior officers present, they would laugh at me. I had to live with the threat of my intestine rupturing along with my aorta aneurysms bursting. If that isn't very stressful what is? The worst thing that you can experience when you are trying to recover from a demented state is trauma and too much stress.

But know that the Supreme Court has stated that deliberate indifference to the serious medical needs of a prisoner constitutes the unnecessary and wanton infliction of pain prescribed by the Eight Amendment to the U.S. Constitutions. Also, the failure of the medical staff to respond to the ongoing complaints of chronic debilitating pain would constitute deliberate indifference even though the prisoner received other medical services. It is also considered medical malpractice. In spite of eight letters to the warden's office, a letter to Director of the Department of Corrections Rick Raemisch, a letter to the State Attorney General Cynthia Coffman, two letters to Lieutenant Governor Donna Lynne, and five letters to the Governor John Hickenlooper nothing was done to alleviate my pain and suffering. Not one answer to all those letters. Not even a simple telephone call by even a lower staff member to my sisters in New York who in their letters to Governor Hickenlooper were pleading to have mercy on their brother. In a so-called civilized age to leave a man in the United States with his guts literally hanging out of him is at the very least uncivilized and inhumane. It is barbarous!

This is something that you would expect to happen in a very poor third world country not the United States of America. That is not considering the fact that I am a very honorable served veteran who volunteered to serve his country in a time of war. Was my veteran' benefits of continual health care suspended because I was incarcerated? I wasn't told that when took the oath to serve and defend my country. Is this the way Colorado government officials treat the elderly, veterans and mentally ill? Are these the wishes of American or Colorado Taxpayers? This is another case of just like my story about Solitary Confinement where government officials say one thing but practice something else. It is so hypocritical.

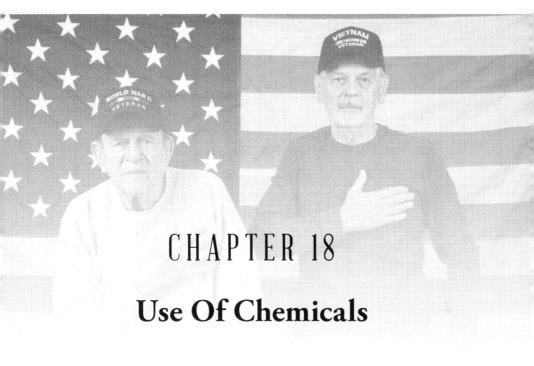

CHAPTER 18

Use Of Chemicals

We criticize the Syrian government and the Russians for condoning the use of chemicals on its populace but at an average age of 71 years I was sprayed with chemicals again despite Federal Court Rulings to the contrary. I was sprayed twice with oleoresin capsicum, twice right over where I had skin cancer. It causes a burning sensation on the skin and eyes. It had a very negative effect on me because suffered from skin cancer and sinusitis. It causes temporary blindness and can cause respiratory failure. It can also cause serious life-threatening complications in people with heart disease like myself.

Chemicals were sprayed twice directly in my eyes while in terrible pain because my inguinal hernia was strangulating. On a daily basis since being sprayed with chemicals in my eyes I'm cleaning sand-like particles from my eyes. I also have had to use much stronger eyeglasses since the spraying. My left eye is still sore when touched. Those chemicals can hasten the development of cataracts especially in the elderly.

The skin of the elderly is more sensitive to chemicals and subject to intense burning sensation because as stated before the top layer, the epidermis, becomes thinner as we age. Therefore, the skin is more prone to blood clots, bruising, and is more sensitive to pain such as burning sensation. The last time I was sprayed with chemicals the pain was so excruciating that I became self-destructive and wanted to take my life. I'm sure the security tape will show that I was pounding my head off the concrete. I was so desperate to do anything to stop the pain from several areas of my body. The courts have ruled the use of chemical agents against a prisoner with mental illness who engages in disruptive behavior as a result of their illness violates the Eight Amendment of the Constitution. The courts have also ruled that once chemical agents used that the prisoner be allowed the opportunity and the means to decontaminate with the proper decontaminates. Each time that I was sprayed I was thrown back into solitary confinement without the proper means to decontaminate for several days while the chemicals ate away at my skin and eyes. This is just another example how Department of Corrections personnel ignore court rulings when it suits them to do so. These are the same people who are employed to not only to enforce the law but to comply with it.

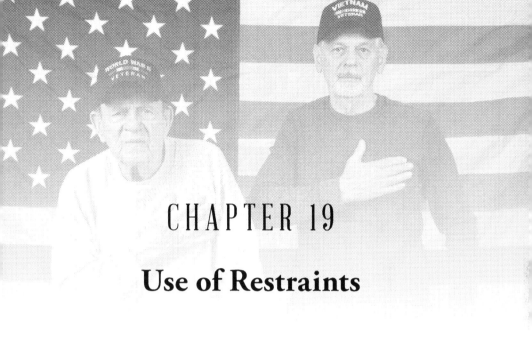

CHAPTER 19

Use of Restraints

As stated before the skin of the elderly is very susceptible to bruising. You can't put restraints on the elderly as you do the young without causing bruising and pain. Whenever I was taken on day trips my body was chained, I was cuffed up with the cuffs stacked in spite of the fact that I had arthritis in my wrists which made stack cuffing very painful. The handcuffs were placed so tight that it created wrist wounds because of the thinning epidermis. The same is true for the leg shackles around my ankles. This happened at least fifty times during my stay at Sterling Prison or the Adams County Jail. It also occurred every time I was taken out of my cell at Centennial Prison and Territorial Prison Infirmary. My skin, wrists and ankles would be very sore and painful for days. There are court rulings against placing an individual in shackles and handcuffing if it causes pain and suffering.

I used to show the guards the large hematomas on my hands, wrists, ankles and abdomen after I was chained up. It made no difference to them especially the older ones as to how old you were or what you may be suffering from. The older ones seemed calloused from the years as guards. As stated, the chains extended into my groin and painfully pushed and rubbed over my inguinal hernia. Try walking with that pain. I also had to endure the defamation and pain of having to be stripped naked over thirty times with a stretched out and extended scrotum which is painful. It would place pressure on the testes and squeeze the intestine.

CHAPTER 20

My Federal Prosecution

It surprises me that the justice system either the prosecution or my defense lawyer didn't recognize my deteriorated mental health condition because as stated I'm prone to dementia in fifteen ways. I was demonstrating so many symptoms of dementia. I found out the hard way from experience that a person isn't going to be properly diagnosed for any condition in the penal system especially and unpublicized ones or uncommonly known ones like pseudo dementia or disassociative amnesia. Whenever you are being evaluated in the penal system at best you are going to experience what I term the "bums rush." They don't have the resources or commitment to properly diagnose as manifested in my medical record and experiences. When it comes to mental health care to say the least, they are overloaded. That is why the prisons and jails are overflowing with inmates. That is why the United States has twenty-five percent of the world's population of prisoner with only 4.5% of the world's population of people. I believe as stated earlier that they would save a lot of money and resources in the long run if they spent the time and resources up front to properly diagnose and evaluate. It is very confusing because what the mental health people say is contradicted or ignored by the legal people in the justice system who see mental health conditions as an excuse not to be prosecuted or convicted.

I started to regain my cognizance and later began to establish new memories, but I still couldn't recall memories of the later twenty-five years of my life. I wondered how I was prosecuted for crimes? Also, this was confirmed after being examined and diagnosed by psychologists, neurologist and psychiatrist. How could they not have given weight or credence to the fact that I suffered from four major psychiatric diseases and five major circulatory systems diseases contributing to poor mental health? How could I remember or relate facts for my defense when I had no definitive memory of them? A lot of what I said was either a guess, assumption or even delusional. Being delusional is a side effect of my mental health disorders. After hearing their diagnoses and comments I was left to conclude that they prosecuted and imprisoned a mental invalid. Think about it how do you fairly prosecute a man who has no memory? Just writing about what happened to me brings me to tears and causes me to become depressed when I read my notes and sense how much I was abused by the system. My children related to me how the judge publicly chastised me for my crime which they found humiliating since I was so incognizant. No one bothered to inquire not even my defense attorney why was I in such a stupefied state like I was on a drug trip. Instead of properly treating me for my disorder or taking them into account they prosecuted me, shouldn't the legal counsel from both sides have properly informed the court of my very tenuous mental state? As soon as I got to the Federal Prison in Texas, they realize something was very wrong. My mental health disorders were present for years and took years to develop. Why else did the staff at that prison want to transfer me to an appropriate mental institution? When I was extradited to Adams County Jail I was immediately placed in the psychiatric unit and was diagnosed with pseudo dementia.

As I stated earlier about my mental health history, I have no memory of my stay at a Federal halfway house in Denver, my first stay of six months at the Denver County Jail or the inpatient stay at Denver Health Hospital, three weeks Federal Regional Detention Center for Federal placement and hospitalization in Oklahoma City and my first seventeen months at the Federal prison in Big Springs, Texas. I couldn't describe one feature of any of them if my life depended on it which it almost did. As stated, I still don't know why I was hospitalized in Oklahoma City. When I was admitted at Denver Health in 2016 almost four years later the staff told me that found precancerous lesions in my rectum which they ordered to be removed but weren't. The Federal penal system just chose to ignore my maladies especially my heart disease except where it was absolutely necessary, and they had no choice.

I started slowly to regain a small part of my cognitive ability and a was able to retain some small number of memories during my last two months in the Federal prison. I regressed back into the very demented state for eight months, when I was extradited by Adams County on January 16, 2014. Most of what I have just written has been taken from notes, records and loved ones not my memory.

CHAPTER 21

Federal Prison

At the Federal Prison in Texas I remember the nurse who catheterized me so I could urinate. Plus, I had to wear a urine collection bag. I do barely remember the nurse saying that she didn't like touching a man's private, but she demonstrated so much care when she did it. Needless to say, I'm very appreciative of her efforts. She also placed me on food supplements because I lost a quarter of my body weight, 46 pounds and was continuing to lose weight. I had lost the ability to do things for myself, so I had to depend on others to do things for me. I am so grateful to the very compassionate nurse and two inmates who assisted in my recovery and the things they did for me that I could no longer do for myself.

I do vaguely remember a male nurse or mental health worker telling me that they believed that I had Alzheimer's disease because of how I acted. I didn't remember at the time what Alzheimer's disease was and neither did I care. Nothing had significance to me. After I found out what Alzheimer's was and its symptoms that I was manifesting I asked myself how was I declared mentally competent to stand trial? I understand that I underwent a psychological evaluation before my Federal Trial at Aurora Mental Health, so I say to myself: how did they miss or overlook my demented state? As stated, I'm prone to dementia in so many ways and I was demonstrating over twenty symptoms of it.

I do remember two inmates. They told me how I was in a comatose type of state and all that I wanted to do was just lay in my bunk all day and not do anything. I barely but vaguely remember them walking me and nursing me back to health. They also said that they talked to the warden about me and my condition, the warden said that they were looking to transfer me to an institution where I could be properly treated. The staff knew of my misery and pain but not much was done to help relieve it such as appropriate drugs and therapy. I can only assume that they were not staffed or equipped to do so. I wasn't even issued a hernia belt. They just chose to ignore my skin cancer which wasn't operated on until my incarceration at the Adams County Jail. They also ignored and didn't treat my cardiovascular disease which I believe exacerbated it and made me very susceptible to another heart attack which occurred just nine months later. By not properly treating my hypertension it made me very vulnerable to aneurysms developing.

I do remember that walking was very painful because of the inguinal hernia hanging out of me. When I asked a male health care worker about the hernia at the medical clinic, he just said we don't fix those things here. I don't remember doing or saying anything more about the hernia until I got to the Adams Jail and started to become conscious and aware of my physical state again. I can't emphasize enough how important it was for me to walk and exercise mentally to help control and bring me out of my demented state. Any physician will state exercise is necessary for cardiovascular disease.

The two inmates said how they would yell at me to get up and do something. They claimed that one day when they yelled at me that I got mad at them for yelling at me, but I started to function. How incredible that anger was key in my recovery from that demented state. I understand that there was such a dramatic change in my cognizance level people would ask me what happened. Out of nowhere I don't know where I got the idea or information, I just said severe major depression. Because of the dramatic change in my consciousness, they nicknamed me the "miracle man." I understand that even the warden asked me what happened to change me from that vegetative state that I was in. Unfortunately, there was no change in my memory, and I couldn't' begin to establish new memories until 3½ years later until about mid-2017. I started to become aware again and slightly cognizant some time in November of 2013.

I do remember the two inmates telling me that Adams County wanted to extradite me. They had me sign some papers for my protection, but I didn't know at the time what the papers were. I didn't care because of my demented state. Later at my hearing at Adams County Court Judge Ensor said if he was competent enough to fill out those papers, he is competent to stand trial.

I remember calling my girlfriend and she told me that my mother died but I didn't care about anything at that time. I was in a very narcissistic and passive state. Now that wasn't typical of the sensitive, kind, loyal and loving John Walshe that I used to be. My girlfriend sent me a letter written by someone else saying that she didn't want to hear from me anymore and that didn't bother me. We had lived together for at least a year. I started the business with her, yet the breakup didn't bother me if that is any indication of my state of mind. You don't demonstrate much intelligence without a memory to rely on. Now I wonder if those events did bother me, but I just repressed my feelings about them because I couldn't handle those feelings at the time. The mind does have a way of protecting itself, consider disassociation. I understand that one of the inmates during my incarceration and before I started to recover called my oldest daughter Rene' because they didn't think I was going to live because I was continuing to deteriorate.

I understand from my research that when they thought that I had Alzheimer's disease that I should have been hospitalized for it. I also understand that I should have been put on at least one of four existing drugs at that time for memory loss. Without a question the inguinal hernia should have been operated on because I was in chronic acute pain from it. The prison records said that I would just urinate when I could without being catharized, I just urinated wherever I felt like it no matter where I was or who was watching. It is a wonder that my fellow inmates didn't get mad at me and beat the hell out of me instead of taking pity on me. Prisoners are not known to be sympathetic or compassionate, but they were with me at the Federal prison.

When I started to become conscious and aware again my notes tell me that when I looked in the mirror at my teeth because they were very sore. I noticed that they had dark spots on them. One of the inmates was a dentist so I asked him to look at and he said that my teeth were rotting. I don' think that I even brushed my teeth when I was in that vegetative state. I asked to be examined by a dentist and after examining me the dentist stated that I had eight cavities. When I asked to have them fixed, he stated that he was only authorized to pull teeth if the pain got very bad. By not having the necessary dental care it just weakened the teeth so over that next five years five of the teeth broke when I used to grit them to endure the pain from my inguinal hernia. Also, for the next five years I had to endure the pain of the very sore teeth and gums especially when I ate besides the pain of the hernia. The courts have ruled that tooth pain should be attended to if the pain becomes debilitating. The Courts have also ruled that deliberate indifference to serious dental needs is unconstitutional. The presence of serious dental needs may be based on pain and suffering by the prisoner and the deterioration of the teeth due to the lack of treatment. Limiting care to pulling teeth that could be saved has been held to be unconstitutional. Again, let me state the failure to provide reasonable and prompt care violates the constitution. Please keep in mind I was assured medical and dental care when I joined the U.S Air Force. I discovered when it comes to running a prison the prison staff doesn't pay much attention to what the court say or other commitments if they even know court rulings. Most are not budgeted or staffed to comply. Lawmakers and taxpayers are not very compassionate towards prisoners even if they are veterans they are treated just like fellow inmates.

There was so much that could have been done and should have been done in the Federal prison to ease my pain and suffering. By not treating my heart disease escalated it. This is especially true when you consider that I was housed in a Federal institution, and I was an honorably served veteran but they didn't care. The penal system staff are only going to do what they absolutely have to do. They have little respect or fondness for prisoners and neither does the public as a whole. Prisoner's well-being doesn't matter much to most taxpayers. That is just reality. Before going to prison I didn't give a dam about prisoners. I learned the hard way to be careful about what you don't care about. Today we seem to have compassion for the Afghans who helped us but little compassion for homeless veterans who fought for our freedoms.

CHAPTER 22

The Adams County Jail

When I was extradited to the Adams County Jail, I regressed in recovering my demented state that I was in at the Texas prison. I have no memory of my first eight months in the Adams County Jail. I believe that I fell back into the demented state with little if any cognitive ability. Upon arriving at the jail instead of going through the regular booking procedure I was immediately sent to the psychiatric unit. I remember writing a letter to myself when I started to regain my cognitive ability. I wrote in the letter that the way you endure in jail is realizing that no one gives a dam that I was in jail, that I had no rights and was entitled to nothing. I wrote that nothing here is fair or would be fair. That statement would be proved to be factual by coming events. Several of my cellmates were very prone to spontaneous violent eruptions which that very stressful atmosphere made me very prone to a heart attack or a stroke.

The abuse and suffering that I endured at the Adams County Jail as you will read was without a question the most painful time of my life. Some of those deputies saw their duty as not to contain but to punish. I used to wonder if I was just a victim of an experiment to see how much pain and suffering an old man could endure. One of the Deputies by name of Sparks liked to get in my face with our noses almost touching to berate me. He seemed to love emulating a military drill sergeant. I used to plead for him to please leave me alone. Because of my sensitivity to noise his yelling was very abusive to me. I remember saying to deputies who abused me at the Adams County Jail "Why don't you pick on somebody your own age?"

In my case besides suffering from several disorders, I suffer more from more intense PTSD and its numerous complications. Some officers and officials couldn't satisfy their responsibilities to their employer, colleagues and their God to do what was proper and right. As I inferred they knew that no one gave a dam about prisoners except for some of their loved ones outside of jail or as the prisoners term it "on the street".

As a result of the torturous incarceration that I will describe with all the abuses I have a panic attack which can evolve into dangerous angina pectoris attacks. It may not have been in the deputies' job description to understand and demonstrate some empathy, but it is implanted in their God given common sense of what is right and what is wrong. The panic or angina pectoris attacks can be so overwhelming and controlling that they caused me to become a danger to myself but thank God not to others. The attacks cause a tremendous surge of anxiety where I want punch or slap myself so I used to pound the concrete walls or floor so I wouldn't hurt myself. I had to relieve a huge amount of very frightening and painful anxiety. When panic attacks occurred, I needed to flee the scene and be reclusive so I wouldn't lose control do or say the wrong thing to another inmate or deputy. Imagine how dangerous that can be in jail or prison? To say the least self-control in prison or jail is critical and not to maintain self-control is suicidal. Fleeing the scene isn't always an alternative in prison or jail. It may appear to others that I'm angry, but it is actually overwhelming anxiety based in fear. My attacks would get so bad that they frightened other prisoners so they would be afraid of me and most would leave me alone.

The attacks started and increased after assaults at Adams County

Jail. The panic attacks increased to almost a daily basis because of the stressful environment. I believe that they cause neurological damage which accounts for their increase in number. I never fully recovered from the previous one before the onset of another. When I encounter people who look like the ones that assaulted me, I relive the event and become prone to a panic attack. The same is true when I encounter similar circumstances of the assaults or events.

We hear how people who suffer from similar diseases and their accompanying attacks take their aggression out on and harm others. I for some reason which I didn't understand at the time I wanted to punish myself. It may be that I hated myself for the hurt I caused others by the demise of my company while in a demented state. I will discuss this more in another chapter.

CHAPTER 23

Adams County Attacks

The following will describe several vicious attacks that I endures during a fifteen-month period of 2014 and mid-2015. Please keep in mind that I have no memory of what happened to me during my first eight months at the Adams County Jail. If it was anything the last eight months, it would have been pure hell.

The lack of knowledge, understanding, respect and overall ignorance caused some of the staff in the penal system to expect me to endure at 70 years of age like I could when I was 20 years of age. We recognize in professional sports how our professions or life take their toll on our faculties. A professional football player only has a career averaging 3½ years. The military has retirement ages of 20-years and 30-years equivalent to the ages of approximately 41 years and 51 years, why? Social Security starts at either 62 or 65 years of age, why? The mortality rates on the elderly who are afflicted with the coronavirus are a manifestation of what I write. Forget about age, after you read some of the abuse and assaults that I endured ask yourself should any human being or even an animal have to endure such treatment at any age? Think of the added burden of my mental and physical health profile on my being?

Heart Attack August 31, 2014

Sometime around August 30 or 31, 2014, about 12:30a.m. Deputy Tapia barged into my cell and started harassing and threatening me and my cellmate without provocation. Again, I have no memory of my stay at the jail prior to that date. At the time I had been incarcerated at the Adams Jail for over eight months, so my physical and mental condition was known to the jail personnel. Deputy Tapia was part of the jail staff so he must have known my health profile. I was still struggling to recover from a very demented state. Just nine months before at the Federal prison in Texas I was so demented that I couldn't find the restroom, dining hall and had to be placed on food supplements because of my undernourished state. I would forget to eat. At the time I was still suffering from severe major depression, acute anxiety and was still considered to be bi-polar. I had a history of cardiovascular disease, type II diabetes, kidney disease, hypertension and high cholesterol plus I was 69 years of age. I was suffering from a total of nine major health disorders. To say I was very vulnerable to a heart attack or a stroke is an understatement. By any standard at I was a weakling trying to emerge from a vegetative state. Stress and trauma were my enemies in my quest to recover to a normal state of being.

Deputy Tapia invaded the cell and started throwing my possessions and my cellmate's around the cell. He harassed me for a receipt for a thermal undershirt that I had purchased from the canteen. Two days earlier a female deputy searched my cell and all of my belongings. She discarded all of my receipts for any purchases and many of my notes that I depended on because of my poor memory. A thermal shirt was hung up by a vent to dry after being hand-washed by me. Deputy Tapia literally tore the shirt down. He was making threatening remarks. The incident and Deputy Tapia's harassment frightened and traumatized me so that it brought an angina pectoris attack where the whole right side of my torso seized up. It felt like my chest above my heart was being compressed in a vise or someone's hands. As stated before, the attacks are like very severe panic attacks, mimic heart attacks and precede heart attacks. Like epileptic seizures the heart convulses. I was terrified. I was taken in a wheelchair to the medical clinic, and they diagnosed it as a panic attack. A few days later Dr. Clower at the medical clinic thought it was a heart attack, but I wasn't treated for it even though I had cardiovascular disease. At a later date after another assault when I was rushed to the Platt Valley Medical Center with the same symptoms, they claimed that it was a heart attack when Dr. Khan, a cardiologist, performed an MRI and other tests.

There is a medical and jail record of the incident because two deputy sheriffs from internal affairs went over it with me when they met with me at Sterling Prison. I had written a formal letter of complaint about the incident along with another incident to the county board of commissioners which my son had delivered to the county board of commissioners.

When I returned to the unit after being hospitalized, I was assigned a new cellmate who was going through illicit drug withdrawals and would verbally harass me. There was no consideration given to my cardiac condition or history even though my heart function had dropped to a mere seventeen percent. At best as my weak and fragile memory serves me from that point in time, I started to experience more frequent panic attacks and in particular angina pectoris attacks which I'm very susceptible to because part of my heart's circulatory system is dead. When I told another deputy about what Deputy Tapia had done, he stated that Deputy Tapia loves to harass inmates and has a reputation for it. It is my firm belief that Deputy Tapia to say the least is a bully who takes advantage of weaklings. Any man who gets pleasure in harassing a senile old man in the condition I was in is the type of man that would also abuse children. It appears he likes to pick on weaker beings who can't adequately defend themselves in a penal environment. I suppose it was his way of to feed his ego and lift his poor self-esteem when he was actually doing the opposite.

Assault by Deputy Born

Please keep in mind as you read the following that Deputy Born like Deputy Tapia was part of the jail staff. Consequently, he knew of my psychiatric and physical condition. At this point in time, I had been housed in the jail for almost nine months. I wasn't new to the jail. On October 3rd I was still recovering from Deputy Tapia's harassment and the heart attack. Deputy Born called me out of my cell into the pod and started to harass me for supposedly asking my cell mate too many questions. I didn't realize that the cellmate was going through drug withdrawals. I was just trying to make friends with my new cellmate. When I tried to explain what I was doing to Deputy Born he grabbed my shirt collar which wrenched my neck and threw me back into the pod. I believe that it injured the thyroid gland and pons area of the brain which triggers the startling effect in you. Since that attack, I have hypothyroidism which contributes to heart problems and mental health disorders. Consequently, ever since that assault I have become even more sensitive to loud noise. I'm very easily startled especially when the noise is unexpected. Being startled triggers panic or angina attacks which made my years of incarceration following Deputy Born's assault more torturous. I was very frightened and traumatized by Deputy Born's actions because he is a very tall and large man as compared to me which intimidated me. He just towered over me.

When he harassed me my whole torso, especially my abdomen and intestines seized up out of fear. It caused both of my hernias to protrude out of body more and very painfully than they had before. The inguinal hernia became very sensitive to touch, and it was too painful for me to push the inguinal hernia back into the abdominal cavity. From that time on I couldn't push the right inguinal hernia back in. Because of intense chest pain and my cardiac history, I was taken to the medical clinic where I was diagnosed with an angina pectoris attack.

The panic attacks started to occur almost on a daily basis because of the stressors in the jail. I was in a very weak and fragile mental and physical state. Plus, there is no necessary recovery period from previous panic attacks. I just had to learn to endure and tolerate them. I asked for but didn't receive any treatment for them which is a violation of court rulings to the contrary. From that point on my incarceration became more torturous because my increased sensitivity to noise.

Attack And Heart Surgery

A few days later Deputy Born invaded my cell and harassed my new cellmate, Mr. Fetzler, who was about 21years old. My cellmate seemed to be mentally retarded and said that he suffers from cerebral palsy. I asked Deputy Born to stop harassing the man because of his mental and physical state. Mr. Fetzler was shaking and trembling uncontrollably during and after Deputy Born's onslaught on him. Deputy Born then started to harass me instead of my unfortunate cellmate even though I was still recovering from a heart attack and his previous assault. I was overcome with chest pain and because of my cardiac history I was taken to the medical clinic. Because I was experiencing neck, chest, shoulder, back pain, severe heart palpitations and my cardiac history I was rushed to the Platt Valley Medical Center Hospital by paramedics. It was presumed that I was having another heart attack. I believe that I was given a nuclear stress test during my stay. I was highly stressed and in severe pain, so I disassociated. As it was very typical for me at that time it was difficult for me to recall dates, times and even many of the events at the jail. I was suffering from major memory loss. At the time it had to very significant for me to having any chance remembering the event. I had to rely on my writings. At the time I was just starting to recover from the demented state that I regressed into when I was extradited to the Adams Jail.

When I woke up in the MRI tube at the Platt Valley Medical Center, I was told that the cardiologist Dr. Qaisar Khan had operated on my heart to perform angioplasty surgery. He inserted two metal stents to open up my artery from my heart. He attempted to do the same with another artery which was totally blocked, but he could not clear it. Consequently, that part of my circulatory system according to Dr. Khan is dead which made me very susceptible to angina pectoris attacks. He also told me that my heart function had dropped to seventeen percent. A normal heart function is sixty-five percent. Needless to say that frightened me. At that time, I didn't know what even more frightening events were in my future and how traumatic they would be. Vasoconstriction of the blood vessels can be caused by severe stress which I was subject to at the jail. I was still recovering from the state of severe major depression which is caused by overwhelming stress. It was also confirmed that Deputy Tapia's assault did cause a heart attack. Deputy Tapia denied his harassment of me but it's on security tape and there is a record of it. Before being released from Dr. Khan's care he told me because of the very fragile nature of my heart if I experienced any chest pain to immediately seek medical help. This occurred just four months before my trial. Dr. Khan said that my heart was too weak to stand trial. I asked in a letter to Judge Roybal that Deputy Born be made to stand next to me in court so a jury could see his size compared to mine and what a bully he was picking on a senile old man suffering from nine major health disorders. It makes you wonder what kind of man would pick on an old man who was recovering from a heart attack. There was no provocation for Deputy Born to enter the cell except for him to feed his ego by picking on two weaklings.

The presiding judge Thomas Ensor with little cardiac knowledge as compared to Dr. Khan's a board-certified cardiologist with his extensive cardiac knowledge decided to ignore Dr. Khan's opinion and proceeded with the trial. Judge Ensor ignored Dr. Khan's recommendation just like her ignored Dr. Bradley's preliminary findings about my mental health. It made no difference to Judge Ensor that I was the victim of two heart attacks at the jail and had to have heart surgery. As was typical of Judge Ensor with his extensive cardiac and psychiatric knowledge said that I looked alright to him. Please excuse my sarcasm because of the pain and suffering I endured at jail I thought I had earned the right to some liberty.

Please keep in mind that after three assaults one by Deputy Tapia and two by Deputy Born the jail personnel continued to put me in harm's way by housing me in the general population. There wasn't any consideration given to my cardiac history or my psychiatric profile. They completely ignored the fact that my heart function had dropped to a mere seventeen percent as a result of a second heart attack in just two months which almost ended my life. It was manifested through the jail's personnel's conduct and of the justice system's personnel that elderly lives no matter what their condition do not matter to officials of Adams County. That was just like the Loveland police officers which you will read about. You would think with my history at the Adams County Jail that the management of the jail would inquire as to what is going on there. Who reviewed the hospital bills and records? You would think that Judge Ensor who is an elderly man himself would have known better. After three assaults which resulted in two heart attacks and having to have heart surgery you won't believe the following assault.

Assault Post Heart Surgery

After I was released from the hospital and returned to the jail, I was housed in the medical clinic to continue my recovery. One day I started to have chest pain. I went out of my cell because of what Dr. Khan told me plus I was trained as a medic in the Air Force. I worked in a hospital for almost four years. I knew how weak my heart was. I asked Deputy Yesin if I could see a nurse about the pain. He told me no. When I tried to explain my concern, he became very inpatient with me and grabbed by my right hand and twisted it behind my back. He then pushed me back into my cell in spite of pleas for medical care as advised by Dr. Khan. He twisted my right hand behind my back so hard that it sprained my wrist. Consequently, my hand turned black and blue. Here was a deputy assigned to the medical clinic who must have known why I was housed in the medical clinic. If he didn't know what common sense indicates when an old man complains of chest pain. This guy either has a very low IQ or he can't control his mind and actions. Since that time my hand and brain coordination deteriorated where it became very hard to control my hand movement when I write and to lift my right arm. I showed it to Dr. Clower on my next visit with him. Dr. Clower worked for a contractor and not directly for the jail. When I told him what happened he just shook his head in disgust and disbelief.

There is no question in my mind that what that deputy did was criminalistic in nature. What did he think I was housed in the medical clinic for? I told him that I was suffering from chest pain. He could have easily checked the medical record to see why I was housed in the clinic, or he could have checked with the attending nurse. What kind of man assaults an old man who is recovering from a heart attack and heart surgery? It is an indication of the violent culture that exists among the staff at the jail. I was traumatized by the deputy's actions. I was already in fear of my life because of my heart attacks.

The following morning after the attack by Deputy Yesin I became very shaky and dizzy. I was so unstable that I kept falling down in my cell. A nurse with a foreign accent was summoned to aid and examine me. She accused me of faking it so in disgust I asked her to just leave me alone. I was never properly examined or treated for chest pain or dizziness both are sure signs of a heart attack. What kind of a health professional was that nurse? Talk about negligence or incompetence. No wonder that I was bound to suffer more severe cardiovascular complications in the future. What would anyone expect?

After my stay in the medical clinic, I was returned to general population with a heart function of only twenty-six percent of normal. At this point you may wonder why I didn't report these incidents to the proper authorities? For one thing I wasn't cognizant enough to totally realize the brutality of what was happening to me. I did realize how the culture in the jail allowed for assault without and repercussions. That staff knew how to cover their misdeeds with me as the future would indicate. At that time in my recovery all I could do was to endure and survive to live another day. I just wasn't strong enough at the time! I had to just keep moving ahead as I learned to do in the Federal prison. Wait until you read about what happened to me on or April 3, 2015, then on April 17, 2015, and finally on November 25, 2015. I finally decided to complain about how I was being treated by writing a letter which I learned to regret after the incident on April 17th.

Assault on April 3, 2015

On April 3, 2015, all the inmates had to leave their cell and line up in the day room so our cells could be searched. Two hours earlier I had delivered a letter to the deputies in charge of the pod complaining about how I was being harassed by the deputies at the jail. That turned out to be a big mistake, but I wasn't cognizant enough at the time to realize dangerous that action could be. You don't complain about the treatment at the Adams County Jail. When we were lining up in the day room the inmates said I was acting very confused and incognizant which I was still emerging from a demented state. That was typical of me at that time of my incarceration whenever I got too stressed, I became incoherent. I believe that I was suffering from aphasia which is common with demented state. According to the other inmates when I didn't properly understand and react to what a deputy was saying to me the deputy grabbed my right hand and twisted it behind my back. That was the hand that was sprained by the assault by the deputy when I was confined to the medical clinic. It was very painful. The inmates later relayed to me that I wasn't resisting but that two deputies pushed me very hard into the concrete wall. The inmates said that I hit the wall very hard because a deputy charged into me. I hit the wall so hard that I fell unconscious on the floor. When I was laying on the concrete floor according to the other inmates the deputies pushed my head and torso to the floor with their knees. I assume that my head was pushed into the concrete floor so hard that a large hematoma appeared right over the left frontal lobe area of my forehead. The hematoma was at least an inch in diameter. When I woke up on a stretcher in the medical clinic Nurse Eva told me that I fell down. I just accepted what she said. She also stated that I was restricted to the medical clinic because the seriousness of my head wound. My head ached very intensely where the hematoma was located. The wound was right over the frontal lobe of the brain where the pre-frontal cortex is located. That is the executive center of the brain what you might term the "True heart of the matter." When you injure the pre-frontal cortex you are risking that the victim will fall into an animalistic or vegetative state. The size of our frontal lobe is what separates us from the animals. I was never examined by a qualified physician even though they thought my head wound was very serious to cause me to be restricted to the medical clinic. There was no consideration given to my cardiac history or my physical profile. I just lied in the bed trying to heal. I can only assume that the deputies didn't want to draw attention to the assault so that is why I wasn't examined by a physician. As stated, the medical clinic is run by a contractor of Adams County. The next morning when I woke up in the medical clinic, I looked in a mirror and saw that both of my eyes had turned black from the blunt force trauma. I looked like Sylvester Stallone after he was made to look beat up after a fight in one of his Rocky movies. I also realized that my vision out of both eyes was blurry, and I had hardly any vision at all out of the left eye. I remember that I couldn't maintain my balance and I would trip over my feet when I tried to walk. My sinuses would leak causing congestion in my throat. It caused me to gag and choke until I could clear my throat by coughing and spitting to expel the excess mucus. My sinuses continued to expel excessive amounts of mucus from then on until the present day. I understand that head trauma can cause the sinuses to leak. I had been diagnosed with acute sinusitis in the Air Force. I learned the hard way not to complain about being harassed by deputies at the Adams Jail. They could care less how old you are or your psychological and physical profile. By pushing my head into the floor with their knees it mimicked what the Minneapolis Police did to George Floyd. Please allow me to state again I learned the hard way that if you complain you will regret it as I did when I woke up from an unconscious state on a stretcher in the medical clinic. I still bear the scars on my left temple.

A few days later was I returned to the pod without being cleared by a physician. I talked to my fellow inmates in the day room. The inmates told me that I did not fall down, and they described the way the deputies treated me. Please allow me to restate for emphasis the inmates related to me that we were getting into line when they were going to search our cells. They said that I was looking around acting very confused. At that time, I was still struggling to regain my cognitive ability. The inmates said that a deputy said something to me and I replied. The deputy grabbed my right hand and twisted it behind my back. The inmates said that I wasn't resisting but that two deputies pushed me very hard against the jail wall. I hit the wall very hard because one of the two deputies charged into me. I hit the wall so hard that I fell unconscious. When I was on the ground unconscious the deputies pushed my head into the concrete floor with their knees and then pushed my torso into the floor. Pleases let me state again for emphasis it was just like what the Minneapolis police did to George Floyd, but I was very fortunate to recover whereas Mr. Floyd wasn't. I understand that my wound and two black eyes were caused by severe blunt force trauma which in my case caused further memory and difficulty in concentrating. It was difficult for me to keep my balance when standing or walking. It is still very difficult for me to concentrate and maintain it. It exacerbated my sinusitis, so I still cough up blood in the mucus from the sinuses bleeding. Imagine the surgeons were very reluctant to operate on my inguinal hernia because my heart was too weak even though not operating could be fatal if the hernia strangulated and ruptured. They were afraid that I wouldn't recover from being anesthetized. That didn't concern the deputies. They had no reluctance to slam me against a concrete wall, and then pushing my head into the floor. I asked two of the inmates if they would give me statements as to what the guards did to me and two of them signed the statement that they dictated to me. After a cell search by deputies the statement was missing but I have the names of the witnesses. They also told me that when the inmates would complain to the deputies about how they were treating an old man, me, the deputies threatened to beat the hell out of them. The incident was caught on the security cameras according to the internal affairs deputies who later visited me at Sterling Prison. Those deputies from internal affairs tried to convince me that I just fell down.

A few days after the incident where I was slammed against the wall a deputy came to me and asked if I wanted to make a deal about the assault and I was so annoyed that I told him no. When I told another inmate about the deputies wanting to make a deal, he said that you will regret your decision not to because these deputies know how to get revenge and cover their tracks. I later found out that the inmate was right.

As stated earlier, when I wrote to the County Commissioners about the incident on April 3rd, Deputy Born's assaults, Deputy Tapia's assault and other incidents two internal affairs deputies visited me at Sterling Prison. They said that I fell down on April 3rd and when I told them that I had witnesses that refuted that one of them asked "Mr. Walshe, what would it take to settle this matter?" What do the security tapes indicate? They knew the truth and a were attempting to coverup the deputies' wrongdoing. It indicates how systematic violence is among some of the deputies. At that time, I still was incognizant to reason about what had happened so I said that I would let them know. I would like to know what it will take for officers who are in charge of protecting the populace to keep them from abusing people especially senile old veterans with my psychological and physical profile? They knew my physical and psychological profile because as stated I was incarcerated at the jail for fifteen months. It was well known that I was hospitalizes for heart surgery. By the way after they slammed me against the wall, they wrote me up for failure to obey a direct order. They know how to cover up their wrongdoings.

Think about it a man is recovering from a very demented state, he is also recovering from two heart attack, heart surgery and suffers from nine major health disorders and deputies slam him against a wall so hard that he is knocked unconscious. They then push his head into the concrete floor with their knees. There is nothing worse for mental health disorders than head trauma. This man wakes up in the medical clinic and is not attended to by a doctor. He shows up in court with not one but two black eyes and not one justice system official bothers to ask why. What kind of penal and justice system is that? They don't give a dam about the elderly or veterans. Read the court records. If the Adams County Justice System isn't a disgrace, what is it?

One day at Sterling Prison one of inmates who had witnessed the assault on April 3rd came up to me and he told me what he had witnessed. The inmate told me that he felt sorry for me because of my age, the condition I was in and that I was always very nice to him. For his safety I will not state his name or the other witness's names. Let's see if the security tapes were destroyed to protect the guilty.

Incident on April 17, 2015

It was well known to the deputies at the Adams Jail that I was prone to panic attacks that were caused by my sensitivity to noise. When I had one, they had to take me to the medical clinic. No matter how much that the deputies at Adams County saw me suffer from the noise there was never any attempt in my 15 months of incarceration to shield me from the noise or to control the noise in spite of my PTSD. If I objected to a cell mate's pill popping in the cell in my presence, the inmate would punish me by continually flushing the toilet. When I would object to one of my cell mate's talk about female children, he would punish me by yelling and hollering in the cell. My pleas to the deputies to be moved were ignored.

It was a big mistake on my part not to make a deal because on April 17, 2015, the deputy in the tower or control room announced over the P.A. system for me to pack up. The announcement was unexpected and so loud that it caused a panic attack which initiates the fight or flee mental syndrome in me. I automatically and instinctively yelled back instinctively at the deputy who made the announcement from what they referred to as the tower to stop. The deputy in the tower continued to make the loud and painful announcement even after I left my cell and the day room as the security tape indicates. What was he attempting to do? I assume he did it to antagonize and torment me. As soon as I packed up, I went out of the pod as the security tape shows and pleaded with Deputy Ezekiel Spotts, who came out of the pod office, to get the deputy in the tower to stop antagonizing me. Let me state again the deputies knew how sensitive and vulnerable I was too loud noise. They knew that I had an anxiety condition and PTSD. I was still suffering from the two black eyes and the wound over my pre-frontal cortex, home of volition ability and self-control. My wound had been bad enough to restrict me to the medical clinic.

I was scared because I was experiencing a panic attack as manifested by chest pain. I was scared because of my recent cardiac history. I was probably very loud and aggressive because the noise was intensifying my panic attack. I was experiencing severe anguish and chest pain. I was desperately trying to protect myself from the loud noise. I was very afraid of having another heart attack. I understand that some saliva spray came out of my mouth when I pleaded with the deputy to get him to stop the deputy in the tower to stop shouting. It is very common for the elderly not to properly control their saliva especially if they are missing front teeth or a large space between the teeth as a geriatric specialist or dentist can state. Since my head injuries from assaults at the jail especially the one on April 3rd my sinuses leaked excessively, and my throat would become clogged with mucus containing blood. It would cause me to gag and choke from the buildup of mucus which is common when I'm experiencing a panic attack. It is embarrassing to talk to someone especially when you're excited to spray saliva on the other person. I don't know how to control it. You can't talk very well with your mouth closed. When inadvertently sprayed Deputy Spotts automatically stated that I was going to be charged with assault for spitting on him. I'm sure an analysis of the security tape will demonstrate that I did not intentionally spit on the deputy. I started to fall into a disassociative state. Again, that it was very common for me to disassociate when I am highly stressed and enduring a lot of pain. Please keep in mind that I already experienced five major assaults, not even considering the daily harassments in subtle ways, by deputies which resulted in two heart attacks and having to have heart surgery. Plus, my guts were very painfully protruding out of me. I was shocked and desperate by Deputy Spotts' accusation. In my opinion I was just falsely accused of a crime. The thought of having to spend more time in that jail horrified me and why wouldn't it? I had a history of panic attacks and PTSD dating back to my military career.

When Deputy Spotts accused me of assaulting him my body automatically tensed up. As inferred, I was so terrified that I gagged probably from my leaking sinuses. By accusing me he in essence was assaulting me because it meant more assaults and abuse. Also because of the excruciating pain in my hernia and abdomen, I accidently spit the phlegm or mucus caught in my throat on Deputy Spotts. It wasn't intentional nor was I conscious of it. It happened before at the jail when I would choke on excess mucus since the first assault by Deputy Born. Plus, I suffer from sinusitis which causes me to choke and a lot of cough up mucus. I build up excess fluids in my lungs. When a person chokes, gags or does anything to cut off the air supply to the brain the brain out self-preservation instinctual behavior takes over and goes into an automatic reflex action. That is because the brain's neurons can't go more than three to six minutes without an adequate oxygen supply to avoid brain damage or death. The brain uses three times the amount of oxygen as the rest of the body. It is called the "Breath of life." Try and cut off your air supply by holding your breath and see what happens. The brain will take over and instinctively do whatever is necessary to survive. It is completely natural and instinctual. You can't stop it without force. The brain will get the body to evacuate or expel whatever is blocking, clogging or cutting off the vital air supply so the brain can receive the oxygen which it absolutely needs. When I'm highly stressed my intestines and abdomen tighten up which because of my guts hanging out of me was very painful. I became very bloated; there was an immediate need to relieve the bloating sensation. I just instinctively gag and choke.

Stress also causes excess salivation and what is more stressful than jail? A close inspection of the security tape will show that I was having a panic attack and was in a desperate state. Inspection of the security tape will also show that I didn't do what Deputy Spotts accused me of. It was an inadvertent spray. So, what was he trying to do? Was he trying to provoke me? At my age ninety-five percent of my behaviors are instinctual. At 70 years of age, you don't start spitting on people or assaulting them in anyway especially law enforcement and especially when you are in jail. I'm not strong enough even if I wanted to, I wouldn't consciously dare to attack a much younger and stronger man. I was still recovering from two heart attacks, heart surgery and five assaults by deputies not considering the harassment by inmates in the last seven months. In the previous four years especially the 15 months at the Adams Jail while I was incarcerated there was no incidence of bad behavior even with all of my mental health disorders. The same can't be said for the deputies. Again, I'm sure an analysis of the security tape and my medical record will substantiate what

I write. Let the tapes show how a group of deputies took a man with my cardiac history, dangerous heart function of a mere 17% to the floor after I supposedly spit on Deputy Spotts. That was the second time in just two weeks that I was knocked to the floor by deputies. I hadn't recovered from one assault when I was taken to the floor again. I still was the bearer of two black eyes and a dangerous head wound. I have no memory of the events after I was forced to the floor.

Later on, I said to myself that I should not have refused to negotiate some kind of deal over the assault on April 3rd where they slammed me against the wall. I realized that these deputies knew how to cover up their wrong doings. It surprises me that the so-termed innocent ones feel an obligation to help cover the wrong doings of the perpetrators. They know who the wrong doers are because when I asked the deputies about how some of the deputies like to abuse inmates, they readily admitted who had a reputation for abusing inmates. Deputy Spotts' partner in the office that morning was one of the parties to the assault on April 3rd. At the time I was almost 70 years of age, and I had no history of assaulting anyone especially law enforcement. Consider at my time in my life, I had been incarcerated for almost four years with fifteen months of that at Adams Jail with no history of bad conduct especially assaults on anyone even though I had been so badly mistreated at the jail by deputies and inmates. I don't remember spitting on Deputy Spotts but in the disassociative or a semi-conscious state that I was in I can't say for sure. I can only remember choking on my saliva which the excess mucus was caused by the assault on April 3rd. Let truth about this matter lie in examination of the security tapes which are part of the court record.

Transfers to Adams County Jail

Please allow me to jump ahead temporarily to describe another assault at the Adams County Jail so you may be able to perceive the cumulative effect of all the assaults. Each time that I was brought from Sterling Prison to the Adams Jail it had a very negative effect on my mental health because I had been assaulted as stated by deputies five times in just fifteen months not considering the assaults and harassments by inmates. Consequently, just the thought of having to be returned and housed at the Adams Jail had a traumatic effect on me. When I was being moved or transported for court appearances, I was not allowed to take any personal possessions with me especially my notes.

Again, in just last seven months at the Adams County Jail I can remember enduring many assaults to my being by inmates and deputies. After an assault on Thanksgiving Weekend 2015 whenever I was extradited to the Adams Jail, I was placed in solitary confinement for a week at a time. Supposedly I was placed in solitary for my protection. The cells were filthy and dirty as a city sewer. I wrote a letter to Judge Roybal in asking just to be returned to Sterling Prison the same day as the court appearance, but it was ignored. I was very afraid of being assaulted again at the jail and experiencing another heart attack.

Talk about irrational behavior; what about bringing a 70-year-old man with my psychiatric and physical profile from Sterling Prison six different times for a week at a time on a charge for spitting on a deputy. That accusation was done to get revenge for me not wanting to negotiate a deal for the assault on my person on April 3, 2015. I will leave to the taxpayers of Adams County to judge if that is a judicious use of their tax dollars and if elderly lives matter to them.

Assault On November 25, 2015

After I appeared before Judge Roybal just before Thanksgiving Day in 2015 on the following Sunday I walked out to the day room which was vacant. I saw the Sunday newspaper sitting on a table. It wasn't addressed to anyone, so I took it back to my cell to read it. About ten minutes later while in my cell I heard another inmate say, "thanks for stealing my paper." I automatically picked up the paper and took it back to the day room. I apologized to the inmate stating I didn't know it was his paper. I remember that inmate chastising me and then he swung at me twice, so I thought to myself just return to your cell; so I did. I didn't want to get into any type of physical altercation with anyone if for no other reason but my weak physical health. A little while later while in my cell I looked and there was blood all over the left side of my body from a wound on my left elbow. I also noticed that a pain in my right side of my jaw was escalating. I thought that the pain in my jaw was from sleeping on it. I went out to get the guard's attention. As I walked out of the pod the inmate continued to verbally threaten me from the window in the cell door. At that point I knew that I couldn't return to the pod. I just sat on the stairs by the office door and waited for Deputy Slettin to finish his rounds. He took me to the medical clinic to be attended to. Deputy Slettin asked me if anyone assaulted me or did any inmate touch you and I said no. At the medical clinic they cleaned and dressed my wounds. I remember on the way back from the medical clinic Deputy Slettin again asking me if someone touched me and again, I said no. I was moved to solitary confinement.

About an hour later Deputy Slettin came into my cell and said, Mr. Walshe, the security tape shows that you were punched in the right jaw and knocked unconsciously to the floor. That accounted to the severe pain in my right jaw. It also loosened some of my teeth on the lower right side. It made it painful to chew my food which it still is because my jaw is out of alignment. Those teeth have since been removed. This is typical of what happens to me when I become highly stressed, traumatized or I'm in severe pain; to endure I fall into a disassociative state. I disassociate from reality, and I don't realize what is happening to me and around me. This is what happened to me on April 17th when I supposedly spit on Deputy Spotts.

A few days later an inmate who goes by the nickname of Black Night told me that the inmate who assaulted me was known to be very violent and that the deputies told that inmate to assault me. The courts have found prison and jail officials to be deliberately indifferent if they fail to protect prisoners who are obvious victims or have been identified as "At Risk". It also applies to if they place a prisoner in a situation of danger from others who are known to be aggressive and violent. The law talks about protecting inmates who are very vulnerable to harm. According to court rulings I was not to be housed with offenders who are known to be violent. Nothing was done to the inmate who assaulted me, but I was brought back from Sterling Prison six times for supposedly spitting on a deputy. If that isn't a "double standard what is?

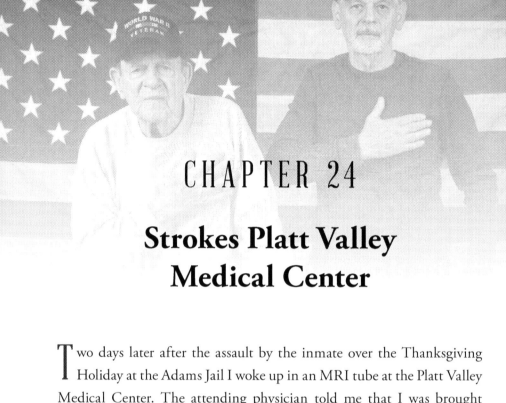

CHAPTER 24

Strokes Platt Valley Medical Center

Two days later after the assault by the inmate over the Thanksgiving Holiday at the Adams Jail I woke up in an MRI tube at the Platt Valley Medical Center. The attending physician told me that I was brought there because I was supposedly having a grand mal seizure. Those seizures started after an assault at Sterling Prison on October 7, 2015. The attending physicians detected not just one but two strokes. They attributed one of the strokes to the trauma of being assaulted by the inmate after Thanksgiving Sunday and the other I attributed to an assault at Sterling Prison on October 7, 2015. This was the second time in a little over a year that I found myself in an MRI tube because of assaults at the Adams County Jail. So now in about a years' time I had to overcome the negative effects of two heart attacks, heart surgery, two strokes and at least seven assaults at the Adams County Jail. Even though I was diagnosed with two strokes I was never treated for them with the proper medication or housing. Is should have at the very least been placed on blood thinners. Did they think I was some kind of superhuman or did they just didn't care? I think that the latter is the case. It is unheard of to endure all of that suffering at 70 years of age with nine major health disorders in just eight months. Please keep in mind that I have no memory of the events during the first eight months at the jail.

To my knowledge no action was taken any of the men who assaulted me. Why wasn't there any accountability for the inmates and deputy's actions when the incidents were captured by the security cameras? What about the deputies who assaulted me on April 3, 2015? What happened to the letter that I gave to the jail staff the morning of April 3rd? Once again, I learned the hard way the consequences of not making a deal with the deputies when asked to make one. It is also an indication of the criminalistic culture that exists at the Adams County Jail. Some of the Jail personnel perceive that they have immunity from any accountability for their actions because it is a jail.

Treatment At The Adams County Jail

I would describe my fifteen months stay at Adams County by the deputies as atrocious. They have absolutely no regard for senior citizens, mentally ill and veterans as manifested in their actions. As stated, some of the deputies are very prone to violence and like to harass inmates especially those who they perceive to be weaklings.

I heard in the news how Senator Bernie Sanders had to scale back his campaign for the presidency because of the seriousness of his heart surgery, heart attack and therefore frail health. I had the same type of heart attack and had to have the same type of heart surgery, but part of my surgery failed to open some arteries of the circulatory system which is very dangerous and could lead to another heart attack. According to the surgeon and cardiologist part of my circulatory system is dead. What is simply outrageous during the next seven months at the Adams County Jail in spite of my frail health I had to endure at least four more assaults and abusive behavior at the Adams Jail.

After one of the assaults which occurred during the Thanksgiving Weekend of 2015, I was diagnosed at the Platt Valley Medical Center with two life threatening and diminishing strokes which were probably caused as a result of abuse. They knew that I had cardiovascular disease when I was extradited to that jail. The abuse wasn't scaled back because of my two heart attacks and heart surgery. It served to exacerbate my circulatory system weakness. Just like in Senator Bernie Sanders case two stents had to be implanted in me. Let the records state as they do that the abusive behavior wasn't scaled back but was actually escalated while I was incarcerated to what I consider uncivilized and savage levels. It is manifested by the fact that less than two years later I suffered two triple "A" aorta aneurysms. I have since had a heart defibrillator implanted in my chest because of the weakness of my heart. I'm still inflicted with the ascending aorta aneurysm and a abdominal aneurysm if they rupture it will kill me. There are no statues of limitations on physical and psychological limitations because of my atrocious treatment at the Adams County Jail. Unfortunately, I will wear those scars to my death. They exacerbated my posttraumatic stress disorder which I was inflicted with a half century earlier during my military service to my country. At no time was any consideration given to the PTSD or my service to my country. In initial and later placement at the jail there was no consideration given that I had cardiovascular disease. As a result of improper placement, I had two heart attacks and had to have heart surgery. Also, there was no consideration given that I was considered "At Risk" or my demented state.

We hire and give people authority to police us and yet they can't police themselves. As stated, when I would complain about deputies and guards to their colleagues, they would tell me that he or she has a reputation for that, or they like to harass or assault inmates. Their response would make me question to myself, why don't you do something about them because their bad behavior will overshadow goodness in others? I wouldn't dare speak that to them because I learned the hard way that will lead to further abuse. There is no justice in jail or prison, just lessons to be learned. I was so abused by some deputies at the Adams County Jail that it caused me to shamefully write to one of the deputies at the Adams Jail that I regretted volunteering to serve my country and serving it honorably. That statement demonstrates that times I was so despondent that I became delirious and irrational. Please keep in mind while incarcerated at the jail I was emerging from a very stupefied or retarded state and the worst thing for me to experience was too much stress and trauma.

As inferred earlier the deputies and guards who abused me, a man of 70 plus years, fighting to overcome the negative effects of four major psychiatric conditions and five major circulatory conditions are akin to the type of people who would abuse children. Some law enforcement officers use the excuse that they are following rules, regulations and procedures; so were the Roman soldiers who performed the crucifixion of Jesus. They forget that God gave them a brain and mind to produce common sense. There are no rules, regulations and procedures that cover a hundred percent of the situations. That is why we hire law enforcement officers with adequate IQs and intellects. Hopefully that intellectual ability will keep them from allowing their egos to get out of control.

CHAPTER 25

Angina Pectoris Attacks

By the time that I left the Adams County Jail after more than fifteen cumulative months of incarceration there I was having daily panic or worse angina pectoris attacks. The latter are characterized by frightening tachycardia, heart palpitations, shortness of breath and a gagging or choking sensation. It is a paroxysm attack which is so overwhelming and frightening because it is so hard to maintain self-control over your actions. You think and feel that your death is imminent. The gagging sensation is like a marble rising up from my stomach and getting caught in my throat. It cuts of my air supply if I don't expel the ball of phlegm or mucus. I believe the attacks are made worse because part of my circulatory system is dead, and my heart doesn't get enough oxygen. My heart is prone to convulse because of a lack of a normal amount oxygen supply.

If you ever had an angina pectoris attack, at least my type, which mimics a heart attack and can precede a heart attack, you wouldn't wish one on your worst enemy. An overwhelming very stressful and tense feeling overcomes you. You lose and have little if any control over your mind and body during the attack. My first reaction is suicidal in nature then I want to slap and punch myself. My entire right torso and sometimes both left and right sides seize up especially where I had artery stents implanted and the circulatory system is dead. It feels like my heart is in a vise and the vise is being tightened up. You swear that you have reached the end of the line and your life is over. Your chest tightens up so much that you have to lie hunched over in a fetal position. You can't straighten out. Let me state again part of the reason is that your heart convulses, and your heart does not have enough oxygen which is so critical for the heart and brain. The pain and chest tightness lasts about three hours and there is nothing you can do to ease the pain in the chest without proper medication which wasn't administered in jail or prison. You just have to endure the pain. It is so frightening because each attack weakens your will, heart and your brain. There are medications that can be administered for the attacks, but they were not administered in my case to ease my pain and suffering. I have since been given those medications by the Veterans Administration that ease my pain and suffering.

I have substantial reason to be frightened since my heart function was a mere seventeen percent and thirteen months later my heart function was a mere twelve percent when it was measured at Denver Health Hospital. How close can you come to death than that? I had little volition ability of self-control. Some days I was having multiple panic and angina attacks. In my opinion these attacks were intensified in nature since I have PTSD. I found out through experience that nothing is going to be properly diagnosed in jail or prison. Courts have ruled that prisoners must be provided with shelter which does not cause their degeneration or threaten their mental or physical wellbeing.

CHAPTER 26

My Psychological Competency to Stand Trial

I understand that upon being admitted to the Adams County Jail I was sent immediately to the psychiatric unit of the medical clinic because of my demeanor. I didn't even go through the regular booking procedure. At my preliminary hearing Judge Thomas Ensor ordered a psychological evaluation. A forensic psychologist by the name of Dr. Max Bradley was engaged to perform the evaluation. Dr. Bradley was late in starting the evaluation because he was nursing and attending to his mother who was suffering from terminal cancer. Dr. Bradley completed part of the evaluation, but he needed more time to finish it before I was to be tried. When my defense counsel asked for a continuance so Dr. Bradley could finish the evaluation he was refused because according to Judge Endor my case was the oldest on his docket. The case was the oldest on Judge Ensor's docket because of the assault on my person by Deputies Tapia and Born which cause two heart attacks and my having to have heart surgery. Dr. Bradly was not given the opportunity to finish his evaluation of me by Judge Ensor refusing a request for a continuance on October 1, 2014. How ironic, Judge Ensor was the one who originally authorized the evaluation.

If that isn't a big contradiction what is? Why extradite a man from another state if you're not going to properly evaluate and try him? Just six months after my trial a psychologist and neurologist diagnosed me with four major psychiatric conditions that just didn't pop up overnight. Some of those disorders were diagnosed back in the early 1960's as manifested the Veterans Administration's evaluation completed post my incarceration. People from the defense or prosecution didn't bother to properly investigate or research my mental health.

When my legal counsel for my appeal talked with the forensic psychologist Dr. Max Bradley about his discussions and his interviews with me, basically, what he was able to preliminarily determine at the time that I do appear to suffer from pretty significant depression and anxiety issues, those appear to have been present at the time of the alleged allegations and they continue to persist to some degree to this day. He wrote those mental health issues that he suffers from, some of the symptoms can be lapse of memory, can also be impaired judgment and concentration in decision making, et cetera, et cetera.

During legal proceedings the same judge said that if I had the mental ability to file what is called an IAD request from the Federal prison that in essence I had the mental competency to stand for trial. Witnesses can state that they filled out the request since I didn't have the mental capacity to do so. I ask since when does a man's ability to fill out a form prove his mental competency? All Judge Ensor or the prosecution had to do was ask how did John Walshe fill out the form in question?

I was charged with supposedly not giving an investor information. The medical record states that I couldn't remember things such as the location of the bathroom or the dining hall in the Texas prison. A psychiatrist Dr. Fohrman at the Adams County jail diagnosed me with a form of dementia which drastically affects a person's psychological ability. Why wasn't that mentioned at my trial?

Judge Ensor simply stated in court that this man, meaning me, was nothing but a "Con Man" and that "I looked alright to him." I may have looked alright to him, but a learned man would realize that ninety percent of the people who commit suicide which is the height of depression look alright right up to the moment that they commit the act. He said that I was just stalling which was ridiculous because that meant a longer stay in jail for me and be subject to more abuse that I was enduring in that jail. Judge Ensor would be the envy of the great Austrian neurologist and psychiatrist who was the founder of psychoanalysis Sigmund Freud. Even Dr. Sigmund Freud didn't dare to or attempt to psychoanalyze a patient by just looking at him.

The jury never heard of Dr. Max Bradely's initial findings of my psychological evaluation that Judge Ensor ordered. The jury didn't hear that Judge Ensor would not approve a postponement so Dr. Bradley could complete his forensic evaluation or why Judge Ensor wouldn't postpone the trial.

I wonder how the jury would feel conned after they read the transcript of my court appearance on October 1, 2014. Couldn't they have been presented what should have been known to them? All they had to do was to review or have someone review the medical record. Dr. Bradley could have revealed his preliminary findings to them.

In October of 2015 which was six months after my trial for securities fraud a neurologist, Dr. Melisa Johnson and a psychologist Dr. Bryce Willson diagnosed me as having the acute anxiety, major depression, bi-polar disease and dissociative amnesia. Those diseases take years to develop and didn't as stated pop up overnight. Three of those diseases dramatically affect the memory. That was only five months after arriving at Sterling prison. Two of my diseases were diagnosed while I was in the U.S. Air Force when I was in my early twenties. I had five inpatient psychiatric hospital stays even one at the world-renowned Karl Menninger Clinic.

The question is should I have ever been prosecuted or tried? Please let me ask again what gave the judge in both my Adams County Trials the right to deny any testimony as to my mental health and state of mind? Who or what gave Judge Ensor the right to deny a postponement so that the evaluation that he ordered to be properly completed? The postponement would not have been necessary if two of the deputies at the Adams County Jail had not triggered my heart attacks and heart surgery by harassing me. This is the same court where I showed up at my sentencing with two black eyes and a large head wound for all to see including my granddaughter with tears in her eyes. Not one justice or law enforcement official during that court appearance asked why I had two black eyes and a very obvious head wound.

The actions of Adams County justice and law enforcement personnel demonstrate how wrong it is to take advantage of the weaknesses of an elderly man, disabled veteran, father of five and grandfather of seven with nine major health disorders. To have a man like that to stand trial at that time was like having a paraplegic to run a marathon. There is no way I could remember facts to be presented to my counsel, court or jury.

What is even crazier that even after the jail got rid of me by sending me to prison the prosecution brought me back to the jail six more times After some of those visits, they had to house me in solitary confinement for my own protection. If that isn't ludicrous what is? I was in a real dangerous state with a heart function on a mere 17% and a history of not one but two strokes and two heart attacks.

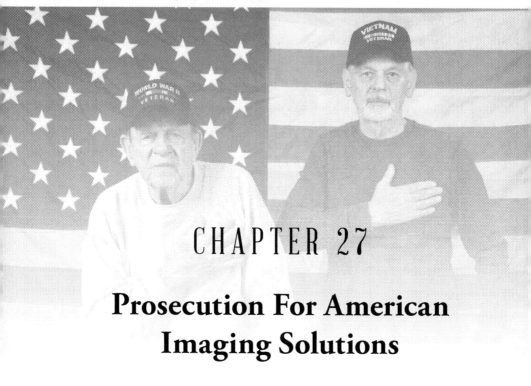

CHAPTER 27

Prosecution For American Imaging Solutions

It didn't make much sense for the prosecution to extradite a man who was suffering from all the disorders that I was at the time. As stated earlier the officials at the Federal prison were contemplating placing me in an institution that could better treat me for my demented state. The prosecution was so eager to score a conviction that they didn't consider my very tenuous health profile. They extradited a man with little if any cognitive ability and no memory. When I got to Sterling Prison post-conviction at Adams County, I still couldn't remember basic things like my cell mate or my cell. When you consider the facts, the prosecution extradited a burden to the county. What did they gain by their actions? The Federal prison was glad to get rid of me. Let me state again the medical record from the Federal prison states I couldn't even find the bathroom, dining hall or my bunk. All they extradited was a big liability for the sake of a score.

When I was down and out because of losing my business which took a quarter of a century to build and operate I spent minimal amount of time sitting around moaning and staying depressed about it. I did something productive to replace all those jobs that were lost. I developed a business plan to start a new company. Since I put all of my capital into saving my former company. I had to raise capital through outside investors so I advertised for them in the Denver newspaper. When I started the company, I was not conscious as how much my mental health had deteriorated. That is very common with my mental health disorders because you lose your ability to be self-conscious. You deteriorate and go downhill in a state of oblivion.

The only thing that you are assured of in starting a new business is a lot of stress which as it turned out severe stress caused disassociative amnesia the main cause of my memory loss. The business wasn't started to use the vernacular of the gutter to screw anyone out of money as the district attorney claimed.

My girlfriend at the time was the owner and only stockholder in the company. I figured we could just work something out at a later date when the company was successful to compensate me for my efforts. I wasn't too concerned about being paid for my efforts. I don't believe that I even took any kind of remuneration out of the company because I was living off of my social security.

As stated, I was not a stockholder or the legal owner of the company. Legally I was not entitled to any monetary or otherwise gain from it. It was my idea to start the company. My main goal was to create jobs, to build a great company again and opportunities in the economy. To become wealthy again would be a secondary benefit of that goal. I had a history of being a humanitarian.

I advertised for investors in the new company in the Denver Post. An investor over a period of time which I believe was almost a year, invested $205,000.00 in the new dealership. He was paid an interest rate of eighteen percent because any new venture is very risky. He was issued a promissory note. I personally guaranteed the note even though I wasn't the legal owner of the business. That is how confident I was in the company's success. My contribution was as unpaid general manager.

I did contact the Colorado Department of Securities and I followed their instructions in issuing the note. I was confident in my ability to make the new venture a success and my relationship with my girlfriend the same. The inherent risk to me personally guaranteeing the note didn't matter to me.

When I was indited for nonpayment of business taxes for the company that I had owned the new that company I was starting, American Imaging Systems, had to be shut down since I was the key man in the company and the company couldn't raise more operating capital. Obviously, the investor lost money when the company was shut down. That is when all the finger pointing for blame was started.

I understand that in early in January of 2014 I was extradited from the Federal prison in Midland, Texas, to the Adams County jail on a charge of securities fraud. As previously inferred, it is surprising that Adams County wanted to extradite me at that time because when they called the prison to express their intentions they were informed of my tenuous mental and physical health. Supposedly, I neglected to tell an investor in new copier company that I was starting how I lost my previous company or other information about it. I don't remember what I told him. I gave that investor a promissory note. I had a law firm who did the incorporation and registration of the company American Imaging Solutions, Inc. develop the note so I would be in compliance with all state laws concerning promissory notes.

Our lives are made up of traditions, customs, and habits especially in the later stages of our life. Again, in my previous 64 years there was no history of deception, deceit or lying. There was no history of John Walshe attempting or taking advantage of anyone. My history was one of honesty and integrity and that is why I was so successful prior to my mental breakdown. I believe that as my history both personal and professional is examined holistically it will be found that I'm no more of a criminal than I am an astronaut. I'm not perfect and I'm not a saint but I'm not a criminal. I did make a lot of mistakes in my life like most people. What I am is a man who was inflicted with four major psychiatric diseases that were not self-imposed by any immoral or illicit behaviors. I overcame the negative symptoms of most of them for at least four decades but they eventually overcame me. As stated previously, half the American public at some time in their lives will suffer with some type of psychological disorder. The older you get the more susceptible you are to mental disorders.

I did become a multi-millionaire by founding and developing very fine companies. In essence I was accused of and prosecuted for taking the risk to start a new business. That is something that made this country the greatest nation in the world that there ever was especially economically. I took the risk of starting another new business after losing my former company to my ex-wife.

My previous companies underwent annual audits by independent auditing firms to satisfy requirements of the lending institutions for twenty-five years. Nothing relating to fraud was ever found. In any business venture there are plenty of negatives, but you invest because the negatives are overshadowed by the positives. If the venture fails, then the finger pointing starts and all the "should haves" arise. At my trial and sentencing hearing the district attorney stated that the company didn't exist and was just a front to milk funds from investors. False, the company existed for over a year and had eight employees. The DA referred to it as Mr. Walshe's company. Yes, I was the key man but technically I was an unpaid employee to the company. The district attorney said Mr. Walshe was just trying to extort money from an investor. I had no personal monetary gain from the venture. Neither of the two assigned public defenders presented one instance or word of my honorable four-year military career and very successful business career or my humanitarian activities. The District Court never heard that I wasn't the legal owner of American Imaging

Solutions because I wasn't cognizant enough to tell them otherwise. I was in too passive of a state to even care what the court heard. They should have learned that when they extradited me. If the crime concerned me remembering, then why wasn't the jury allowed to hear testimony about my memory and the diseases that affected my brain and memory?

A new business has a twenty-five percent chance of being successful. Let me state that I successfully started the following companies:

- Finzer Imaging Systems Inc. of Washington
- Finzer Leasing Inc. of Washington
- Finzer Leasing Inc. of Colorado
- Finzer Imaging Systems Inc. of Colorado
- Finzer Holding Inc. which owned Olympic Copiers Inc. and Copyco Inc.
- I also participated in the founding of Tech National Bank

With only a one out of four chance of success I would judge my success rate to be pretty good. If we assume that I was legally and actually responsible for the failure of American Imaging Solutions, Inc. I still had a success rate of eighty-three percent.

I ask you to consider what the originals explorers, the captains of industry, immigrants, pioneers and the original settlers did? They took big risk in their undertaking. They weren't sure or had any guarantees. When Columbus sailed, he wasn't even sure that there were the two continents of North and South America. He was looking for Asia not the Americas. Bill Gates one of the richest men in the world failed at his first venture. Where would this country be if people like me were not willing to take large risk? Maybe my risks weren't as large, but it was still big risk for me as they say, "I put everything on the line."

If I was trying to extort, I wouldn't have knowingly personally guaranteed the note to the investor? I was trying to be a productive citizen as I had always been as substantiated by my resume. They claim that I didn't fully disclose my business history to the investor. Unfortunately, I don't have any memory of what disclosed to the investor. You might say that was a convenient excuse but the psychiatric professionals' evaluations support what I have stated about my memory.

May I state that President Abraham Lincoln is rated to be one our greatest presidents and in world recognition of the greatest people he ranks with Jesus and Mohammed. President Lincoln in his campaign literature and speeches never disclosed that he had lost eight elections, the business that he failed at or his mental breakdown due to major depression which he overcame. Thomas Jefferson filed for bankruptcy. I tried to do the same and I successfully overcame the negative effects of my psychiatric disorders for years, but they eventually overcame me. If anyone thinks that I deliberately succumbed to my psychiatric disorders where I lost all my worldly possession and my mind than they are crazier than I.

The trial occurred in February of 2015 a mere four months after the cardiologist said my heart was too weak to stand trial and after I had two heart attacks, heart surgery and my heart function was barely seventeen percent. I asked my counsel for copies of cancelled checks to aid in my defense, but I never received them even though I was being accused of executing a bad check and extracting funds from the corporation for my personal use. The Sheriff's department refused me access to materials that I wrote which would have aided in my defense. They said that they were a fire hazard. Because of my failed memory those documents were critical in my prompting my memory. As stated, many of my notes were missing after cell searches. The jail staff frowned on me taking notes.

It is strange that Mr. Earle's one of my public defenders doubted mental disability because I was able to remember that his wife was pregnant with a child that they were going to name Alexander. I remembered because I named my youngest son Alexander. Mr. Earle and his partner also doubted my mental disability or deficiency because my disease was referred to pseudo dementia and to a layman pseudo means false. Why didn't they research it? How good of a defense can your public defenders render when they are not convinced of your innocence? Neither of my two children who had worked for me at the Colorado company, Rene' for twenty-two years and Christopher for seventeen years were never called as witnesses to testify as to my honesty and integrity. They could have been asked in all the years that you worked for your father in the business did you ever hear of or witness him committing an illegal act? My son Alexander who worked in the new business could have and would have attested to the businesses existence which the prosecution denied. I may have made a lot of errors in developing the business, but it was a legitimate and operational business. It was my fault that the business failed.

Instead of being admired for trying to start a new business I was prosecuted. I do know that the company had a clearly defined business plan which is one of the reasons the investor invested. It had an inventory of color copiers, trained service technicians, a telemarketing staff, salespeople and an administrative staff. To say that it was just a front for fraud is a falsehood. To say that I made many bad decisions unknowingly because of my poor mental health is probably the truth. You fail your way to success in a new venture. Do we prosecute people for mismanagement?

Was I a defrauder or a man who was taking the initiative to start a new business which would provide opportunities for many as I did in the past? What does my history indicate I was attempting to do? If I was so greedy for money, why was I so generous? I did this at the age of 64 when most people are retiring or considering it. I did what most sane people wouldn't consider doing at my late age. I started all over again by starting another business as my contribution to society even though the odds were against my success like they were before. I took the initiative and had the courage to move forward and do something productive.

It was never disclosed in court that I had personally guaranteed the note to the investor. It makes me wonder about a witness and a so-called plaintiff not disclosing vital information in a trial? If you are going to defraud someone you don't personally guarantee the note. I understand that the investor wrote checks five different times over a period of several months as his investment in the company. Why would he have continued to invest more funds if he wasn't pleased with the company's progress? The district attorney stated that there wasn't really a company, and it was all a fraud and there wasn't even any inventory. I don't believe that she properly investigated as to the company's existence. I admit that I would have been very disturbed if I had lost money as the investor did. I can understand his anger.

Maybe I did not properly disclose how I lost my previous company, but I rather doubt that because the investor supposedly invested because of my previous success and not my so-called failure in losing my company. There was over two and a half decades of dynamic success in me starting four companies and operating six companies. Why did I have to raise outside investor capital instead of using my own? As inferred if he did not like the progress that I was making in developing the new company why then did he continue to invest? Any person of my age at that time in my life of sixty-four years has had their fair share of failures in achieving success. I had very successfully developed and operated six companies. I had very successful previous business career of forty years. I did not allow my mental health disorders inhibit me from achieving my previous success. I had attended to those mental health disorders to minimize their effect on my career without knowing that I had been misdiagnosed at the time.

If there wasn't inherent risk, why else was I willing to pay eighteen percent interest and personally guarantee the promissory note? The higher the interest rate the less credit worthiness of the borrower. If I wasn't willing to disclose information about my previous company then why was the investor willing to lend the funds? If there wasn't a good business plan, why would someone be willing to invest?

I was also accused and convicted of check fraud which I don't understand since I don't believe that the checking account was in my name since it was a corporate account. I have no memory of it or the supposed overdraft which I understand amounted to $3,426.00. There is very little success without failure along the way. If Thomas Edison was still alive, we could ask him. He failed more than 999 times when inventing the light bulb. I wasn't afraid of risk; that is why I accompanied my brother on a health care mission to rural Nigeria where we had to be guarded twenty-four hours a day by soldiers with a machine guns. If I was so greedy, why did I give money away especially to unfortunate children's causes? Why did I adopt children, a complete unknown but I didn't care? Why was I willing to volunteer to serve my country in a time of a very unpopular war? Being a person with my psychiatric profile and history should have automatically caused questions that were never asked during my prosecution and consequently never answered. The district attorney's office besides being a prosecuting unit of the government is also considered an investigative unit.

Let us say that I was absolutely guilty of everything that I was accused of did that give the court the right to withhold vital evidence as to memory or mental health disorders. Did that give the jail personnel the right to allow me to be abused by other inmates? One of the assaults resulted in a stroke. Did that give some deputies the right to inhumanely assault a senile old man which resulted in two heart attacks and having to have heart surgery? Did that give deputies the right to assault a senile old man with a history of two heart attacks and assault him in almost the same manner as George Floyd? I didn't die as George Floyd did but my heart function was a mere seventeen percent. If the district attorney's office was concerned with upholding the law, why didn't they ask why did I show up in court with a large head wound and two black eyes? It was obvious to all my loved ones in that court room that I had been beaten up but not to the district attorney. Some of my loved ones were brought to tears when they saw me. How often does an old man show up in court with a large and very obvious head wound and not one but two black eyes?

I would describe my treatment by their so-called justice system as a charade. As the records will demonstrate there was no pursuit of justice and truth but a game of who was going to win no matter how much truth and justice was trampled on. To my public defenders they just wanted to get the case over with and to hell with justice. I assume that they were just too taxed with cases. It is obvious that my life didn't matter to the justice or penal system.

Probation Report Adams County

The probation report submitted to the Adams County District Court by Probation Supervisor Lindsay Gooden contained numerous errors and false information such as it listed numerous addresses where I never resided or worked. It cited a personal bankruptcy that was filed but not followed through on and no debt was forgiven. It cited incorrect employment history for nineteen years and did not mention my earnings and income levels for thirty-eight years. It named the wrong business partners. It cited that I had a pool of victims which was totally false. One investor lost money in the new company I had started not a pool of investors.

The report implied that I wasn't successful in a career which is another falsehood. I was continually successful in the U.S. Air Force and promoted three times in four years. I was continually promoted at Xerox Corporation and Savin Corporation in all the corporations that I worked for. As an entrepreneur I became a multi-millionaire. Consider the fact that the divorce court awarded my ex-wife Rebecca Walshe in today's dollar values approximately $61,000.00 per month along with other benefits such as our home which she sold for about a million dollars and new automobiles.

I don't know how much weight those distortions of the truth carried in my sentencing. For a white-collar crime I was sent to a maximum-security prison. Ms. Gooden one of the authors of the report should have researched my court records and consulted my siblings and children. Not one word was mentioned about my humanitarian deeds. I was convicted of not properly disclosing information what about the officials of the court? It listed me as living in Reno, Nevada. I've never been to Reno even for a stopover or a short visit.

Again, I was prosecuted for not giving information to an investor, but Ms. Gooden's actions were very similar in that she submitted false information to the court. You would think that it should have occurred to Ms. Gooden why did Mr. Walshe fail after over four and a half decades of success? It makes me wonder if Ms. Gooden would have been more diligent in her department's efforts if I hadn't appeared to be a used up senile old man. I was at the time an elderly man of 64 years who used up all of his financial resources and mental being in trying to start a new enterprise without any immediate gain personal gain. Twenty-five percent or one out of every four new businesses fail in the first year. I would like to believe that my life mattered too but it is obvious that it didn't matter to Ms. Gooden or the Probation Department. It appears that my life was very cheap to them.

Sentencing Hearing Adams County

On April 16, 2015, there were numerous representatives of the justice system and the law when I appeared with a large head wound with not one but two black eyes and my guts were protruding out of me. As stated not one representative or officer of the law enquired as to what happened to me. It is like it was common for a senile senior citizen especially one with my disabilities to show up in court beaten up in the county jail. My sister and my sons were very disturbed when they saw my wounds and my guts protruding out of me bulging in my pants. My granddaughter was brought to tears when she saw her Papa so battered and wondered what had happened to him. It makes you wonder about a double standard in enforcing the law. There is one standard for the accused no matter what their circumstances or profile and one for law enforcement. The jail staff can't police themselves. What about a standard for the elderly, disabled veterans, mentally and physically ill? At Adams County my eyes were opened as to how cruel and mean people can be who are charged with justice and law enforcement. I was left with the impression and justifiably so that life is very cheap in the Adams County Justice System especially for the elderly. The incident was akin to what happened to the lady with dementia in Loveland, Colorado.

If anyone from my past life believes that I should have been punished for misdeeds they got their wish from how I was treated at Adams County and later at Sterling Prison. It causes me to wonder what did the ancient Greeks knew when they questioned if we should prosecute the elderly? You don't have to be a mental giant to realize that the body and all of its vital organs which includes the brain deteriorate with age. We are just not capable of enduring in our golden years what we were in our younger years. Ask those who administer to the elderly in nursing homes if you doubt what I write and proclaim. Why do we place the elderly in nursing homes? As indicated earlier in this writing the older you get the more susceptible you are to being afflicted with demented state and its complications. It appears that in Adams County as manifested through their abuse and negligence that elderly lives don't matter no matter what good they have done in the past. It was the great philosopher Emerson who believed that a man deserved to be judged by his best not his worst.

By the way after my trail and before my sentencing on April 16th for some reason a psychological evaluation was ordered again but it still was never completed. Why was it ordered? I was still placed in solitary confinement when I was transferred to the Region Detention Center. A psychological screen was done by a person who was not considered by the law to be an expert for formal forensic evaluation purposes. It is my understanding that those evaluations are not done at the Adams County Jail. One was done six months later at Sterling Prison where I was diagnosed with four major psychiatric disorders. Please keep in mind as witnesses will state for months after I got to Sterling Prison, I still couldn't remember my cellmate or the location of my cell. My cognitive ability did gradually improve but not my memory. That took two more years for me to establish new memories but until this day I still have no memory of those missing twenty-five years of my life. Three years after my release from prison, I'm still regaining cognitive ability. I thank God for that.

CHAPTER 28

The Denver Regional Detention Center

The next thing that I have a memory of after being taken to the floor at the Adams County Jail is waking up in solitary confinement in the Denver Regional Detention Center on April 18, 2015. I don't know if I lost my memory or was knocked unconscious again at the jail because my head ached severely. While at the RDC I remember waking up on the floor in solitary confinement in a torn jump suit. I remember a guard was kicking me in the shoulder to see if I was still alive like I was just a piece of meat. It demonstrated how much respect the guards have for the elderly especially veterans. He couldn't bother to bend down to check on me he had to kick an old man. I also remember being chained up and being taken to see a neurologist, a Dr. Melisa Johnson who was analyzing me at the center. I was issued a blanket with holes in it the size of golf balls. It was dirty and full of human hair. After Dr. Johnson's analysis she came to see me at my cell and said that my memory was fine. When I asked her why I had no memories of the last twenty-five years of my life especially my youngest son's birth or upbringing she simply said, "Mr. Walshe, I don't have time to stand around and talk to you" and she walked away. Needless to say, I was very disturbed by that comment coming from a highly educated mental health professional. I'm sorry that her schedule to be so taxed as all the mental health professionals seem to be at the Department of Corrections.

What I asked must have made an impression on her because six months later Dr. Johnson agreed without seeing me again with Dr. Bryce Willson's diagnose of me. They said that I had dissociative amnesia which accounted for the loss of memories of the latter twenty-five years of my life. If Dr. Johnson didn't have time to stand around and talk to me then how could she properly diagnose with me or confer with Dr. Willson? I don't have any other memories of being at the RDC. I had regressed again after being moved. I needed to be in a stable and stressless environment in order to progress in my recovery from a demented state. Being transferred and moved many times was detrimental to my recovery as manifested in my regressions when I was moved. Being moved so much mimicked the repercussions of being placed in solitary confinement. The records state that I was housed there for three weeks in a manner synonymous with solitary confinement. I still don't know why I was placed in solitary confinement for such a long period of time in spite of Federal Court rulings which banned it for a 70-year-old man with a psychiatric condition. Dr. Johnson must know the negative effects solitary confinement has on the mentally ill and the Department of Corrections regulations concerning it. I was never given a reason as to why I was housed in solitary confinement. I don't recall receiving any health care in spite of my cardiac history.

I did not know why I had no memory of being transferred to as they term the RDC. It was frightening to keep regressing into a demented state when I was moved. Understandably I didn't want to fall back into the animalistic state again when I was struggling so much to regain my cognitive ability and ability to remember. I was struggling to learn and become cognitive again. The first book that I read when I started to regain my cognitive ability was on learning.

CHAPTER 29

Sterling Prison

As was common with me at the time I still couldn't establish new memories when I arrived at Sterling Prison so what I write come from my notes. One of my cell mates told me that I was a "big pain the ass" as he put it because I couldn't remember him or where my cell was. At Sterling Prison with my large intestine handing out 12" like a banana they thought it best to assign me to a top bunk. At times I was housed on the third tier so I would have to painfully climb upstairs. I would stumble and fall climbing in and out of my bunk. When I fell it was against the metal furnishings which made it more painful. When I suggested that I sleep on the floor so I wouldn't fall, Lt. Hoffman thought best to threaten me if I did as if that would solve the problem. Courts have ruled that prison authorities must take the prisoner as they find him and provide facilities with his physical condition that meet a civilized standard of decency. Unfortunately for me the staff at Sterling chose to ignore that ruling or other rulings. They had their own standard of decency. That was borne out in a recent ACLU suit against the prison concerning the pandemic and the treatment of prisoners. From a worldly and legal point of view the Supreme Court of the U.S. has stated that deliberate indifference to serious medical needs of prisoners constitutes the unnecessary and wanton infliction of pain as proscribed by the Eighth Amendment to the Constitution. But who cares about prisoners? I admit that I didn't care before I was a prisoner.

CHAPTER 30

Attempt On My Life
Denver County Jail

About May 23, 2015, a little over three weeks after arriving at Sterling Prison I was taken to the Denver County Jail for a court appearance. I spent all day in the waiting room which was very taxing on my nervous system because it was a relatively small area for the number of prisoners that were in it. Being confined in a small area for a long period of time causes the inmates in the room to become very anxious and boisterous. The noise from all the loud talk and hollering was taxing on me. I did everything that I could to control my thoughts and feelings so I wouldn't initiate a panic attack. I would close my eyes and cover my ears to block out the noise and the chaotic atmosphere. Later in the evening I was taken to a multiple man cell that at the time contained about seven men. The guards when assigning me a bed noticed how much my inguinal hernia was bulging in my pants which indicated to them that I couldn't be placed in a top bunk as they made me do at Sterling Prison. My guts hanging out of me was that obvious to the guards. They had a black man move from a bottom bunk to a top bunk to accommodate my disability.

After the guards left the cell three black men, who I presume resented me entering and disrupting their domain, came up to me and said "we hate white men". I said to myself oh my God what is going to happen now? They stated we are going to kill a white man tonight and it's you. I became terrified. I said to myself and to God, it's all over and my life is at an end and I'm in your domain Lord. I was in no condition to defend myself against the onslaughts of what seemed to be three very large men. I was still recovering from assaults at the Adams County Jail.

I vaguely remember, because I started to disassociate, one of the three men grabbing me by the throat and all three pushing me backwards to the floor. All of a sudden and miraculously another black man stepped in and in the chaos of the moment I escaped to the guard station for refuge. I told the guards what was happening to me. The guards went into the cell and removed the three black men. Very inquisitively and gratefully I asked the black man who stepped in to save me why he stepped in to help me? I believe without a question that his actions saved my life. He said that he remembered me from the Adams County Jail and that I had told him that I had been in his home country on a Christian health care mission. I asked him what country that was and he said Nigeria. I said that I had been there and thanked him so much for saving my life. I felt very grateful to God and that man. I was so surprised that anyone in that environment would risk harm to their being to save me. I couldn't believe the so-called coincidence because Nigeria is the country with the largest population in Africa of over 200 million people and the U.S. has a population of 331 million people. I said to myself, when you do good it is sooner or later it returns to you. Now if that isn't the hand of God, what is? I don't know what the exact odds are of that happening, but it is unbelievable. I'm writing this with tears of gratitude streaming from my eyes.

A couple of years later I was walking the track at Sterling Prison; a black man came up to me and said I don't know if you remember me but I was there the night in the Denver Jail when those men as he put it were bullying you. I told him about my memory disorders and apologized to him for not remembering him. He told me his name and that he was 59 years old. I asked him if he remembered the man who saved my life. He told me the man's name and that he saved me because he knew that I had been in his home country of Nigeria on a health care mission. I couldn't and still can't believe the coincidence. To me there was no coincidence but the Hand of God for my past good deeds. Here was another incident just like with my son Chris giving me a home fifty years after I gave him a home. It had been two decades before when I accompanied my brother on a Christian health care mission to Nigeria. It was a dangerous mission where we under the protection of an armed guard who carried machine gun and watched over us for twenty-four hours a day. There I was putting my life in danger for others and here I was two decades later a man putting his life in danger for me. The good I did two decades earlier came back to me. By the way no one from the district attorney's office ever showed up for my court appearance. It was just a big waste of time without any regard for my physical or mental well-being. Yes I do believe in divine destiny and in miracles. Wait until you read what I experienced while walking the track at prison. Now my oldest grandson, a marine, is stationed at the American Embassy in Lagos, Nigeria.

CHAPTER 31

Adams County Assault Trial

I was brought back to the Adams County Jail to appear in court for on an assault trial for supposedly spitting on a Deputy Spotts on April 17, 2015. My court appointed attorney Mr. Steven R. Barnes had written to me that he requested that an investigator by the name of Mark Carlson be appointed to properly investigate the incident but that never happened. I didn't even meet my attorney, Mr. Barnes, until the evening before the trial. I had not talked even on the phone or met with him before. How was he able to properly prepare my defense? The case couldn't have been properly investigated. At this point in my incarceration because of my psychological and physical disorders proper investigation and preparation was essential. Now if that isn't considered ineffective assistance of counsel what is? I can only assume that Mr. Barnes wasn't being paid enough for his efforts by Adams County, so he treated my case accordingly.

As stated earlier being transferred from the prison to jail was very hard on my disorders especially my heart disease. I was recovering from a heart function of only twenty-six percent of normal. As stated, I was brought back to the Adams Jail from Sterling Prison six times for the assault charge. In my later visits to the jail after I was assaulted by an inmate, I was housed in a dirty filthy cell in solitary confinement. Even after my stroke

I was housed the same way. At that time of my incarceration at the jail or Sterling Prison I couldn't even remember my cell or cellmate. At the trial I was found guilty but not sentenced to any more time in prison or any other penalties. I understand from my notes that with my lack of cognitive ability that I just made a fool out of myself when I testified in my defense. The trial was a charade. Even my defense attorney, Mr. Barnes, criticized my conduct to the court and jury. I understand that I just ranted on and on in desperation when giving testimony in my defense.

I believe at this point in time that Judge Ensor realized my deficient mental abilities and that is why he didn't increase my sentence me to any more time in prison. He stated at the trial I've known Mr. Walshe for years. What did he know?

The trial and the six trips from Sterling Prison to the Adams Jail turned out to be a big waste of time and resources. Unfortunately, during one of the transfers from Sterling an assault on November 25, 2015, by an inmate caused me to have another stroke and to lose more of my memory that I had struggled so hard to regain. I had previously pleaded in a letter to Judge Roybal to no avail to be returned to Sterling Prison after my first court appearance. For ample reason I was very afraid to be housed at the jail. It causes you to wonder if the district attorney gives any consideration to an accused mental and physical profile and even the cost to prosecute. They knew of my cardiac history at the jail, but they insisted on extraditing me as they did when they did when they extradited me from the Texas prison. They extradited what could be considered a mental invalid six times from the Sterling Prison. By the time of my trial the Department of Corrections had evaluated my mental health and had diagnosed me with four major psychiatric disorders, but that evidence was not introduced at the trial except in my ranting while testifying. What kind of a lawyer would withhold that type of evidence from the court? Probably one who wasn't being paid enough to properly investigate.

In this case they went to all that expense to prosecute me, but nothing was done to the deputies who assaulted me and caused two heart attacks and having to have heart surgery during my fifteen months of incarceration at the jail. What about my being assaulted and treated in a similar manner as George Floyd was? Anyone especially the internal affairs people who later visited me at Sterling could view the security tape of April 3, 2015 and see that I didn't fall down as the deputies claimed as an excuse for being knocked unconscious by them. If the security tape of April 3rd is missing which it may be the case other inmates could have been interviewed. The other inmates told me what happened when I was returned to the jail pod. Some of the inmates wound up at Sterling Prison and they told me what happened to me on April 3rd. They had been threatened for protesting to the deputies for how I had been treated. The inmates had more moral standards than the deputies at the jail.

In my opinion if I had been willing to cut a deal as I was asked to do concerning the assault on April 3rd the incident of April 17th would have never happened. The assault on my person on Thanksgiving Weekend would not have occurred and maybe the stroke on Thanksgiving Weekend wouldn't have occurred. Stress is a huge risk factor for strokes. The taxpayers of Adams County were made to pay for all what is best termed as negligence, a charade and a complete waste of taxpayers' money to cover up criminalistic misdeeds by deputies at the jail. My history at the Adams County Jail and the Justice System there indicates that the deputies' lives matter there as they should but not the elderly especially ones who dare to complain.

CHAPTER 32

Assaults at Sterling Prison

On October 7, 2015, at Sterling Prison I was told to pack up that I was being transported to the Adams Jail for a court appearance. I complied and was sent to what they called the receiving area even though I was being transported. When I arrived at receiving, I waited to be chained, shackled and cuffed up for transportation. Being cuffed up was very painful for me because I have arthritis in my wrists and hands. I knew the trip would be painful because of how I would be shackled. When I was cuffed up, it hurt more than normal because the cuffs were placed with them what is termed "stacked" which makes your wrists and hands immobile in an awkward position which in my case strains them. My wrists and hands are not as mobile as a younger person's. Being stacked became more painful ever since the time when Deputy Yesin twisted my wrist behind my back when I went to him with chest pain at the Adams County Jail Medical Clinic while recovering from a heart attack and the assault on April 3rd.

I was very fearful of going back to the Adams Jail because of the number of times that I was attacked there by the deputies and inmates. The deputies who were supposed to safeguard me were responsible for six assaults and ignored my pleas about harassment by inmates. Please keep in mind that I only remember the assaults by the deputies that took place my last 7½ months there. I have no memory of ninety-nine percent of the events of my first eight months of incarceration at the Adams Jail. That amounts to one assault about every 5.7 weeks that I can remember. That does not include any assaults or harassment by prisoners. As stated, it resulted in me suffering two heart attacks and having to have heart surgery while incarcerated there. Needless to say my stay at the Adams Jail had a very traumatic effect on me as it would any human being. That isn't considering my treatment from the so-called justice system there. My history taught me not to have any faith in the justice system there. Who wants to go back to a place where he had the hell beat out of him? Who wants to be judged in a court system where vital evidence is not allowed to be presented? I almost died in that jail. All of a sudden, I had a panic attack in the transport area which elevated to an angina pectoris attack. I found myself lying on the floor. Subconsciously I must have been terrified to go back to that jail. I had every right to be because of inhumane treatment there and what happened just six weeks later on November 25th and the 27th. I was taken to the medical clinic where they performed an EKG and a blood pressure test. Both tests proved to be abnormal, but the medical staff still approved me to be transported to Adams County even with my tenuous cardiac and neurological profile. If that isn't medical malpractice what is? That concerned me and why wouldn't it? Would you go back any place where you were assaulted multiple times and almost died? If my heart function dropping to seventeen percent and a heart attack isn't frightening, what is? It was like being sent to death row.

The Courts have ruled that prisoners may not be transferred if their medical conditions make it dangerous to their health. When I was sent back to receiving to be transported to the Adams Jail, I had another angina pectoris panic attack. I was very susceptible to those attacks since part of my circulatory system was dead. Again, as stated I must be very afraid of being taken back to the Adams Jail as I had every right to be because of the treatment there at the jail and court system. It is like being sentenced to a beating. Please remember prior to originally arriving at the Adams Jail at the Federal prison I couldn't even find the bathroom or the dining hall. The brain and mind have a way of protecting its life. You naturally lose your volitional ability under the circumstances that my brain was in. At the prison instead of being taken back to medical I was placed in solitary confinement or the "Hole" where I passed out on the bunk. Because there wasn't an adequate refractory period while in the "Hole" as stated I had another angina pectoris attack which was so painful that I fell on the cold and dirty concrete floor. Please keep in mind my blood pressure was abnormal and so was the EKG. While lying on the floor I started to disassociate. I fell into what I believe to be a semi-conscious state and was trying to understand what was going on. When the guards couldn't arouse me to their satisfaction when I was lying on the floor, they opened the slot in the cell door and sprayed me with oleoresin capsicum chemicals. When that didn't work to arouse me, they sprayed me a second time right over where I had been operated on recently for skin cancer. It burned my skin intensely especially over the incisions from skin cancer operation. When the second spray with chemicals didn't work to arouse me three guards wearing helmets and bearing shields opened the cell door and attacked me. I was still in that semiconscious state. One of the guards reached down and ground his knuckles into my chest right over where I had heart surgery, where metal stents had been implanted in a vital artery. It was also where I was experiencing severe chest pain. That hurt so much that for the first time in my 70 years I hollered and screamed out loud in pain. I was so traumatized that I lost control of my bladder and bowels and shamefully soiled myself. At that point to say the least I was terrified and in tremendous pain. I remember the guards stripping the clothes off of me. Then they threw me naked into a cold shower which further traumatized me. I vaguely remember a female guard videoing the attack. It didn't matter to her or the other guards that I was naked. I remember saying out loud this is somewhat what it was like for my brethren at Auschwitz Concentration

Camp. I know that was an exaggeration and could not compare with the horror that those poor souls suffered but that's how traumatized that I was. I believe that the stress on my mind and body caused me to become delirious. I was experiencing severe chest pain which terrifies me because of my recent heart surgery and heart attacks just a year prior. Plus, the chemicals were intensely burning my eyes and skin as they were meant to. At the same time besides the chest pain my intestines were very painfully hanging out of me. The cold water of the shower did little do alleviate the skin from burning because on an elderly person as stated before the epidermis is very thin and very susceptible to burning from chemical spray. Plus, I was sprayed twice right over the tender surgical incision. As stated, the pain from the residue of the chemicals was especially intense where I had recently been operated on for skin cancer over the left temporal lobe. The scar from the incision swelled up and felt like a raw carrot and a big lump on my temporal lobe. It felt like a burning poker was being forced into my skin.

The courts have ruled that officers may not use chemical agents against a person who poses no risk. I was lying on the floor in solitary confinement in an unresponsive state at no risk to anyone. The only thing that I was bothering was Captain Long's ego. Here was this senile old man in an unresponsive state and not obeying his orders to get up, how dare I be so obstinate? He demonstrated to me and the guards his authority and how to deal with disobedient inmates no matter what their age or condition. I wonder if Jeff Long would be willing to relate the incident to his father or grandfather? I wouldn't dare show that video to my three sons and six grandsons. Would he be willing to show his loved ones the video of the attack and describe to them my mental and physical profile? I wonder if the warden viewed the video?

The courts have also ruled that once chemicals are used the prisoner should be allowed a reasonable opportunity for decontamination. I couldn't believe how I had to holler out in pain in order to endure the pain. I had never before hollered out in pain before or lost control of my bladder and bowels because of pain.

After that attack I was thrown back in the "Hole" for nine more days. I wondered what the purpose of was arousing me from the cell floor just to be thrown back into a cell. I wasn't allowed to shower for three days to remove the chemical residue with soap and hot water. My skin and eyes burned for that period of time. The prison officials completely ignored court rulings such as of Walker vs. Bowersox where chemicals were used and proper decontamination wasn't allowed as deliberate indifference. To endure, I remember saying to myself what the German philosopher Nietzsche said, "That which does not kill me only makes me stronger." Ultimately, I did grow stronger even with a very weak heart and eight other major health disorders at 70 years of age. I was determined to endure, survive and rise up again no matter how painful it was and would be. You can beat me but not defeat me only I can do that through disbelief in myself.

Federal Court Rulings prohibit the use of chemicals on the mentally ill or those that are considered "At Risk." Those rulings don't seem to inhibit some of the guards at Sterling to act as if they are immune to the law. A few days later after being released from solitary confinement when I was walking the track, I met up with Captain Jeffrey Long the man who initiated and led the attack on me. I asked him how he felt about abusing an old man. He claimed that he sought and had the approval of medical and mental health personnel. That statement caused me to lose respect for Captain Long who is now the Warden Long. If you are going to commit a wrongful act, at least be man enough to admit it and if appropriate stand by it. To cover their tracks, I was accused of refusing to be transported to Adams County and was given ten days in the "Hole." I experienced severe chest pain for months after the assault where the guard ground his knuckles into my chest. Right after that assault I started having grand mal seizures for almost two years. Grand mal seizures are a sign of brain damage and abnormal electrical activity in the brain and can be deadly to a person with a weakened heart. They are frightening!

I wrote to Warden John Chapdelaine about the assault. When he met with me, he stated that he was afraid to empower me. I said to him: it is your people who empower me with their malicious conduct. I believe that Warden Chapdelaine ordered a psychological evaluation because shortly after the assault I underwent an evaluation by a staff psychologist Dr. Bryce Willson. He diagnosed me as having acute anxiety, bi-polar disease, major depression and dissociative amnesia. He conferred with Dr. Melisa Johnson at the Regional Detention Center who confirmed his diagnosis especially dissociative amnesia. The courts have ruled that major depression and bi-polar disorders to be extremely serious diseases.

Two months later on December 30th I was ordered to the medical clinic for a colonoscopy. I asked that it not be done because my rectum hurt too much. My hemorrhoids were very swollen, they were bleeding and consequently very painful. The medical personnel saw my request as a refusal, so they ordered me to be placed in solitary confinement. When Nurse Ryder visited me in solitary confinement, I asked him if he approved the attack on October 7th; he said that he did approve it. When I asked him if that was proper, he said it was up to the proper medical board to judge his actions. A mistake or wrong not admitted in a timely manner only grows in size. It wasn't proper for Nurse Ryder to approve the attack because court rulings state that chest pain especially someone with an acute cardiac history requires a qualified physician's attention.

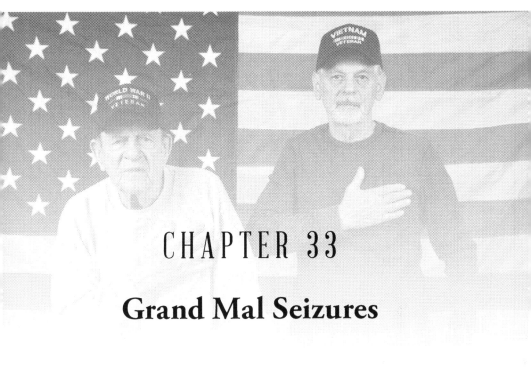

CHAPTER 33

Grand Mal Seizures

After an assault on October 7, 2015, I started having severe grand mal seizures. I would be found unconscious lying on the cell floor foaming at the mouth biting my lips and tongue causing them to bleed. I would lose continence in my urinary track and would embarrassingly wet myself. My body would shake all over from violent muscle contractions. My seizures got so bad that they would frighten the guards and even the emergency personnel. Seizures are usually caused by tissue damage in the brain. Abnormal electrical activity in the brain can lead to strokes and I already experienced two strokes. They usually occurred when I was sleeping so I wasn't aware of their onset. When I first started having scizures Dr. Christner requested neurological testing for me. Her request was denied even though I had to have seven stitches in my head from falling on the floor which split the scalp on my head open when I had a seizure. Grand mal seizures are life threatening especially when not properly treated. Plus, as stated, I already suffered from two strokes. The prison dealt with my problem by ignoring it. The seizures lasted about two years and I had at least forty of them. They were terrifying! Seizures have been proven to weaken the heart and the brain which just added to my issues with those organs. As stated, the seizures would even frighten the emergency personnel who were supposedly trained to deal with them. I would go to sleep not knowing more than most people if I was going to wake up, where I was going to wake up and in what condition I would wake up. It was difficult and painful for me to talk or eat for days after a grand mal seizure because my lips and tongue were very sore and swollen from the bruises from me biting them. I thank God that they stopped because people with a history of grand mal seizures as I did are at risk for sudden death from them.

CHAPTER 34

More Assaults Sterling Prison

My Gay Cellmate

On May 27, 2016, I was moved to another a cell and my new cellmate claimed that he was gay. He stated that to move me into his cell they had to relocate his lover not only to another cell but to another unit or building where he and his lover couldn't have any further contact. He told me that before he ever laid eyes on me, he hated me because he blamed me for the breakup of his relationship with his lover of three years. He was continually critical of my actions no matter what I did. He used every opportunity to harass and criticize me. He enjoyed telling me how he beat up other inmates and cell mates. He was incarcerated for murder. He described to me how he shot a man in the head and just to make sure that the victim was dead he fired two more bullets into his head. He told me what he would do to me if I didn't comply with his wishes. Needless to say, I was very fearful of what he would kill me. It made the atmosphere in the cell with him very stressful. One day for no reason he grabbed me by the throat and pushed me up against the wall. He kept on verbally harassing and telling me how much he hated me for the breakup of his relationship. He continually punched me in the abdomen which was already sore because of my protruding hernias. It served to intensify the nausea and chronic severe pain from the hernias.

I told Sgt. Snyder what was happening to me, but he refused to move me. He didn't believe me because I had no wounds or scars. Needless to say, my stay in the cell with this man was pure hell from the continual verbal and physical harassment. I was always on edge because I never knew when and what would cause him to attack me. While incarcerated in that cell I suffered from chronic chest pain. There was no consideration given to my physical or mental health profile in housing me. Finally, two other inmates talked to another correctional officer about what I was enduring and thankfully that guard moved me to another cell.

Massive Heart Attack Sterling

The morning of September 24, 2016, all the inmates were being moved from unit two to unit three, so all the inmates had to evacuate their cells and wait in the day room. The move was particularly stressful for me because I had just changed cells the day before. I waited in the dayroom day room with about ninety-seven other inmates who were acting very anxious, boisterous and irritated because they had to move. The day room became noisier and more chaotic with inmates talking very loud over each other so they could be heard in the chaotic and very loud atmosphere. The atmosphere became very turbulent and riotous. You could tell from their demeanor that it was even affecting the guards negatively. I started to feel pressure and tightness in my chest around the heart from tachycardia and heart palpitations. I felt an angina pectoris attack starting as the pressure and tightness in my chest kept escalating especially in that part where the arteries are blocked. The pain and pressure in my chest around my heart kept on increasing and I was experiencing shortness breath to the point where I could hardly breathe. I sensed another heart attack starting and I was terrified. I just had a stroke only ten months before. There was just too much frightening exposure to the chaotic and rowdy atmosphere in the dayroom for me to tolerate it. The more boisterous the voices got and the more riotous the atmosphere got the more the pressure in my chest increased. I thought that my death was imminent. I knew how low my heart function was and that the surgeons at the Platt Valley Medical Center were afraid to operate on me because it.

I suddenly uncontrollably fell to the floor in a fetal position with my arms clutching my chest trying to endure the intense chest pain. I felt paralyzed because of the tremendous intense strangulation pain in my chest. I thought that I was going to die because of the tremendous pressure and pain surrounding my heart plus the nauseous pain in my abdomen. Again, I remembered that my last heart function was measured at a mere seventeen percent. I was in too much pain and agony when Lieutenant Sherwood ordered me to sit up straight when I was placed in a wheelchair to be taken to the medical clinic. When I couldn't straighten up it was like I was paralyzed in a fetal position because of the intense pain. There was no way I could straighten up it was too painful when I tried. Lt. Sherwood started yelling at me very loudly to straighten up. I just couldn't straighten up as much as I tried. Lt. Sherwood kept yelling at me, but I could no longer understand his commands. He kept yelling and harassing me. Lt. Sherwood then he yelled out according to witnesses that he was going to teach a f-cking old man how to respect a correctional officer's orders. When I couldn't respond he grabbed me from behind the wheelchair by the shoulders and then he put me in a choke hold. The pain in my entire torso was still too paralyzing for me to straighten up. When the choke hold didn't work Lt. Sherwood grabbed me by the ears and pulled on them to get me to sit up straight. I just instinctively knew that I had to endure the pain and agony of the choke hold and the pain of being pulled up by the ears. I was enduring the pain of my ears being stretched besides the intense chest pain plus and the pain in my groin from the hernia hanging out of me. Even during Lt. Sherwood's abusive and tortuous actions I was in too much paralyzing pain to straighten up. When Lt. Sherwood's very painful actions didn't work, he finally let go of my ears, but he kept on yelling and verbally harassing me. He kept chastising and castigating me all the way to the medical clinic. The medical clinic was about four city blocks away but it seemed like miles because of my very painful state. Lt. Sherwood was very determined to teach a f-cking old man as he termed it a lesson for supposedly not respecting his authority by not obeying his orders. He lost any signs of common sense. He seemed to lose all self-control of himself and his emotions. Who in their right mind would pull a 71-year-old man by the ears when he was having paralyzing chest pain? The guards go through training for that type of circumstances. Here I was fighting for my life and Sherwood was fighting to protect his ego. At the medical clinic I was so despondent and desperate to save my life that I finally said to Lt. Sherwood: "You idiot, will you leave me alone." That response seemed to bring the lieutenant to his senses. He verbalized more to me, but I was in too much pain to understand what he said. He finally left me alone and left the medical clinic. After Lt. Sherwood left the clinic Nurse Nicole said to me, you shouldn't have said that to the lieutenant. Here I was having very bad heart spasms and the nurse decides to lecture me about how I addressed a guard. I wasn't examined by a doctor even though the law required it and I had a history of two heart attacks, a heart function of only seven-teen and two strokes.

I was taken to Denver Health Hospital a few days later to be treated for another matter of which I don't remember. When they examined me, I was immediately sent to the emergency room. After I was examined and initially treated in the emergency room, I was sent to the Intensive Care Unit because of my very weak and tenuous condition. At Denver Health Hospital the cardiologists diagnosed it as a massive heart attack where my heart function was measured at an average of twelve percent. They questioned my survivability which is very reasonable when you consider that a normal heart function is sixty-five percent and mine was only nineteen percent of the norm.

This was my third heart attack when you consider Deputy Tapia's and Born's assault on me at the Adams County Jail. I had just turned 71 years of age just a month before when this outrageous inexplicable assault occurred. I was diagnosed with a triple A aorta aneurysm, but the doctors were very reluctant to operate on it because the heart was too weak. It is an ascending aorta aneurysm which is 3.9 centimeters long and an abdominal one of 5.0 centimeters long. It turned out that I had two very dangerous aorta aneurysms one ascending and the other an abdominal aneurysm. If those aneurysms rupture I will bleed to death. They didn't think that I would survive surgery and neither did I, but in any case, I was determined to do whatever I could to live on no matter what it took. I started to believe that I could survive and recover because I had such a strong meaning and purpose in my life. There aren't many things that are stronger than a belief. I wouldn't entertain any thoughts of death. I knew that I would live on to write about what happened to me and bring attention to elderly abuse.

If I was attempting to challenge Lt. Sherwood or his orders or authority, I would have found a less painful and frightening way of doing it. Did Lt. Sherwood think it was pleasurable for me to lie curled up on the dirty day room floor among ninety-seven other riotous inmates? I would have done anything to alleviate that terrible pain in my chest and my groin like I was attempting to do on March 7, 2018. On that day I was unbelievably sprayed twice in the eyes with chemicals directly in my eyes.

To my knowledge nothing was done to Lt. Sherwood even though I sent a letter to the warden, and I'm considered "At Risk". Captain Cole interviewed me about my letter to the warden. Warden Mathew Hansen couldn't take the time to talk with me about the incident, but the Colorado Department of Corrections thought it to be appropriate to promote him and condone negligence. It is an indication how he feels about inmate abuse which creates bad feelings in the inmates and in a way causes guard abuse by the inmates. Abuse attracts abuse and is not discriminating. Consider the incidence of guards being assaulted at Sterling Prison. Many of the guards consider Sterling Prison a hell whole and look for other jobs in law enforcement. They work at Sterling to enhance their resume' and then move on as soon as they can. Consequently, Sterling is short of competent guards. Sterling is located in an area where there is a shortage of economic opportunities or else the guard shortage would be worse. I witnessed guards running like rabbits for their lives because of gang assaults.

Lt. Sherwood has since been promoted to a captain. Let me state again the cardiologist told me that they were reluctant to operate on it because the heart function was too low and, therefore, the heart was too weak. The heart was too weak to operate on it but wait until you read what happened to me just one year later. If I may term the aorta aneurysm a major disability is an understatement. The aorta is the main heart artery. It is accentuated by the fact that I suffer from hypertension which taxes the aneurysms by increasing the pressure on the heart and the walls of the aorta. The hypertension is exacerbated since I have been diagnosed with and suffer from acute anxiety and other circulatory system diseases such as kidney disease. Please keep in mind that my guts were still very painfully hanging out of me while I endured the consequences chronic abuse. None of those diseases or disorders were properly treated at Sterling Prison.

When I was discharged from Denver Health, I was housed at the RDC to recover further. My cellmate told me that he was blind because he had been stabbed in both eyes with a pencil by prisoners. In spite of my very weak heart and susceptibility to another major heart attack I was returned to the most dangerous unit of the prison. Obviously, they didn't give a dam if I lived or died but I did. My life didn't matter as much to the prison staff as much as Lieutenant Sherwood's career did. In spite of Lt. Sherwood's outrageous behavior, he got his promotion. Lt. Sherwood is an experienced guard that is part of the reason he was made a lieutenant.

Considering his experience, he should have immediately declared a medical emergency when I was experiencing severe chest pain but instead, he puts me in a choke hold and then pulls me by the ears. If that behavior by Lt. Sherwood is totally outrageous, please tell me what is. By tolerating that type of behavior by a guard, prison officials are essentially instigating more abusive behaviors by other guards. It creates and maintains a culture of abuse. Who in their right mind puts a man in a choke hold who is exhibiting the symptoms of a heart attack? Consider the American Public's reaction to how George Floyd was treated by law enforcement. Lt. Sherwood now Captain Sherwood has a reputation for harassing the inmates but obviously the Warden Hansen didn't care. Instead of being counselled for his wrongful behavior Sherwood is promoted. That only serves to perpetuate the culture of violence and abuse. What does this tell the others such as Lt. Reeves? Captain Sherwood loves to play tuff guy, but I say stupid guy because of his outrageous behavior is criminal in nature and cast a negative dispersion on other guards. He is like a time bomb waiting to go off. He and some of his fellow guards which are a minority are as much of a danger to society as some dangerous prisoners. The incident is a manifestation of the violent and harassing culture towards inmates no matter what their condition at Sterling Prison.

My life mattered to me and obviously not to some of the prison staff. I was determined to do everything possible not to just survive and recover to tell the story how elderly and mentally ill are treated in the Federal and Colorado penal system. It is my belief that this is not just about John Walshe but many elderly prisoners especially ones who suffer from mental illness and sadly some are veterans. Neglect is essentially synonymous with an assault.

Prior to my surgery for the inguinal hernia at Saint Thomas Moore Hospital in Canon City, CO, they performed a heart scan and said that I still had the aneurysms which made them wary to operate on me, but they didn't have much of a choice. An emergency room nurse at Centennial

Prison with thirty years of experience said that she had never seen a person survive my type of heart attack. That frightened me. I came very close to dying with a heart function of a mere twelve percent. Keep in mind that my guts were still very painfully hanging out of my groin. Needless to say, I didn't think that I would survive my surgery and had come to the end of my life. I just placed my life in God's hands to do what God wished for me, but I already knew what that was. It is obvious that God wanted me to live to profess God's will for the elderly and mentally ill.

Assault October 6, 2017, at Sterling Prison

Please try and remember that I previously referred to a Lt. Reeves in my writing. Also keep in mind what I said about guards being assaulted by inmates. On October 6, 2017, and just one year after I had a massive heart attack that created the triple A aorta aneurysms, I was walking laps in the yard to relieve the pain and stress from an angina pectoris attack. I had a stabbing pain in my inguinal hernia which is a side effect of untreated inguinal hernias. My right leg seemed to collapse and I fell flat on my face on the concrete walkway. As stated, before because of the inguinal hernia it was very painful for me to walk, stand or even sit especially for long periods of time. I had no choice I had to walk if I was to continue to recover from my demented state and treatment for my cardiovascular disease. I wasn't administered any medications or therapy for either. When I fell flat on my face, I struggled to stand up again. When I stood up a female officer by the name of Officer Spence came up to me and asked why I had fallen down. I told her that it was because of my inguinal hernia that the prison was supposed to operate on for the last three years. Officer Spence didn't like the way that I answered her, so she had me turn around and she handcuffed me with my hands in the back in spite of human decency standards. As stated, before it was painful for me to be cuffed up with my hands in my back. I was in pain from being cuffed up, the fall, the inguinal hernia, and the angina attack but as the DOC report states I complied with her instructions.

All of a sudden, a male guard by the name of Lt. Reeves came along with a smirk on his face. He was acting in a macho man style, so he pushed me up against the prison wall right under the security camera. I asked him his name and he spelt it out very distinctly as Reeves. All of a sudden, I felt him grab my head by the right temple and he slammed my head against the prison wall like a pancake. I was traumatized and startled by the assault as is typical with me I disassociated. I don't remember but the inmates who witnessed the attack said that Lt. Reeves slammed my head against the wall two more times for a total of three slams.

Where Lt. Reeves slammed my head is the temporal lobe of the brain where dementia usually starts and memories are formed. At that time, I had spent over six years in trying to recover my ability to establish new memories and recall the older ones. Let me state again the worst thing for mental disorders is head trauma. After the assault by Lt. Reeves some other guards strapped me into a restraining chair. I was taken without any medical attention to the "Hole" for four days. I didn't receive any type of medical care in spite of my pain from the hernia, from the fall and my head being slammed against the concrete wall. Imagine the surgeons were reluctant to operate on me but Lt. Reeves thought nothing of slamming my head against the wall not once but three times. He may not have known about the hernia, my heart, my strokes and my other disease but at the time I was an old man of 72 years. As much as I wish otherwise, I don't look like a young man. I experienced severe headaches right over the left temporal lobe all the time that I was in solitary confinement and for months after being released. I still experience a throbbing pain in that area and bear the scars of it. At times the scars bleed. As stated, the assault occurred under the security cameras. Please allow me to state again mental health professionals state that the worst thing you can do to a person with my mental health diseases is to cause head trauma. Why did Officer

Spence have to intensify the pain by cuffing me up especially in the back when I was already experiencing pain from the fall, the hernia and from the angina pectoris attack? Why did Lieutenant Reeves think it was proper and humane to slam my head against the wall not once but three times? If that is criminalistic please tell me what is? The Department of Corrections written report stated that I was complying with Officer Spence' orders. By the way very unfortunately recently Officer Spence was severely beaten by inmates. Remember what I said about abuse attracting abuse which was very unfortunate for Officer Spence. No guard deserves to be beaten when in their minds they were just doing their job especially a female guard. It is due to the culture of inhumane actions at Sterling Prison. Now a person who was guilty of abuse is the warden and another for ignoring the abuse is Deputy Director of Prisons.

I noticed when I got to the "Hole" that I had open wounds from the handcuffs being so tight. While in solitary confinement I experienced another angina pectoris attacks. Plus, I continued to experience pain from the inguinal hernia, severe headaches from the assault plus my wrists were very sore. I could not digest food, so I skipped meals. The guards would become angry when they couldn't arouse me or get me to eat meals. To further punish me Lt. Wirth and other guards would kick and slam the steel door which would cause a very loud agonizing noise which served to make the headache more intense. My head would just keep pounding as if the brain was trying to emerge from the skull. I remember being on my knees having to hold on to the toilet for hours. I would vomit any food that I tried to eat because I had the dry heaves. I was very nauseous as a consequence of the hernias. After the assault and harassment while in the "Hole" I experienced chronic ear, neck, chest and more head pain besides the abdominal pain from the hernias. I was very afraid that the trauma was causing the metal stents in my arteries to rupture the arteries because of the severe pain in that area and the ascending aorta aneurysm. I always experienced a crushing chest pain in that area right over the blocked artery when having an angina attack but this time it was more intense than usual. At my age with health profile, it causes parts of me to regress to childlike state because my toleration of pain is diminished. To assault a person with my profile is synonymous with assaulting a child and is criminalistic in nature.

When I was released from solitary, I found out that Lt. Reeves and Officer Spence had accused me of sexual harassment to cover their misconduct. Officer Spence evidently when I referred to my hernia as being the cause of my fall Officer Spence said that was sexual harassment because I referred to my inguinal hernia as large nuts and testicles. I doubt that because I wouldn't use those terms with ladies and the hernia was my large intestine and not testes. Is that a cause to slam an elderly man's head against a wall not once but three times when he was already in a very painful state? What it was a way to cover their misdeeds because the security camera would not show anything else except for me complying with their orders. In my state Officer Spence should have at least taken me to the medical clinic which was only a few feet from where I fell down.

Please keep in mind that I was in pain from the angina attack, my hernia and from falling. If I still had a sexual urge after all that I would be the envy of most of mankind for my so-called manliness. I must be very manly to survive my head being slammed against the wall, to endure the pain from an angina pectoris attack, stabbing pain from my hernia, the pain from falling flat on my face still think and talk in sexual terms. I still don't know why Lt. Reeves had to slam my head against the wall when Officer Spence's report said that I was complying. I believe Lt. Reeves had a great need to demonstrate his male prowess to Officer Spence. I was suffering from and in tremendous pain, but Lt. Reeves had to slam a 72-year-old man's head not just once but three times to demonstrate his manliness. To call Lt. Reeves a bully and a coward for picking on an old man who was already restrained is nothing but cowardice and criminalistic in nature. His actions demonstrate that he is a danger to others and not just prisoners.

Lt. Reeves is on overweight man with a long and bushy beard. Even now when I see a man with that type of beard and physical profile even on TV, I relive that attack. That attack caused me to lose a lot of memories that I strived for years to recover. I lost a lot of my hearing because the temporal lobe is also the home of auditory perception. I believe that it also further damaged the pons area of the brain and the thyroid gland because my sensitivity to loud noises increased. I sense that attack aged me at least a decade. May I say again what Lt. Reeves did was criminalistic in nature and to say the least as idiotic as Lt. Sherwood's behavior. Both of those men act like common criminals and mimic the behaviors of many of the men housed in maximum security. Ask yourself if you would want those type of men to associate with your fathers or grandfathers? I was placed on restriction for ten days which had a negative effect on my mental health as did the assault. As is usual at Sterling Prison nothing was done to Lt. Reeves for slamming a senile old man's head against the concrete prison wall not once but three times. By not making Lt. Reeves accountable for his criminal behavior, it only served to perpetuate that type of uncivilized behavior by guards at Sterling Prison. It also serves to foster attacks on the guards by inmates. The gang members and especially the gang leaders would tout look how the guards treat old men. Let me infer again that just don't treat John Walshe that way but I assume from their actions that they treat many prisoners that way. You can never forget what is in a man's heart and what that makes them capable of doing. We lock people up not just for the crime they committed but what they have demonstrated they are capable of doing. It only demonstrates the lack of regard for human decency in the Colorado Department of Corrections. It is no wonder there is such a high turnover of guards and a shortage of them at Sterling Prison. Guards who have resigned and taken positions at other law enforcement agencies should be interviewed as to why they no longer want to work at Sterling Prison.

Assault on March 7, 2018, Sterling Prison

The evening of March 7, 2018, my hernia seemed like it strangulated again. It was so painful that I could not stand up straight up or walk. I had to crawl to my bunk and lay in a fetal position because I couldn't straighten my leg. When my cellmate noticed how much pain that I was in he called the guards. When the guards saw my predicament, they summoned medical. I was on my bunk when they came to my cell with a gurney. The medical personnel and the guards asked if I could walk out of my cell to the gurney. I told them that I could crawl which they allowed me to do. The severe pain in my inguinal hernia wouldn't allow me to straighten the right leg. I crawled out of my cell to the gurney in the day room even though it was very painful to crawl. I was placed on the gurney and a strap was placed over my upper torso. When they tried to place a strap over my thighs they couldn't because I couldn't straighten my right leg. I couldn't straighten my leg because of the strangulated hernia was very painful. The attending guards and medical personnel continued to push the leg down and they wouldn't stop in spite of my pleas not to push on my right leg. I was secured to the gurney with the upper torso strap. They could have placed the strap over my left thigh to further secure me to the gurney. The pain got so severe from them trying to straighten my right leg that I decided in desperation to roll off the gurney about three feet onto the floor to relieve my pain. I was willing to do anything to stop the pain much of which was dictated by self- preservation instincts. When I landed on the floor a guard took it upon himself to spray chemicals directly in my eyes not just once but twice consecutively. I was in severe pain because of the stabbing pain from the hernia, from falling on to the concrete floor and now the intense and severe pain from the chemicals burning my eyes and skin.

To endure the pain, I pounded the floor with my fists. The pain intensified so much that I pounded my forehead off the floor to end the pain by ending my life. I was that desperate to relieve the excruciating pain. While I was pounding the floor with my fists the chemicals blinded me which they are supposed to do. I inadvertently struck a lady officer's foot when she moved it to where I was pounding the floor. Let me state again, I couldn't see her or her foot because I was blinded by the chemicals. Plus, if you are going to purposely assault someone you don't hit them in the foot while you are lying face down on the floor in excruciating pain while blinded by chemicals. Then as I understand from the inmates who witnessed the assault several officers jumped on me while I was incapacitated on the floor. So now I had to endure the pain of being pushed into the floor and the guards laying on top of me. I was placed in handcuffs so tight that it created open wounds on my wrists. Here I was a 72-year-old inmate with a life-threatening aorta aneurysms a history of three heart attacks and two strokes with my guts hanging out of me while medical personnel are standing by while several guards jumped one me. If that scenario isn't barbaric and savagely cruel what is? My memory is vague about what happened after I rolled to the floor because the terrible pain caused my memory to fail, and I disassociated.

I was taken to an observation cell in solitary confinement instead of the medical clinic where I lied on the floor because I was too weak and in too much pain to climb up onto the bunk bed. Two lieutenants kept on yelling at me to get up on the concrete bunk, but I just couldn't because of the excruciating pain from my hernia, burning sensation from the chemicals in my eyes and skin plus the pain in my torso from being jumped on by the guards. The two lieutenants came into the cell when I couldn't respond to their orders and with my hands twisted behind my back, they grabbed me by my hands and lifted me up. It was very painful to have all that weight placed the joints of my wrists, elbows, shoulders and hands. I already had wrist wounds from the handcuffs being placed on me too tight. Plus, my eyes and skin continued to burn from the chemical spray. All the while I was enduring the stabbing pain from my strangulated inguinal hernia.

Since the lieutenants lifted me up by my wrists and hands, I lost a lot more of the coordination between my hands and brain. My right wrist was still healing from the assaults at the Adams County Jail. Since being lifted up by my hands behind my back it is hard and painful for me to control the movement of my hands when I write or hold my hands in a still position. Put your hands together behind your back and push them away from your back and see how that feels. Now imagine doing that will all the weight of your body being place on your wrists, elbows and shoulders. It's a wonder they didn't cause a sprain in the joints like what happened to the 73-year-old lady with dementia in Loveland, Colorado. Even now more than three years after the incident in March of 2018 when I see the video of the lady in Loveland being assaulted, I start to intensely cry. It is like I was feeling pain that unfortunate lady felt.

After being held in the observation cell I remember being placed in a caged cold shower where I knelt on my knees because I still could not stand up straight on my legs. I kept trying to splash cold water in my eyes from the water on the floor which was leaking into the drain while on my knees to get rid of the chemicals in my eyes. Three guards stood outside of the caged shower socializing while I was crying out in such severe pain wishing for my death. You do strange things in desperation to relieve pain. I asked the guard for some soap to clean out the chemical residue on my skin, but I was refused. I remember saying to them go home and tell your fathers of grandfathers how you treated an old man tonight. Once again, I had to stay in solitary confinement with my eyes and skin burning from the residual from the chemicals for days without any opportunity to decontaminate.

To mask their wrong doings, I was accused of assaulting an officer because I inadvertently hit the female officer's foot when I was blinded by the chemical spray. Those guards know to mask their wrongdoings. I did not receive treatment for the hernia and just suffered for days from the severe strangulating pain. I was too nauseated to eat whole food or anything I tried to intake. I would just vomit it back up when I tried to eat. I can remember kneeling on the floor literally hugging the toilet so I wouldn't fall over while vomiting. When I couldn't respond to the officer's commands to get up from the floor. The lieutenant would slam the slot in the steel door and kick it to punish me. Keep in mind I was restricted to a solitary cell and was a danger to no one but myself. To say that it was torturous and barbaric to abuse me when I was in a painful state is an understatement.

When I was returned to general population after my stay in the "Hole," I was placed in the maximum-security unit four again, the most dangerous unit. As stated just a few months after my release from Sterling four guards from that unit had to be hospitalized after being attacked by a gang. As stated before one of the guards was hospitalized with a crushed skull. Once again if that isn't frightening to be placed in that unit, what is? You don't screw around with those inmates, or you will pay for it. You exist with people who are guilty of some very heinous crimes. I still have visions of guards running for their lives like rabbits. What causes the inmates to attack the guards when they know they will be severely punished? I believe that part of the reason is the violent culture in the prison caused by people from both sides of the walls; violence attracts violence.

CHAPTER 35

Centennial Prison

I was originally sent to Centennial Prison for a psychological evaluation which I welcomed to determine the basis or cause of my issue with loud noise especially sudden ones. When I got to Centennial Prison, they claimed that I was in the wrong place. They said that it was a program for rehabilitation for drug and alcohol abusers. Needless to say, I was disappointed because I was yearning for some relief from the tortures of loud noise. I was locked down in cell for twenty-seven days and twenty-four hours a day. My housing was synonymous with solitary confinement and was very taxing on my mental health disorders. Now because of coronavirus we are finding out how taxing isolation is on people's mental health. The only time I wasn't locked down and chained to the bunk is when I was taken to Saint Thomas More Hospital to have my inguinal hernia operated on.

At Centennial and Territorial Prison, I met a lot of guards who had worked at Sterling Prison. They all said to me that they couldn't wait to get out of as they put it "Hell Hole". They said that they couldn't believe how some of the guards abusive and inhumane behaviors were tolerated by the prison officials. When I was taken somewhere for treatment or evaluation, I was always chained to something like such as a wall as if I was a wild animal on a collar. It was so humiliating. When I got to my destination, I was chained to a wall again. The chains would press on and rub against the hernia.

My inguinal hernia got worse and worse where I could no longer walk and was restricted to a wheelchair. A doctor from Ethiopia was so amazed by the size of the hernia and how far it protruded out of me that she measured my hernia for the record. She thought it would have to be spliced in order to get it back into my lower torso. Because I could no longer expel my human waste my ability to intake and ingest food was very limited. Finally, when I could no longer intake food for nine days in row, I was taken on an emergency basis to Saint Thomas Moore Hospital in Canon City because my kidney function was failing and very perilous. I was getting weaker and weaker and less cognizant from lack of proper nourishment. I got to the point of delirium. Keep in mind I was already suffering from kidney disease and was recovering from type II diabetes. At first the physicians were reluctant to operate on me because of the very dangerous aorta aneurysms. They realized that they didn't have a choice because of my failing kidney function besides my perilously very low heart function. I had been placed intravenously on a special type of plasma for my kidneys. I thought that I wouldn't survive the surgery, and I was getting weaker and weaker as each hour and day passed without being able to intake whole food. I couldn't believe that the Department of Corrections let me suffer so much for so long. They chained me like an animal and neglected my medical needs like a useless wild animal. My life didn't matter to them. I wrote much more about this in a previous chapter describing my inguinal hernia.

CHAPTER 36

Prison Guards

Some of the guards would have made great recruits for the Nazi death camps. As stated, I wouldn't dare to say then what I thought publicly but I will now in my late age. In my so-called "Golden Years" my fear is diminished, and my courage has increased so I will state what I experienced because I experienced the worst of the worst. What else could they do to me? Some of the personnel in the penal system did every negative thing that they could do to me except place me on death row. The gold in my "Golden Years" became very tarnished until I found God. Thereafter I learned to tolerate the worst of the pain. I developed the attitude of do what you will do to me I can handle it as I did with God as my mentor.

I will state that those who have knowledge of abuse or observe another weaker human being abused, if those people have the ability to do something about it and don't, they are narcissistic and as negligent as the actual perpetrators. If they have the authority and ability and don't, they are just cowards. Their character is too weak so consequently they are too afraid to rock the boat. Being too calloused from years of service is a poor excuse not to speak up. They have an obligation to themselves and fellow humans to renew themselves. Consider what is happening to the officers who stood by while George Floyd was killed. The years should demonstrate wisdom and not weakness when it comes to character. Too many of them just want to play politics by saying nothing or it's not my job. Those who say or act like it's not their job shouldn't have one.

There is a saying that God helps those who help themselves but it very true that God helps those who can't help themselves. Why does God bestow more on some than others? God expects to help and share with our fellow humans especially those who become disabled in some way by age, diseases, and circumstances. As an example of my plight guards, deputies and their seniors would make me strip naked because they saw bulging in my pants. They would assume I was hiding contraband. When I stripped and they saw my guts hanging out of my groin like a huge banana they would ignore my plight and how I was suffering. When they saw me having to walk and hold my scrotum up to control the pain so I could walk, they ignored it and some would laugh. Imagine having to exist for five years with your guts hanging out of you. When they saw me holding on to my right torso to try to minimize the chest pain over where my cardiovascular system was not functioning because I was having an angina pectoris attack, they would ask me what was wrong. When I told them that I was having an angina attack they would ignore it.

Let me state with knowledge, ability and authority comes responsibility. Responsibility to act in a God-like and civilized manor. If you, don't you are cheating yourself as well as your fellow humans. When our lives our examined by our Lord and Savior and God asks what you did with the abilities that I bestowed on you especially the extra ones, we can answer in confidence that we used them in our Loving Savior's Manner in service to our fellow humans. We can also say when we did use them in a God like manner it made me feel so good when I did. A life void of service to others is indeed a voided life.

The other inmates used to say to me that these people think that you are not going to survive so they won't have to answer for their abusive ways. Some would say, "Johnny, you're still here, they haven't killed you yet?" They said that you are only going to leave here in a body bag. They were almost right because I kissed death four times while incarcerated. As an example, on one occasion my heart function dropped to seventeen percent on another time it dropped to twelve percent. My kidney function became perilous and my large intestine almost ruptured. I was knocked unconscious four times. I did survive and now I'm writing about it so the world can see how we treat the elderly when they have a mental illness regardless of regardless of age.

CHAPTER 37

Life Threat Sterling Prison

On June 29, 2018, when I was walking through the lunch line with my tray. I was suddenly verbally attacked by a gang member which caused me to have a panic attack. That meant real trouble for me. Because of the trauma on my neurological system, I automatically dropped my tray on the floor which drew attention to the incident. I tried to leave the dining hall, but the door was locked. I asked the guard to let me return to my cell, but he refused so I went to the most distant part of the dining hall away from where the gang was sitting. When I asked the officer in the dining hall to be taken to the medical clinic the guard asked why. He also asked who threatened me. I looked to the inmate which was a huge mistake because as it turned out that inmate was a prominent gang member. I don't think rationally when I'm having a panic attack. The inmate started yelling out in the dining hall for all to hear that I was a rat. When lunch was over I along with the other inmates was allowed to return to my cell.

A couple of hours later an inmate came to my cell door and stated that the gang had a meeting and that based on my actions they determined that I was a snitch. I never named who verbally assaulted and threatened me, but it was obvious who it was based on my actions and the perpetrator yelling at me. The gang member said that they were going to get me for snitching on a gang member. In prison that meant that I was as good as dead. I was terrorized another life threat. How many could I endure? I could just imagine a shiv penetrating me as it is all too common in prison especially in the maximum-security unit.

The threat caused an angina pectoris attack, so I asked to go to the medical clinic. At the clinic Nurse Karen took my blood pressure and it was 160 percent of normal. That frightened me because of my aorta aneurysms and my cardiac history. My heart was pounding in my chest. It felt like it could explode. After being medicated with nitro glycerin tablets, I was sent back to the same maximum-security unit. I was very fearful of returning to the maximum-security unit but I complied. The nurses told me that if I was threatened again, I should refuse housing so I could be placed in solitary confinement for my safety. I took their advice and asked to be placed into segregation or the "Hole". The officer in charge of the unit said that he would have to write me up for refusing housing but I didn't care. My concern was saving my life. It was now a matter of self-preservation. The guard in charge of the unit agreed so I was escorted to solitary by two guards. On the way to the "Hole" I said to the guards that it appears that the gangs run this prison. Their retort to me was "you are exactly right, Mr. Walshe." Their lives were subjected to a constant danger as I witnessed many times. When I got to solitary one of the female guards said jokingly, you're hear for another vacation, Mr. Walshe because I had been placed there so many times. It is like the improper or unlawful was considered ordinary. When I laid on my bunk in my cell in solitary confinement it felt like I was laying on a beautiful beach in the Bahamas. It dawned on me to the extent of fear of being killed that I felt was so large that it was a pleasure to be in solitary confinement. It was a relief to be in solitary confinement. I realized that I had never that I was aware of having been in so much of a fearful state. It was the continual exposure to fear that had been building up in me over the years of confinement especially in a maximum-security prison.

When I was released from solitary about a week later a detective interviewed me as to what happened. I dared not to tell him because he told me that I was being sent back to the same maximum-security unit in spite of the danger to my life. When I confronted him about it, he said that nobody would dare to bother you because it would be considered a "Hate Crime." Just a month before on two occasions I witnessed two officers who were making their rounds being attacked by gang members. They took the guards to the ground and just savagely and continually beat on them. The other guards who were in the day room literally ran out of the unit like rabbits in fear of their lives. Both attacks occurred within ten feet of me. Just witnessing the assault made me feel like I was a victim because I had become so sensitive to violence. That is what can happen when you are exposed to so much violence. I asked the detective how you can protect me when you can't even protect your colleagues. He didn't reply. I had heard that the gang could even cause an attack on your loved ones outside of prison.

I couldn't believe my ears because how could I trust the guards with my safety because of how I had been treated by guards, in particular senior guards. I couldn't even trust the warden, Matthew Hansen, who ignored my three letters to him and my sister's letters about my plight, especially the ones concerning my hernias. His ignorance demonstrated that he didn't give a dam about my plight. If that isn't negligence, what is? Let me state again it just fosters further violence within the prison walls. Matthew Hansen has since been promoted to Deputy Director of Prions at DOC headquarters. This is the guy who wouldn't respond to any of my letters concerning abuse and now he should be controlling it.

A few days later at the noon meal I was threatened again which caused another angina attack. I had become very susceptible to those angina attacks. That tendency lasted until well after I left prison. The chest pain became very severe so that I beseeched an officer to allow me to go to medical. He called medical and shift commander, and both escorted me to medical. At medical my blood pressure and EKG were more abnormal than when it was taken last time. Dr. Bryan Reichert who attended to me after reviewing the tests he ordered emergency blood work because he thought that I was having another heart attack. He wanted to check my troponin level which would indicate if I was having a heart attack. I'm very prone to heart attacks and angina pectoris attacks because as stated before one of my main arteries is totally blocked. The results of the blood work were satisfactory to Dr. Reichert, so I was returned to the same unit. I met with Captain Tidwell, because of the threat to my life. I asked to be moved to a different pod. He agreed with me and said that I would be moved on July 8th but that didn't happen. I returned to the maximum-security unit in fear of my life.

A few days later a detective by the name of Ron Uhrick who had been my case manager, before he was promoted, interviewed me about the assaults on the guards. As stated, I was within ten feet of the assaults when they occurred. When he heard about my situation, he automatically saw that I was moved to a safer unit. I was so grateful to him for that. As mentioned, I had been wrongfully placed in the maximum-security unit without any regard for my safety.

CHAPTER 38

Medical Care at Sterling

To give an example of the type of medical care I received at Sterling Prison on November 13, 2015, I laid in my bunk trying to push my inguinal hernia into my abdominal cavity so it wouldn't hurt so much especially when I stood up straight or walked. Walking had been so beneficial in my recovery from the demented state that I suffered from. I had to walk as often as it was allowed for at least thirty minutes at a time. Plus, exercise at least walking for thirty minutes a day is essential for people inflicted with cardiovascular disease. I had been at times successful in pushing the hernia on the left side back in, so I tried once more to push the right one in. When I pushed on the hernia on the right side it went partially in, and it seemed like the intestine twisted. Needless to say, it was very painful and caused me to choke and gag. I became very nauseated. I started to have shortness of breath which frightened me because of my cardiac history. I tried for over an hour to push it back out so it would untangle and relieve any blockage. I couldn't get it to protrude all the way out to relieve the pain. My cellmate noticed how much pain that I was in, so he called the guards to declare a medical emergency. I was interviewed by Sergeant Bell, and he ordered that I be taken to the medical clinic in a wheelchair. He had experience as a medical technician, so he realized how serious my medical state was. When I arrived at the medical clinic the nurse at the reception desk without trying to diagnose me criticized me for claiming that I had shortness of breath. If that isn't the height of malpractice what is? My blood pressure was taken and proved to be abnormal. I was just sent back to my unit without any further medical care. A guard wheeled me back to my cell where I suffered for two more days until I was able to push the intestine all the way out. I remained in very painful state for a week especially when I tried to have bowel movements. Let me state again that the courts have ruled that a prisoner whose medical needs call for a doctor's attention must receive it. Shortness of breath with a history of heart disease mandates a doctor's attention. If the hernia had strangulated and ruptured, I would have died. The nurse didn't even bother to see if I needed to be seen by a doctor. She just went by her own set of standards. Wait until you read how they treat letters at the clinic.

On June 3, 2016, I had a seizure when it was time for the nighttime lockdown. I have no memory of this incident because that is a side effect of my grand mal seizures so what I write from inmates, prison staff and their records. A Lieutenant Joy Davis attended to me. During the attack or seizure let me state again I have no memory of the incident I grabbed the lieutenant's hand. I understand that I scratched or injured the palm of her hand by pressing my fingernails into it. I believe that it was a consequence of a seizure because I wet myself and bit my lips and tongue which is a consequence of my seizures. I believe that I was probably grasping for something. Like most people who have seizures you do abnormal things like foaming at the mouth when having them. Lt. Davis told the prison officials who investigated the incident that she didn't think that I was trying to harm her in anyway. Lt. Davis stated she had known me to be a nonviolent man. I understand from the emergency room nurses and guards that my seizures are very frightening. Without getting any medical care which is critical in my case I was sent to the "Hole" for three weeks. The inguinal hernia became very sore and painful while in solitary confinement, so I asked for medical care. Three times a day nurses are in solitary to hand out medication but none of them were allowed to attend to my pleas for medical care. I was just made to suffer without any relief. The hernia became so painful that I couldn't even crawl to the cell door for food trays. The Courts have ruled that prisoners in solitary confinement must be able to communicate their medical needs to the medical staff. Nonmedical personnel such as guards cannot be allowed to decide which prisoners will receive medical attention. Prisoners whose medical needs call for a physician's attention must be able to receive it.

Outrageous Behavior by Medical Personnel

On or about January 26, 2017, my cellmate found me passed out on my bunk trembling, foaming at the mouth and all symptoms of a grand mal seizure. He called the guards and they summoned for medical personnel after viewing my state. Nurse Tabatha along with guards came with a gurney to take me to the medical clinic. While I was still unconscious the guards handcuffed me up with my hands behind my back. They placed me on the stretcher with my back down on the stretcher with the handcuffs pressing into my spine like a sharp tool. The stabbing pain in my spine caused me to regain consciousness. It felt like a screwdriver was being pushed into my spine. The pain was excruciating. They also placed a strap across my upper torso. When they placed a strap over my lower torso over the inguinal hernia the strap pressed onto my inguinal hernia which caused tremendous pain and nausea. The hernia protruded out too far to be pushed into the abdominal cavity. At the same time the handcuffs were being pushed into my spine. The pain was so excruciating because the strap was crushing the intestine and pushing it into the testicle. I started screaming and hollering out in terrible pain. Plus, the pain from the handcuffs being pushed into the spine proved to be too much for me to endure. When I tried to lift my torso to relieve the pressure and pain in my spine it would just put more pressure on the inguinal hernia. As I tried to lift the torso Nurse Tabatha and the guards kept pushing down on my torso which caused the handcuffs to further press into and on my spine. The dual pain from the spine and the hernia became so severe and intense that I started yelling out loud from the pain. Many of the inmates in the unit started to yell from their cells to torment and ridicule those attending to me. The inmates continued to yell until I was removed from the pod. I kept trying to lift my lower torso because I was very afraid of the damage to the spine which is vital and critical to the whole neurological system. It was only the third time in my life that I yelled so loud to endure the terrible pain. The first was October 7, 2015.

The tortuous activity and pain continued all the way to the medical clinic and until the straps were released at the clinic. The nurse and the guards witnessed my anguish, but they refused to act in a humanistic way to relieve what their senses were telling of my pain and suffering that their actions were causing. Later on I asked myself what kind of people are these to witness an old man suffering from the pain they were causing and not trying to ease or eliminate it especially trained medical personnel? It is akin to a physical assault on my person to say the least. How can people be so cruel in their actions? It is part of the culture of Sterling Prison where life is considered very cheap even by medical personnel. Even elderly lives didn't matter to them.

It only takes one catastrophic event when one is so powerless to change brain chemistry and cause brain damage. Those cuffs protruding into my back and the large intestine being pushed into my abdomen were akin to bullets doing the same. The pain was so intense and severe that I disassociated and lost my memory. The incident caused me to lose a lot of painless movement in my arms and shoulders for months. Because of the injury to my spine, it has been painful for me to lie on my left side especially when I try to sleep. Again, the courts have ruled the use of restraints may be unlawful if they are applied in a manner that is dangerous, painful, injurious or degrading. Handcuffing may be unconstitutional if it inflicts injury because the cuffs are excessively tight and placed in a way to cause pain. Forget about court rulings as they do at Sterling Prison, what does common sense dictate? I wrote to the warden about the incident, and he had the administrator of the clinic meet with me. The administrator was annoyed with me for writing to the warden and he tried to convince that there was nothing wrong with laying me on the gurney with the handcuffs protruding into my back.

To give you another example on June 8, 2017, I had an angina pectoris attack. The chest pain alarmed me, and I thought that I was having another heart attack. I asked to be allowed to go to the medical clinic. When I got to the clinic, they performed an EKG which proved to be abnormal, and my blood pressure was 150 percent of normal. That frightened me because of my aorta aneurysms. Excessive pressure on the aorta artery wall can cause those aneurysms to easily to rupture and burst. That would cause almost instant death as any cardiac surgeon would state. I waited for a long time the results of the blood work to come back from the local hospital; it seemed like about three hours. There was only one examining room separating me from the room that the doctor occupied. At the end of my wait, I was taken back to my unit without ever being examined or even seen by the doctor. The clinic wasn't busy. I wasn't even given the results of the blood work or any assurances as to my safety from any of the medical staff. After serving in the U.S. Air Force Medical Corps for four years and my cardiac history I couldn't believe how I was treated. The courts have ruled that a prisoner whose medical needs require a physician's attention must receive it. The courts have also ruled that severe chest pain does require a physician's attention especially a patient with my cardiac history. Just a few months before I had suffered from a massive heart attack and my heart function was a mere twelve percent. After writing a letter to the warden about how I was being treated at the medical clinic I met with the clinic's administrator again. I don't recall the administrator's name.

Again, he seemed very annoyed about me writing letters to the warden. Once again, he claimed that the treatment that I was receiving at the clinic including my hands being cuffed up in the back and being laid on handcuffed hands on a gurney was proper medical procedure. It made me wonder where he got his training in covering up wrongful medical actions.

There are many more examples of poor medical care but here is one the most alarming. As mentioned for five years I functioned with my guts hanging out of me. Twice I wrote letters to the medical clinic to express the seriousness of it. One day about the beginning of August 2015 while meeting with Nurse Kautz a nurse practitioner and one of the medical heads of the clinic I asked her why no one appropriately responded to my letters. One of them was just sent back me with a note on it saying return to Mr. Walshe with no appropriate action. Nurse Kautz told me we don't respond to letters. I said to myself that is new one for the medical journals on how to deal with medical issues. Consequently, I suffered on a daily basis for almost three more years with my guts very painfully hanging out of me.

An examination of my medical record for the period of my incarceration will substantiate even more what I have stated in this writing. What I have describe illustrates the culture at Sterling Prison where not only does elderly lives don't matter but inmates' lives don't matter even to so-called trained medical personnel.

Abdominal Attack Sterling Prison June 30, 2016

On June 29, 2016, when I was in solitary confinement, I was pleading for medical help because I was in severe abdominal pain. It started about 5:30p.m. and lasted about thirty-one hours. The severe cramps started in the lower abdomen by the inguinal hernia in the right groin and moved through the digestive system into the stomach. The pain intensified and became intolerable. I braced my abdominal cavity to endure the pain. I could only move my legs about an inch. I could barely move my torso an inch in any direction without it being very painful. The pain was paralyzing. My entire digestive system became as hard as a rock, and it was very painful to the touch it. I had fallen to the floor and remained there because I was very nauseated and wanted to be close to the toilet. I couldn't contain or digest any food. I remained on the floor because it was too painful to crawl to my bed. I continually had the dry heaves all through the night and the next day. I was in too much pain to sleep. I couldn't even drink any water because I couldn't move to reach it and my throat and esophagus were too sore. It felt like I was having an angina pectoris attack because of the intensity of the attack. It was proving to be one of the most painful events of my life.

I remember the cell floor being very cold, grit on it and filthy dirty. All I could do is just lay on the floor in my own urine because I could not raise myself up high enough to urinate in the toilet. I had to endure. I just laid there close to the toilet and the cell door. I pleaded for medical care several times from my position on the floor. I tried also declared a medical emergency to the guards to no avail.

A nurse didn't come by the cell to see me until 11:00AM until seventeen hours after I first asked for help even though they had been in the unit handing out medication three times a day. When she came to my cell just to talk to me it as through the slot in the cell door. Two officers finally took me in a wheelchair to be examined by a nurse in the medical office of the segregation unit. That was twenty hours after I first pleaded to be seen by a nurse. She checked my vital signs and listened with a stethoscope to my abdominal cavity in particular my large intestine. Per my request she ordered a laxative to be delivered to my cell about 4:00p.m. I thought that a laxative would relieve any blockage in the intestine. Now I realize that was the wrong thing to ask for. I thought that it was a blockage since I wasn't able to move. At that point in time, I had been restricted me to solitary confinement for a month.

At times the pain was so intolerable that I would moan and groan out loud to endure it. I finally fell asleep about 2:00AM July 1st. When I woke up about 6:00a.m. I was still very sore and in pain but it was more tolerable. During that ordeal no officer would enter my cell to check on me. They claimed that they had to be concerned with their own safety no matter how much pain I was in. They claimed that they originally couldn't take me for further medical care because my hands couldn't reach through the slot in the cell door to be cuffed up. It was the same reason that I couldn't raise my body up to deposit bodily waste in the toilet. That was very odd since I was scheduled to be released from solitary without handcuffs in just two days after a month's stay. At the time I was 71 years old, sixty-nine inches tall and I weighed 143 pounds not what you would consider a strong man. Considering all my major disorders, I had little ability to harm anyone.

In the early morning hours of July 1st, I was finally able to slide and scoot over to my bunk and pull down my bed pad and blanket to the floor to lay on and cover myself from the cold, dirty and grimy floor. In a few hours later I was scheduled to be released from solitary confinement into the main unit and yard. Any inmate would be very anxious for that to happen. I was still not able to move painlessly. I couldn't even walk and stand upright. I informed the guards of my condition, and I wouldn't be physically well enough to move for a couple of days. They insisted that I be released any way. Just a couple of days before I couldn't be taken to medical no matter how much I beseeched them to do so because it was implied that I was too dangerous. So, they wrote me up for refusing to be moved. Who would want to stay in solitary if they absolutely didn't have to? A guard in the in the segregation unit hollered out just "give the old man two more weeks in the Hole" and they attempted to give me two more weeks in the "Hole". I said to myself, John, you can't get any lower in life than this but now you can start to climb back up. Don't allow these guys of circumstances to defeat you.

I was an old man in a fragile state. The guard's treatment of me made me agree with the inmates when they said, Johnny, the guards don't think you will live to register a complaint. Even if you do live, no one will believe you about the tortuous abuse. Obviously, I did live and even though it makes me sick to think about it, I am writing about it. The guards' propensity for cruelty makes what I write credible. It is not like this is an isolated incident or just me. It is not up to the guards to judge who should be or not be punished or receive medical care. Their job is to confine and not punish. As stated, before isolation is considered by many mental health professionals as the worst kind of abuse. When they extended my stay in the "Hole" for two weeks I was in too much pain to care. The officers in solitary confinement must have thought that I was absolutely out of my mind for not wanting to be released from the "Hole" after a month's stay there especially in my demeaned physical state. Instead of getting a medical opinion they just extended my stay. It should have occurred to them that maybe something was very wrong with me. Life was very cheap and didn't matter to those guards. This incident served to exacerbate my health issues. Finally, when a supervising officer returned from his 4th of July holiday, he took pity on me and released me. After my punishing thirty-one day stay in the "Hole" and in spite of my medical condition Ms. Rynek my case manager and her supervisor Ms. Sims decided to house me in the maximum-security unit again. Their action was akin to the guard's action who hollered out give the old man two more weeks in the Hole. They gave no consideration to my medical or psychiatric condition which was their responsibility.

I was not properly treated for the attack even though it was obvious that I was in so much pain and agony. Why else was I crying out in pain? Why else would I want to stay in that terrible environment? No consideration was given to the fact that I had a history of strokes, grand mal seizures, heart attacks, angina pectoris attacks or panic attacks. No, you don't put a man with my profile in the "Hole" and leave him there when he is in pain without the intent to harm him. To do so is malice or absolute ignorance and negligence. That incident is another illustration to demonstrate the inhumane conditions at Sterling Prison. If you doubt what I have written, consider that this is the same system that placed inmates with covid nineteen to be placed in solitary confinement to languish and die. How do you properly treat someone who is dying of covid nineteen in solitary confinement?

CHAPTER 39

Psychotherapy at Sterling

T he following is an example of the type of psychotherapy that I received while incarcerated. After the attack on my person in October of 2017 when my head was slammed against the prison wall, my anxiety level increased dramatically. A manifestation of that is that I became even more sensitive to noise. I was to the point that at the end of each day I felt like I was going to have a nervous breakdown, so I put in a request for psychotherapy. On January 5, 2018, I was sent to the mental health section of the medical clinic at Sterling Prison. A young lady by the name of Ms. Landers introduced herself to me and said that she had a master's degree in psychology but was not licensed to do therapy. She stated because of my mental health profile and history that she was ordered to interview me to see how I was doing. I had waited three months for some therapy after a heinous assault and was in a very tenuous state, so I decided to cooperate with her. I said to myself that at one time I was a trainee as a young man starting off in my career and people helped me out by tolerating my inexperience. Plus, some therapy at my mental state was better than none. Consider some of the traumatic events that had happened to me while incarcerated. I knew that I needed some professional help.

I went through each of my four major mental health disorders with her and how they were affecting me in hopes of motivating her to get me the help that I so desperately needed. After I described each one, their symptoms and complications Ms. Landers response to me was but "you seem all right now." I found that to be frustrating and it caused my anxiety level to increase because I told her that I felt like I was close to a mental breakdown. I told her how the noise level in my unit was having a toxic effect on me. But she kept saying "you seem alright now." There was no probing on Ms. Landers to clarify what I was stating instead she seemed overwhelmed and perplexed by what I was saying. I got the impression that she wasn't knowledgeable enough to deal with my situation. I said to myself, how can I seem alright when I can't even remember my youngest son's birth or upbringing? I told her that I was in chronic and acute pain from my large intestine hanging out of me. I describe how the pain made me very moody and irritable. I said the hernia was so large that it is the size of two male fists. I demonstrated that by putting my fists together. I told her that the hernia protrudes out of groin like a large banana.

Over five years I described my inguinal hernia to the penal staff the same way by pointing to it. As mentioned, it was so large that it caused a very large bulge or swelling in my pants which made it very obvious. I told her at times I had to hold it so I could walk. Also as mentioned the bulge was so obvious that the guards even female guards would make me strip naked to see if I was hiding contraband in my pants. As mentioned, the inmates nicknamed me "Long John" because of it. I pointed to the hernia and the bulge in my groin trying to get her to understand how painful it was and how negatively it affected my mental health. All of a sudden Ms. Landers ended the interview without explanation and left the room.

A few days later when I met with Ron Uhrick, my case manager, he informed that Ms. Landers was accusing me of sexual harassment. I assume it was because I pointed to the hernia, but I did not refer to it verbally in a vulgar, profane or sexual terms. I couldn't believe what I heard. I was frustrated by Ms. Landers' accusation and what she was accusing me of. To accuse a man in his 70s of sexual harassment with my history and physical profile is like saying that your apple tree is sprouting potatoes. Nothing could be further from the reality or the truth. I'm sorry that Ms. Landers thinking was sexual in nature. I could only assume that she was a product of the prison environment where people from both sides of the walls talk in vulgar and sexual terms. The vulgarity and profanity rage in prison but her superiors should have counseled her. What do you expect to hear in a prison? It is far from being a nursery school. At the point in my life and my physical profile with a very painful hernia I'm no more inclined sexually than I am to swim in a major city sewer.

I judge that I was being harassed by the system. I waited three months to what I thought was some critical and vital psychotherapy after the brutal attack by Lt. Reeves. Instead of therapy I got what to me is a traumatic and heinous accusation. I was shocked by what Ms. Landers accused me of. I judge that I was violated by her. I have two sisters, two daughters, a granddaughter and daughter-in-law plus I spent years in support of abused children's causes. During my career I had over five hundred female employees and seven thousand female customers. I was never accused of any type of improper sexual conduct. My psychological evaluations found no predisposition towards improper sexual conduct. Instead of asking for clarification of what I meant, Ms. Landers abruptly ends the interview without any explanation at the time and just walks away without any concern for my mental health. She later accuses me of sexual harassment without any regard for the effect on me. I said to myself that's what I get for trying to comply with what I assumed was the short staffing of the mental health clinic. I could have protested about Ms. Lander's inexperience, but I was instead empathetic towards a young woman's career development.

When you cut off a person's hormone production, which in my case is testosterone because of the hernia, it creates a chemical imbalance in the brain. It affects more than a man's libido. Ms. Landers' studies should have taught her that a hernia pressing on a man's testicle which can cut off hormone production can cause dementia, memory loss and irrational behavior. Of course, any man would demonstrate many of the symptoms that I was trying to describe to Ms. Landers. Instead of properly conferring with her superiors Ms. Landers made her very inappropriate accusation. I questioned in my mind the professional competency of Ms. Landers' supervisors to have what I termed a neophyte intern performing a psychological evaluation on a man who had been diagnosed and suffering from at the prison with four major psychiatric disorders.

When I was sent to Centennial Prison for a psychological evaluation, I told the therapist about what happened with Ms. Landers. The therapist apologized for the incident, and she stated that by state law it was illegal for Ms. Landers to attempt to conduct psychotherapy without being properly licensed. She also stated that whoever authorized Ms. Landers to meet with me was guilty of malpractice. Consider this, two years prior at this same clinic I was diagnosed with four major psychiatric diseases for which I didn't receive any appropriate medications or therapy. When they finally decide to give me some therapy, they have an unlicensed and inexperienced young lady to treat a man with not one but four major psychiatric conditions. The patient, myself, just months before had a massive heart attack that produced a very dangerous triple A aorta aneurysms. If that isn't a malpractice which reeks with negligence what dose? By the way I was written up and punished for sexual harassment. Instead of therapy I was subject to a very traumatic experience which had a very traumatic effect on my mental health. It is an indication how the staff at Sterling ignores laws and proper procedures. You don't accuse a man with my background and profile of sexual harassment like you're issuing parking tickets.

A few months later when I was complaining to a nurse about my very painful state with inguinal hernia the nurse asked to see it. I refused her because I learned the hard way not to trust the clinical staff and especially its management. I was afraid to make myself vulnerable to another perverse accusation of sexual harassment. If pointing to my groin area is considered sexual harassment, then what about the following incidents? Lady Officer Baird forced me to strip naked to explore what was between my legs. Lady Officer Sexton insisted to know what was between my legs. I mentioned what happened to me at intake when four officers were called over to view the size of my scrotum. Since I was incarcerated at Sterling Prison, I have been forced to strip over forty times and lift up my scrotum which is very painful because it is already stretched and swollen from the inguinal hernia filling it. When I lifted up my scrotum, I was also bending part of the large intestine which was contained inside the stretched-out scrotum. I then have to bend over in an erotic pose and expose my anus. It made me feel so dirty and sexually violated just like when I was a defenseless and helpless little boy and raped continually by an uncle. I still wonder what causes a person especially one studying to be a therapist to think only in sexual terms? What about her supervisors and officials conducting the hearing?

CHAPTER 40

Excuses

Nazis who participated or condoned the terrible and horrific slaughter of six million European Jews claimed at their post-World War II trials said that they were just following orders but the judges at Nuremburg still condemned them. Many tried to plead ignorance, but the court did not accept that excuse and said they should have known. The courts were right because it is a rare organization which the members don't know what their associates and colleagues are doing. You don't keep negative behaviors and crimes a secret from the rest of the group. Members develop reputations for their behaviors especially if they are negative or wrong and people love to gossip. Officers used to confess to me when I complained about being abused that it was known that certain officers had a reputation for abusing the inmates. This was the case in my first heart attack at the Adams County Jail when Officer Tapia invaded my cell late at night and harassed me and my cell mate.

What I don't understand and what bothers me is that when officials of the law and justice system witness or hear of an inmate being abused in some way, they seem not to do anything about it. Yet these people are employed by the taxpayers to enforce the laws and ensure that they are being enforced without prejudice. I experienced this lack of concern even by those who held the highest rank and occupied the highest positions within the system. It seems that any rights that I had earned because I am considered by our Federal Government an honorably served disabled veteran were suspended as soon as I was accused of a crime. This fact is manifested that I was denied proper legal representation, evaluation, diagnosis or proper and necessary health care which I earned by volunteering to serve my country in a time of war. I also served my communities in many ways after my military service. It seems that the statement that "Water under the bridge is soon forgotten" is factual in my case. Did the good that I did go away, and should we ask those whose lives that I influenced in a positive way?

Officers of the law need to police themselves and their associates if the abusive behaviors are going to be controlled and reduced. It has to be controlled from within the organization no matter what type of organization. Officers are not immune from obeying the law just because they are charged with enforcing the law. You can't act oblivious to what is going on within the group or organization. History indicates that wrongful behaviors of a minority will eventually tarnish the reputation of all or the majority. This is true for the individual or even countries. Look what happened in post war Germany. Many innocent German's especially women and children suffered post WWII because of the atrocious acts by the Nazis. Russian soldiers were encouraged to sand in line to take turns raping the women and girls. The communist and Nazi governments taught us how wrong governments and their officials can be. As we became more knowledgeable and learned over centuries many laws had to be abolished, repealed or amended. What about segregation in our own country? Thank God that rightness and goodness ultimately arises for the good of the masses.

When this book is published the individuals responsible for my treatment by the penal and justice system both directly and indirectly will have their excuses. You will hear that Walshe did this and Walshe did that but please let me paraphrase what the Austrian psychiatrist Victor Frankl said when it comes to excuses, he said that no matter what harm was done to him it still didn't give him the right to harm another. Victor Frankl survived the tortures of four Nazi Concentration Camps and lost most of his loved ones who were murdered at the brutal hands of the Nazis.

CHAPTER 41

The Law of Attraction and Guilt

A metaphysician will most appreciate what I have to say about my later life and what I believe influenced and help create my downfall. The ancient Greek philosopher Socrates went to his death proclaiming that one should lead a virtuous life which I believe most of us try to do. He had proclaimed "the unexamined life is not worth living". That is what I wanted to do was to examine my life and figure out how I went from being multimillionaire to laying on prison floor in my own human waste in solitary confinement and subject to so much abuse. How did that happen and what did I do to cause it to happen? How can you go from so high to so low? What did I do to attract so much negativity to cause my downfall and later on to intensify and exacerbate my punishment? I don't believe that things just happen to us. We do things that make things happen to us. Just like I did things to cause my success so what did I do to cause my failure? I'm a very kind, loving, generous, gentle and God loving person. When I look back on my life especially over the last two decades it makes me wonder how and why could I have suffered so much? If I may term it "bad luck" prior to going to prison and during prison. How could a man's life which had been so fruitful for almost four adult decades turn so sour? No alcohol, no illicit drugs, no perverted sex and no gambling. What happened?

When you grow up in a religious household and attend parochial schools you are taught, and it becomes ingrained in you that you have to pay for your sins. That according to the biblical accounts is why Jesus died on the cross for the forgiveness of the sins of mankind. Many religions believe that sins can be forgiven by God. In the Roman Catholic Religion in which I was raised sins can be forgiven by God with the help of a priest through the sacrament of Confession. That said, there leaves your conscience which can be defined as an inner voice which some believe is part of the soul and acts as a guide to rightness or wrongness of one's behavior. Guilt is an emotional experience that a person experiences when a person believes that what they have done violates a moral standard ingrained in them or established by society. Guilt is also related to the concept of remorse or shame. Guilt is a very strong emotional experience that can be so strong as to drive someone to take their life. We feel guilty when we perceive that we have done harm to another person. It can be perceived a self-regulating emotion that can holds someone to a moral standard. It also serves for the human race to perpetuate itself. It could be said the bigger or more sensitive the conscience the more susceptible someone is to guilt and the intensity of it. The guilt emotion is an emotional state which if left unregulated can lead to neurological, psychological and physical damage to a person.

In my case guilt led to my destruction by me, by others and society. Others moved on with their lives after I did unintentional harmful things whether they forgave me or not. That is the smart thing for them to do instead of letting hurt impede their progress. Unfortunately, subconsciously I didn't forgive myself for the harm that I had done whether I was of a right mind or not. Some people will hang on to the harm that you have done to them in order to manipulate you. You owe me because you did this or that to me. In other words, you have harmed me therefore you owe me some type of retribution which could be some type of servitude. Some will hang on to hurtful events in order to use it as an excuse for their own failings. Misery loves company. They continue to use the harm that you caused them as an excuse for their failings in life. If you are going to move on in life on the road to achievement you need to recognize what I will term as the nonforgivers are doing to you. You need to forgive yourself even if others don't forgive you otherwise it will be an anchor in your life in your movement forward. If you don't forgive yourself as I didn't, it can have a life devastating effect on your life. In my case as stated I would continue to punish myself physically or psychologically. Whenever I would get frustrated or angry with myself, I would punish myself by slapping or punching myself in the face or body. I didn't understand why I wanted to punish myself until one day when reading a self-help book on the power of attraction. When I started to regain my cognitive ability and awareness, I started to imagine what I was like and what I did in that demented state that I fell into. It created such intense guilt feelings in me that I would pray to God to take my life. The "what ifs" or the "I must haves" were causing me to fall back into a very depressed and demented state again. It created a very dark cloud or aura which hung over me. When I left prison and I started to hear from loved ones what I actually was like and learning of my misdeeds once again I wished for my death. I realized that I wasn't only causing myself harm, but I was attracting harm to myself by those who were so weak and ignorant to want harm others through their unforgiveness. I believe they did it in order to mistakenly feed their egos or self-esteem by abusing me. They loved to remind me of the harm I had done to them. It was as if their unforgiveness gave them power over me. Before going to prison and while in prison I attracted the negative behaviors by others by broadcasting my own negative very guilty energy which were generated by my beliefs. I created this negative energy field by believing the negatives of what others said about me whether it was logical, right, or wrong. If it was wrong, I didn't reject it. If it was valid, I didn't minimize its negative effect on me by recognizing my psychological weakness because my disorders or an offsetting strength. I discounted the effect of my psychiatric diseases on my behaviors just like the justice and penal system did. What I write does not condone the wrong that was done to me by others because no matter how much negative energy I was broadcasting it didn't give them the right to harm me. The negative energy continually built within me and accumulated to a life devastating state because I did nothing to offset or relieve it through self-forgiveness. I didn't recognize the shortcomings of the unforgivers and realizing how their unforgiveness was harming me. It is like I welcomed their abuse like I did my own abuse so I could pay for my sins as I was taught to as a little boy. Even at seventy plus years of age in some ways I hadn't matured yet and in some ways, I regressed to a childlike state.

For years in my adult life through the cumulative effect of successes I overcame the harm done to my self-image through the negative effects of my upbringing. It was as if I was saying to those who had a negative effect on my self-image, I will prove you wrong. Watch me and see how I will become successful when you didn't think that I had the ability to succeed or to succeed a lot beyond your expectations of me. I rejected other's negative opinion of me and demonstrated to them how successful I could be. I recognized the shortcomings of my parents which all parents have and so do I as a parent have my shortcomings. But as I went along in my adult life, I didn't recognize the short cummings of others that I was counting on to feed my self-esteem. That was a huge mistake counting on others to feed my self-esteem when many of them couldn't feed their own self-esteem. I didn't guard the gates of my mind and allowed others negative statements or opinions about me to affect my opinion of me. I became too overconfident. Instead of looking to myself to filter and assess what others said about me I consciously and subconsciously accepted it. Now as I look back on my life instead of feeding my self-esteem, I allowed the negative opinions of others to help destroy me. A tragic example of that self- destructive behavior at my second divorce I tried to take my life.

I didn't recognize the wrongness in others and the negative effect that they had on me. I automatically accepted the so-called wrongness that others accused me of instead of challenging at least in my own mind. I felt guilty and assumed that I needed to be punished just like when I was a young boy. Instead of looking to myself and my Creator for forgiveness I relied on some people who couldn't forgive or accept themselves. It was like looking for love in all the wrong places.

In prison I automatically accepted the abuses the wrongness that was being inflicted on me instead of asking myself what was I doing to attract so much negativity. I believe that I was broadcasting the belief through my negative energy field that I deserved to be punished beyond the norm because I was so guilty of hurting others through my failings. I didn't realize what I was broadcasting to the world around me. I didn't realize that just the loss of freedom and separation from family and spending years in prison was enough punishment. When being abused I didn't ask myself why me. I just saw it as my necessity to endure and recover instead of saying to myself what am I doing subconsciously to attract this abuse? The broadcasting of negative energy is not as obvious of a cause to being abused like being disobedient obstinate or unruly. Yes, there is the law of attraction where you attract goodness, but I know there is the law of wrongness where you are causing negative behaviors to be inflicted upon you. You may be doing harm to yourself through the perpetuation of negative behaviors and habits. In some people this is manifested in obesity, alcohol or illicit drug use which causes them to age beyond the norm and hasten their death. It demonstrates that you have to be constantly aware of the energy that you are broadcasting to the world around you. If you don't think enough of yourself don't expect others to do the same. If you have not forgiven yourself for your misdeeds don't expect others to forgive you. If you don't forgive others for their part in what happened to you don't expect others to forgive you. I believe that I'm a very kind, loving, gentle and generous person. I also believe that I'm very accountable for any wrong that I have done to others. I now believe that it is more important that you forgive yourself for your misdeeds if you expect to move forward with your life again in a positive way just like you forgive others. If you don't, you never cut the rope or chains to those negative anchors and that will create even stronger anchors. It is up to you to empower yourself and not others. You have to live in the present and not the past. Maybe this is why there is so much recidivism among ex-convicts that makes them convicts again. You rehabilitate people by empowering them not suppressing them which the penal system does. Making people feel guilty disempowers them. If you want people to change you have to empower them to change by seeing the good in them.

Consider this as stated I am a very kind, loving, generous, gentle and rule or law-abiding man. In spite of the foregoing, I was treated in my opinion unfairly by the justice system and was terribly abused in the penal system so much more than my fellow prisoners. I was thrown in the "Hole" eleven times and experienced at least fourteen assaults some of which were major which exacerbated my physical and mental disorders. The abuse caused me to suffer three heart attacks, two strokes, a very dangerous aorta aneurysms and had to have heart surgery. I suffered the pain and agony of my guts hanging out of me for five years, over forty grand mal seizures, numerous angina pectoris attacks and panic attacks. How does a man who tried to do so much goodness even in prison experience so much abuse and a minimum to describe it as an atrocious and barbarous existence? As described earlier when I experienced panic or angina pectoris attack, I would strike myself. Why did I have such a negative and self-destructive tendency?

I believe that it was the law of attraction. Instead of attracting goodness into my life like most people wish to attract, I was attracting a lot more than my fair share of punishment and abuse. Why because as stated when others and society forgave me I didn't forgive myself. I didn't think enough of myself. I believed the misguided persons, and in some cases loved ones who want to take revenge out on me by reinforcing my guilt instead of saying at least to myself that is enough. I believed the ignorant ones who wouldn't allow themselves to attribute my so-called wrongful behaviors were as a result of my four major psychiatric health disorders. I believed the unloving ones who just couldn't find it in their hearts to forgive me. They were the ones who tried to lift their self-esteem by punishing me by withholding their forgiveness and understanding.

I didn't say to myself or others I have experienced my fair share of punishment and unforgiveness. I was broadcasting to the world and those who would take advantage of my mental health disorders I'm so guilty and I need to be punished more. It is like a child or an abused spouse who experiences so much abuse that they believe that they deserve to be abused more and more. It is like they become a battering ram for their abusers. I say this so others can say to themselves and therefore through their energy field that they deserve to be forgiven and loved. They deserve acceptance, love, kindness and success in their live instead of punishment beyond the norm. Now instead of broadcasting through my energy field that I deserve punishment I say I deserve love, acceptance and success. Most of all my forgiveness comes from within me and my God. It no longer matters if others don't forgive me, I forgive me. I paid for my sins over and over again. Now, I deserve acceptance, love and to be very successful again. I visualize my success on a daily basis but most of all I believe it. In summary uncontrolled guilt can cause you to be your own worst enemy. You have to be reborn again each day and leave the negative past in the past. Just practice the positive lessons learned. Now my life is turning fruitful again because my mind believes that I can, and I deserve love, acceptance, and success.

We need to realize that most people live their lives doing the best that they can at that moment in their lives. They make mistakes and have their failures especially when venturing out into the new ground. Sometimes they are strong and sometimes they are weak but most of the time they are doing the best that can. They need to forgive their mistakes and failures and give themselves credit for venturing into new ground. Our Creator created us to succeed but in order to do that we have to make mistakes and fail on our way to success. By the way since writing this chapter I no longer punish myself physically or mentally. If I have the urge to strike myself, I just say "No". It proves the power of the "Pen" in helping to cure yourself.

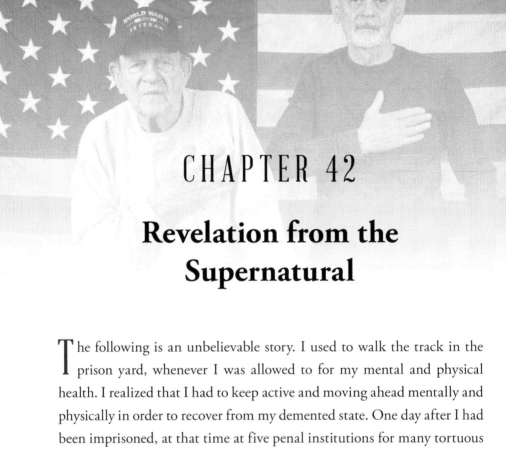

CHAPTER 42

Revelation from the Supernatural

The following is an unbelievable story. I used to walk the track in the prison yard, whenever I was allowed to for my mental and physical health. I realized that I had to keep active and moving ahead mentally and physically in order to recover from my demented state. One day after I had been imprisoned, at that time at five penal institutions for many tortuous years, a voice out of nowhere spoke to me. The voice said, to me and please allow me to paraphrase, John I'm not up there I'm right here walking next to you. The reason that you have been inadvertently incarcerated for years is so you could learn, experience and witness how the mentally ill and elderly are treated in prison. You especially are well qualified to speak for Me because you have no history of alcohol and illicit drug use. So, when you speak for me, they can't say, well he is just some old drug addict or alcoholic. You were very successful in your life and performed many good deeds for Me until your mental health unfortunately failed you as it has for many that are in prison. Your mission now in life is not to become a multimillionaire again but to be My messenger and advocate for the mentally ill and elderly in prison.

From that moment on I felt that I was no longer in a prison but a seminary to prepare me to do God's work. Each torture, assault and abuse were no longer such but a lesson in preparing me for God's mission for me. The heavenly feeling that came over me I can only describe although my description is inadequate. That euphoric feeling was well beyond ecstasy. I would love more than anything to feel it again and would make any sacrifice to do so. Now as you read this story and you wonder how I not only survived so many abuses, tortures, etc. I can only say it wasn't at my hand but God's Hand. I experienced every ill act that a prisoner could experience except for lawful execution but I did so with very honorable meaning and purpose. Each abuse and torture were just another lesson and gave me the ability to challenge and endure any amount of pain or fear. I used to just say to myself you can handle with God's help, it's not so bad and with God's blessing I did handle it. I don't regret one moment of it. From that point the abusers may have caused me physical hurt, but it only made me grow in so many ways. Yes, I would endure all the so-called pain and suffering all over again if it is God's wish for me. I thank God for adding honorable meaning and purpose to my incarceration.

CHAPTER 43

Perpetual Daily Assault

Just being housed in the manner and place that I was housed with my physical and psychological profile on a daily basis is an assault on my person. Almost every person lives with a degree of fear of death but each day all I had to look forward to, was more pain and suffering. It is part of natural and instinctual self-preservation which perpetuates life and causes us to be cautious in our actions. When you live in a hostile environment where violence is so prevalent with my history of assaults, hostile acts and the complications of nine major health disorders fear becomes terror without God as your mentor. Each day that you are housed in that environment with my disabilities is tortuous diminishes your lifespan, your cognizance ability and your memory. Memory deficiency because of the stressful atmosphere causes you to feel very inadequate. Every day that you spend in that environment is a hell of a lot more than cruel and unusual punishment. I challenge anyone to prove otherwise. As I look back as to the condition I was in when I left Sterling Prison all I can say is that each day there took a tremendous toll on my life. To say the least it was devastating. To use terms such as inhumane, barbaric, savage, uncivilized, etc., are inadequate to describe it. All I can say is shame on those who perpetuate that existence on a man whose crime was to fall victim to age and mental illness some of which was developed by honorably serving his country. To allow that to overshadow all the good in his life is wrong and is a crime. To say my existence in that environment is akin to child abuse is an understatement and totally inadequate. The prison staff took advantage of a weaking. Without God as my mentor, I would not have survived and like so many I would have left that prison in a body bag.

CHAPTER 44

My Future Health

The point is that as far as my future life is concerned for me, if I may phrase it, I'm walking on thin ice. Much more than the average person I have much less chance of surviving life's stressors. Without God's sacred mission for me I would not be alive today. I go to sleep most nights with little hope of surviving the night or even the next day. The Colorado Dept. of Corrections knowingly housed me in a maximum-security prison and in the maximum-security section of that prison in spite of my physical and mental health profile. Some guards even senior ones would ask why I was being housed in the maximum-security unit. Just a few months ago four guards from that unit, number four, had to be hospitalized and one was hospitalized with a crushed skull. Now if that isn't elderly psychological abuse what is? Not just me, the guards are in fear of their lives. I exist every day and go to sleep each night with a very dangerous circulatory aneurysms. I've already had two strokes. That is a total four aneurysms not even considering three heart attacks. If that isn't very stressful, what is? The abuse at that prison endures because the culture allows it. People from both sides of those walls are subject to it. That is why they are short of personnel and have such high turnover in a rural setting where there is usually a stable atmosphere. Correctional officers who have left are write in their description of Sterling when they refer to it as a "Hell Hole".

CHAPTER 45

My Prison And Jail Philosophy

When I started to regain my cognizance in jail and prison I didn't see prison as an end but just a temporary detour which I knew that I could and would overcome. Actually, I was full of gratitude when I realized the animalistic state that I had descended into and was emerging from. I was so grateful that I was emerging from that state. I didn't understand how I fell into that state, but I was thankful for emerging from it. Even today when I can urinate and defecate normally, I'm grateful. I was very grateful to those who reached out to help me in my recovery and forced me to start moving forward again. When you emerge from nothing or such a demeaned state you become grateful for everything.

To endure being incarcerated I wrote to myself not to expect anything good from the system. By not expecting anything good any good that was bestowed on me was a gift which I was grateful for. As an example at Sterling Prison, I wasn't issued a pillow so I rolled up my winter coat and used it as pillow and enjoyed it. When I was issued a pillow even though the vinyl casing was torn and full of cracks, I was happy to get a pillow no matter what the condition. The mattress pad was very compressed from use and smelled of old urine but at least it was better than laying on cold metal. The food was tasteless but, in my opinion, there was plenty of it for me. I resolved to myself that nothing was fair and not to expect anything to be fair. When I was abused or treated badly, I saw it as just part of being incarcerated and a lesson. My military experience helped me to endure the structure.

I also resolved to myself that I would be treated as dirt by the system. I said to myself that no one other than your loved ones cares that you are incarcerated. I realized that I would just have to endure and just make the best of your circumstances and not fight the system. I knew that I had fallen down but I had the confidence that good would emerge and I would rise again. I had led a very structured and moral life when I was on what the prisoners termed it "on the street" but prison showed me the total opposite side of life. I don't think that prior to being incarcerated that I had ever knowingly met an ex-convict. It may sound crazy to most, but prison added a completeness to my life. I would have never experienced what I did while on the street. It helped give me a better understanding of the diverse nature of the human race. Learning the histories of many of my fellow prisoners taught me not to be so quick to judge others. Needless to say, being housed in the maximum-security prison and in the maximum-security section of the prison I had to fine tune my human relations skills. I thought that I was learning more about human relations in prison then I had learned in forty-two years in sales and marketing. If you screwed up, you paid for it.

I saw being incarcerated as a misfortune. I did feel very guilty for the circumstances that caused me to be incarcerated. I had my times of doubt and depression, but I felt fortunate as compared to many of my fellow inmates. I might have had it bad but there were so many others who had it much worse. When you hear the story of a person being raped at the age of eight you stop feeling sorry for yourself. At times I might have doubted that I could rise again but I never thought that things would get worse. With dementia you are not fully aware of your circumstances. In November of 2013 I started to regain my cognizance after losing it for at least a decade. It is now over eight years later I'm still becoming normally aware again whatever that is. Hopefully I will continue to recover and will do everything in my power to do so. I would like to regain the memories of my children and grandchildren growing up. Like the universe and I know that I must keep on growing and moving forward again.

As we examine history, we find that good always arises and the bad eventually fails. The human race with God's inspiration has a way of perpetually correcting and perfecting itself which insures its survival. Consider how many life forms have failed because they didn't have the mental ability to correct themselves. We hear about all the endangered species who have to rely on our efforts. When wrong or bad arises through an individual, society or even disease sooner or later when it is recognized and brought to the forefront of our awareness and thinking, something be it an individual or groups of individuals such as organizations and institutions arise to counteract the destructiveness. Consider that Black Lives Mater movement and covid nineteen vaccines. This wrong or danger as stated could be a person, a group of people such as societies, governments, countries or diseases. In the past century these maladies have taken the form of diseases such as cancer, smallpox, polio, and now covid nineteen. In individuals they have been termed murderers, rapist, robbers, drug czars, etc. In organizations they have been called mafia, Nazis, communist, etc. This is what has made mankind to survive the ages and separates us from other life forms. What is very interesting, I have referenced the Nazi Concentration Camps the people who were most likely to survive those camps were those who cared more for others than themselves. They did it God's way! The best way to survive the tortures of a maximum-security prison is to care for others more than yourself.

When the harm or evil is recognized in time something, someone or groups of people organized and used or developed the resources to counteract it. It was miraculous how fast covid nineteen vaccines were developed. That is why the human race perpetuates itself. As we recognize wrong, bad or evil and as long as we continue to initiate action and harness resources to correct the problem, wrong or evil the longer the human race will survive and enhance itself. We need to appreciate whatever or whoever brings these problems, wrongs and evils to our attention because as the old saying states: "a problem identified is a problem half solved or corrected." Think of the major problems or issues that have plagued humans through ages. Where would we be if those problems were not addressed or attacked in some way and solved in a timely way?

We may not like hearing about problems not matter what form they take but where would we be without hearing about them through the centuries? We probably would not be here now. I believe that those who bring problems that plague our societies to our attention are God's messengers to help perfect us. Charles Darwin termed it as "survival of the fittest." Darwin did not consider himself as an atheist but a theist. It is my belief that God's greatest messenger was His Son Jesus whose message was love, goodness and kindness. What kind of society would we have without love which is the strongest force in the universe?

America is the richest country in the world and has so many resources to properly treat the mental illnesses that our societies create through their behaviors. Think of the amount of mass murders and other crisis such as opioids that are a manifestation of mental health disorders. How many resources, material goods, money, etc. does a man need to be happy? The answer is very few even if he shares them. Can we direct some of our riches to bring mental health disorders and the problems that they create to the forefront without the negative stigma as we have and are doing with cancer? The greatest lessons I learned in prison is it takes very few material goods or resources to be happy. Let me say again that I found that I could be as happy in a small cell which I shared with another man as I could in a house of many thousands of square feet. I could be as happy in a prison bunk with a compressed mattress pad soaked with old urine as I could in a very comfortable king size bed. You may be more comfortable in a big house and king size bed, but you won't be happier as long as your conscience tells you that there are fellow humans suffering. Material goods don't make you happy because you will never have enough if you take that path. The proper spiritual attitude and a decision to be happy will make you happy. Consider the type of housing Jesus' mother Mary occupied. I witnessed the shack that His mother occupied in Ephesus, Turkey after Jesus' death. After Jesus was born Mary laid him in a manger which animals would eat from.

Instead of incarcerating the mentally ill or the unfortunate elderly we need to share the wealth that God has bestowed upon us to treat the unfortunate because that is where and how true happiness lies. I was housed with the worst of the worst, but I found that when I looked for the good in them and focused on it that good would emerge. You can't live just for yourself. You must live to do good for unfortunate others and not look down at them because the day may come when you become one of them as I did. Before you criticize your fellow human first learn their histories. True happiness lies in meaning, purpose and love for your fellow human especially the most unfortunate and the worst of the worst. A life lived just of oneself is too terminal and a life lived for others' lives on. When you aren't happy it is time to make someone else happy! That is how I overcame the side effects of severe major depression and my other diseases in the most negative environment known to civilized man. I found happiness and fulfillment through the meaning and purpose that God added to my life.

I believe in my heart considering American History that the American Public doesn't tolerate such things as physical abuse especially elderly abuse and psychological abuse especially when it is brought to their attention. This is especially true for those who suffer from major disorders that have their birth during military service. I'm writing about how I was abused as an elderly person in Colorado institutions, yet Colorado has had a law concerning such since such. It demonstrates that it doesn't matter as much as to what the law says but what is in people's minds and hearts. Elderly lives have to matter in people's hearts and minds which is manifested in the culture and actions of a society in order for it to thrive spiritually.

I wrote this story not to seek pity or for you to feel sorry for me. I write to show how a man can sink from very high to so low but rise again. How a man can endure, survive and grow emotionally, mentally and even recover physically. Most importantly how he can grow and thrive spiritually in some of the worst physical, mental and emotional circumstances. I did this while supposedly with the limitations of age, mental and physical health disabilities. Many said I couldn't and wouldn't rise again. Some called my family and said that I wouldn't make it. Others who had visited me didn't believe that they would see me alive again. My story is meant to show that people who say you can't they may be wrong because if you accept God as your enduring and loving partner you can and you will rise again. God brought me out of a vegetative state that I was in for almost three years to be reborn in so many ways. I was dysfunctional in many ways. You have to grow to endure and tolerate but that takes strength and courage which come from an intimate relationship with God. Then each brutal or terrible act motivates you to endure, grow and recover which is very challenging in a penal environment. I got to the point when people would hurt me physically, I would say to myself, thank you for another lesson. Yes, I would see it as just another lesson to be learned. To me there is nothing stronger to cause you to grow and endure than faith or belief in a loving God.

They say that no man is an island but with God's help and guidance you aren't just an island but a country, continent, planet and even a universe full of God's knowledge, power and most of all love. God can give you strength and courage to overcome any amount of abuse and torturous being by adding very honorable purpose and meaning to you and your life as God did to mine. God has the final word not others no matter how many say you can't; if God says you can, you will. I found that the more my relationship with God was enhanced so were the relationships with others especially my loved ones. I hope that once you read this story when someone tells you that you can't which includes yourself tell them they are wrong because with the right God-given attitude and God as your partner you can. Just learn to remove the letter "t" from the word can't and you will.

If after you read this document if you think that I left prison the way that I entered it as a broken old man, then I have failed you. I left prison as a man that was reborn in so many ways especially spiritually.

CHAPTER 46
Proper Evaluation and Diagnosis

W hen you evaluate a person especially their disability or competency most mental and physical health professionals would agree it should be done holistically.

Please consider that a disability is a disorder, ailment, disease or malady that limits a person's ability, senses, movements or activity. Every additional major disease such as cardiovascular disease creates more disability. Additional diseases especially in the same category such as circulatory system disorders dramatically increase a person's disability. Hypothetically if we say that cardiovascular disease creates a disability of twenty percent now add hypercholesterolemia at ten percent, hypertension at ten percent, kidney disease at ten percent and diabetes at ten percent: the total disability is sixty percent. The VA has rated me as eighty percent disabled almost ninety percent of which is based in just my mental health. Now when you consider psychiatric diseases which amplify the effects of circulatory system diseases such as acute anxiety and major depression the person's disability is increased. When you consider other factors such as the perilous environment of a prison filled with antagonism, hostility, animosity and the sheer propensity for violence the disability is increased even further. The point is the level of punishment or pain and suffering is much higher for a person who is disabled in some way than one of average age with no or minimal disabilities.

I judge that if I had been thoroughly and properly diagnosed and the cases properly investigated the cases would not have gone forward. Once a case does go forward then the need arises for the individuals within the justice system to defend their actions or lack of appropriate actions. It becomes a matter of win or lose and not what it should be a quest for the truth, fairness and justice. No one wants to lose or be labeled a loser. Once an individual is indited for a crime people's egos and reputations are a stake instead of truth and justice. Someone is going to win and someone is going to lose whether it is the prosecution or the defense. Unfortunately, in the justice system lawyers are not rated for how much they pursued justice but whether they won or lost the case. True justice becomes imperiled when people's reputations are at stake. Lawyers whether they represent the prosecution or the defense are rarely rated for how many cases they worked but how many cases they won or lost which places the pursuit of justice at stake. It is like medical doctors are rated for curing sicknesses and saving lives not losing lives. Who would see a doctor if he or she developed a reputation for most of their patients dying?

Once you are charged of a crime and found guilty you are stigmatized which reflects negatively on any future accusations or prosecutions. Your past positive accomplishes are then overshadowed by a conviction and your stigma. People rarely rationalize as to why a man in his golden or retirement years all of a sudden resort to criminal behavior? Contributing disorders and diseases are readily dismissed because as inferred it becomes a game and the challenge is who will win in spite of the truth. In my case just one stroke should have raised a red flag and I suffered from two strokes which effect one's brain and can affect a person's thinking.

The same is true for one inpatient mental hospital stay but I had four, the same is true for a suicide attempt and four major psychiatric disorders. The court record states that the jury heard none of them since there was no mention of any of them in the trial transcript. Why didn't the jury hear of any of them especially concerning my memory and judgement ability?

The focus was on a very small portion of my life that wasn't properly examined. There were so many red flags that were never examined. Just a review of my medical record for no proper treatment of major health disorders raises the flags of negligence and malpractice. How do you diagnose a man with four major psychiatric disorders and then don't treat them with medication or therapy for almost three years? How do you justify having an honorably served veteran to have to live with his guts hanging out for five years? How do you justify similar inaction that a man lives with an extremely dangerous aorta aneurysms in the most hostile prison for almost two years? The answer is pure unadulterated negligence and indifference. It comes down to the fact that once you are found guilty of a crime no matter what the circumstances your life no matter what your age or profile "Your life doesn't matter" anymore.

A major consequence of physical and psychological abuse is to live in fear. This is especially true for psychological abuse. When the abuse is chronic as it has been with me with at least fourteen acts of violence and at least ten very hostile acts, the fear becomes terror. The fear/terror response can be so intense as to cause a permanent chemical imbalance in the brain chemistry and consequently the mind. As mentioned, just one catastrophic experience when one is elderly can also cause permanent brain damage. In my case I was already struggling to overcome the negative effects of four major psychiatric disorders and four concussions. Grand mal seizures are a sign of brain tissue damage. I had over forty of them.

I understand as Judge Ensor said I may look alright but let me state that you don't abuse or bully a 73-year-old man no matter what state of physical and mental health he may be in. This is also true for individuals half my age. You don't abuse any man the way that I was abused especially veterans. I will carry the psychological scars in the form of PTSD, strokes and heart attacks for the rest of my life which unquestionably has been dramatically shortened by the penal system. I often wonder what my granddaughter thought of law enforcement when she saw her Poppa with two back eyes and a large head wound in a court of law? What should she think? If the justice system was truly seeking justice and law enforcement why didn't even one justice system official ask why does this old man have a large head wound and two black eyes? I can only assume that by asking that question they would have sacrificed expediency.

The following is a partial list of just some of the more traumatic events that took place and that I had to endure at Adams County Jail, Denver County Jail and Sterling Prison in a period of just four years. Please keep in mind that I have no memory prior to September of 2014. Also keep in mind that these acts were performed on a man who had a profile of four major psychiatric disorders, five major circulatory systems disorder and was struggling to recover from a very demented state where he couldn't even find the bathroom, dining hall or his cell. Plus, he was enduring the pain and agony of his guts hanging out of him. To say that each of these acts was performed on a weakling is quite an understatement. The list is not inclusive and by any means it begins to describe the pain and agony he endured for not just days, weeks, months but years:

1. Heart attack after being harassed by a deputy.
2. Injury to pons area of brain and thyroid gland.
3. Heart attack and heart surgery after being harassed by a deputy.
4. Injury to his wrist after being assaulted by a deputy.
5. Concussion and black eyes after being assaulted by deputies.
6. Taken to the floor after being provoked by deputies.
7. Stroke after being assaulted by inmate.
8. Attempt on my life by inmates.
9. Assaults by inmates at Adams County Jail.
10. Sprayed with chemicals.
11. Thrown in "Hole" after seizures.
12. Solitary stay extended from gastritis attack.

13. Massive heart attack after being placed in choke hold.
14. Laid on handcuffs into my spine and hernia injured during seizure.
15. Head being slammed on prison wall three times over the temporal lobe.
16. Sprayed with chemicals in the eyes and thrown in the "Hole".
17. Lifted up with wrists with my hands behind my back.
18. Placed in body chains forty times.
19. Made to painfully strip naked thirty plus times.

When you treat a person that his or her life doesn't matter anymore than it is very likely why other people's lives won't matter to them. Whatever you put out sooner or later that is what will return to you. Talk to civil rights lawyers and they will tell you that there are more cases concerning prisoner abuse then they can possibly handle. The penal system is aware of this which lack of legal action can perpetuate the abusive culture. No one will be held accountable for the abuse of someone whose life no longer matter matters. But that life will matter when that person continues to commit crimes while they are in prison and once they leave prison. If lawyers do take those cases on the cases can wallow in the courts forever without any timely renumeration for the legal counsel. Lawyers need to pay their expenses and make a living too. I had a prominent civil rights lawyer visit me at Sterling Prison and he asked are you the man that the prisoners talk about being so abused the guards? When I answered that it was probably me, he told but about the unbelievable number of possible cases for prisoner abuse by the perpetrated by the penal system. We wonder why the high rate of recidivism among ex-convicts. Treat a person like dirt and they will act that way and do more dirty things. Almost sixty percent of ex-convicts will return to prison and that is if they are caught committing another crime. Many continue to commit crimes without being caught again because they learned how to navigate the system. They find refuge in the gang culture.

Since leaving prison numerous people have urged me to take legal action. I say to myself and to those who suggest why should I try and seek justice in a system that treated me so unjustly? There is very little justice for ex-convicts no matter what their circumstances. There is little incentive or relief for all those involved to seek justice. How many ex-convicts have the resources to seek justice? The answer is only very few. Only a tiny minority of the population has any empathy for ex-convicts not matter how they were treated by the justice and penal system. If they can't live justly within the system, then they are left to live criminally outside of the system either way society becomes the victims again.

I don't seek justice for myself or to have any of my cases overturned. I'm serving God's purpose for me by publishing this book at my own expense to bring focus to our treatment of the elderly and the mentally ill. I really don't care that I'm considered a convicted felon. I ask who were my accusers, presiding judge and prosecutors? An appeals attorney stated in my appeal that trial should be a truth-seeking process, but this didn't occur in Mr. Walshe's case. I console myself with the fact that Jesus Christ was considered a criminal by the romans and pharisees, Moses a murderer (Exodus 2:14) and David killed Goliath. My future focus will be to return to that of abused children because that is where so much criminality and social deviance is born. When you talk to prisoner and ex-prisoners about their childhood history you say it no wonder that person resorted to criminal behavior. Most grew surrounded in criminality and was taught it was the way. Yes, many were strong enough to overcome their negative histories, but most were not. It starts with illicit drug use and excessive alcohol use to deal with the pain and agony of their evil and abusive childhoods. I recently heard the story of a so-called "call-girl" who lost her virginity at eight years of age and was continually raped by her mother's boyfriends throughout her childhood and adolescence. If she didn't have a self-esteem issue and felt unworthy who would? Now she is addicted to crack cocaine and alcohol worst of all she is perishing from lung cancer as she approaches her elderly years. She resorted to drugs and alcohol drugs to endure the pain of her abuse. Unfortunately, she couldn't endure her pain without self-medicating before you dare to judge her ask yourself who would be strong enough to change with that type of history. Keep in mind the Cherokee Indian proverb "Don't judge a man until you walk a mile in his shoes." She was treated as dirt and therefore thought of herself as such and chose a wayward way of life. Only a small minority survive that abuse without permanent harm. Now she is left to die without anyone giving a dam from the pain and agony of lung cancer which will probably metastasize to brain cancer. She is the mother of four who have probably disowned her because of her lifestyle unless they followed in her path.

She spent a good portion of her adult years in prison for robbery to support her illicit lifestyle. I ask myself how I would feel and act if I were her. It leads me to believe that the more we properly treat society's unfortunate children the less we will have unfortunate elderly to treat. I was lucky to survive abuse as a child and as an elderly person, but I am among a minority who survived atrocious abuse to live again. I say to myself John dare not to judge but to understand and help wherever you can. Let me say that if you take care of the children, you will have less elderly to take care of and their lives will matter as much as anyone else's life.

CHAPTER 47

Choices In Prison Life

In prison you have one of two choices. You either grow or rot because standing still is synonymous with rotting. In my case I did both. When I first went to prison, I was in a in an incognizant or what I term a stupefied state for almost three years. I regressed until I fell into a vegetative or an animalistic state. As stated earlier I fell into such an animalistic state that if I had to urinate, I would just unashamedly just take remove my private from pants and urinate no matter where I was and no matter who was watching me just like an untrained animal. Now that is by anyone's judgement such a negative state. You can't get any lower than that, but I did sink that low. I had sunk so low that not only did I lose all my worldly possessions, the love and respect of some of my loved ones but most of all I lost my mind. When you lose your mind, you have literally lost everything except for your soul. I got to the point physically where I couldn't urinate without being catharize and had to wear a urine collection bag called a urostomy pouch. I developed type II diabetes, major dehydration kidney disease and hernias besides other major disorders. Mentally I couldn't find the bathroom, dining hall or even my own bunk bed. As stated, I deteriorated and stayed in an incognizant state for about thirty-two months.

Before leaving Federal Prison in Big Springs, Texas I started to regain some of my cognizant ability, but I regressed for eight months when I was extradited to the Adams County Jail, in Brighton Colorado. When I started to regain my cognizance at the jail, I couldn't believe what happened to me. How did I go from being a multimillionaire to a prisoner? Because of my pride and ego, I had to find out. How could that have been my fault when I was such a kind, loving, gentle and overall good man? I couldn't point to alcohol or illicit drug use because I didn't partake in any of those.

Yes, I had been inflicted with mental health disorders over the years, but I had tried to attend to those with inpatient hospital stays, medication and psychotherapy. What happened to me? As stated, earlier Dr. Fohrman a psychiatrist at the jail diagnosed me as having pseudo dementia. Another doctor who was familiar with the disease told me that if I wasn't careful that I had a five hundred percent chance of falling back into that very demented state again. That made me determined not to fall back but to recover. Over the years I tried my best to be a good husband, son, brother, father grandfather and businessman. I had to learn how that devastation happened to me and what caused it. I knew that I couldn't go on and feel sorry for myself. Something told me that I had the opportunity to renew myself and I was going to take advantage of it. The deputies and guards could push me down, but I wasn't going to stay down. I knew that I could endure whatever they did to me no matter my age or condition. I was going to show myself, my loved ones, and the world that I could rise again. I started reading every book that I could on the brain and mental health. Those books are very limited in a jail but one of the first books I got my hands on was about learning which I had to do all over again because of my memory loss.

I also remembered how the two fellow inmates in the Texas prison forced me to get up and start moving again and how that helped to regain some cognizance. That lesson taught me that if I was going to going to get back to a state of normality I had to keep moving not only physically, but I had to keep moving mentally. On a daily basis I exercised as much as possible but that was limited with my intestine protruding out of me. Whenever I got the chance to walk and exercise, I took advantage of it no matter how painful it was. I knew that I would get better and I did. I read everything that I could get my hands on about the brain and anything concerning self-help. To me failing wasn't an option I already did that, but I could learn from my failures. One of my sons, Johnny, sent me self-help books but the jail staff wouldn't let me have them but that didn't stop me. I also started writing about what I was reading because I knew that I had a very limited memory if any at all. I read and wrote so much that by the time I was released from prison my pile of notes was about twenty-four inches high written on both sides of letter size paper. I wrote about four thousand mostly positive affirmations about life. When I was weak in one area God made me strong in another. It seemed what I lacked in cognizance ability I had in writing ability. The one thing that I learned while incarcerated is the power in belief. When I was incognizant, I didn't believe that I could, but I certainly didn't believe that I couldn't. When I was regaining my cognizance not only didn't I complain or speak negatives to my fellow inmates but I knew that I couldn't dare speak negatives to myself. Once again failing or not recovering wasn't an option. Did I have my low and doubtful periods? Yes, but when I caught myself, I would refer to my writings and praying to get myself back up. I had to rely on my writings because my memory was still too weak. I would also get out of my world and do something nice for a fellow prisoner who was abandoned by his family and was down. There were always plenty of them.

CHAPTER 48

How I Overcame Some Of My Demons

Please allow me share what I learned to deal with one of my and man's biggest friends or demons namely fears. While incarcerated I had to learn to deal with my fears so they wouldn't continue to destroy me as they did before. A derivative of fear stress and its consequences had already devastated my life. Fear is a very strong emotion, and in that respect, it is almost akin to love in its strength. In some respects, it is like love because it can protect us from harm like a loved one would try and shelter us from harm. Fear is caused by a perceived danger or threat of danger which can cause a very stressful state in the mind and body. Fear can be an asset to us in warning us of a real danger like pain does. Fear is actually our friend, but fear becomes a liability when it becomes unreasonable because of our imagination. Fear can become a negative emotion instead of a positive one that can give birth to negative behaviors or paralysis. Fear is also a form of energy like anything else in the universe which I will discuss further. Fear can rob us of opportunities to grow and enhance our lives. As inferred fear is meant protect our lives but when fear is not controlled through over protecting our minds it can paralyze us. Think of all the things that you would have liked to have done in your life but didn't because you were afraid of failing or you doubted your abilities. Think of how many times in your life you said to yourself that I can't do that instead of saying I can do that, or I can learn to do that. Fear can be a very uncomfortable state. Humans seek comfort and do what they can to avoid uncomfortable states. They spend most of their time avoiding the uncomfortable and the unpleasant which negative fear can initiate. Uncertainty and a lack of knowledge about a subject can breed fear. Humans are tribal in their nature and are further drawn into organizations and groups to feel secure and safe. In prisons they join gangs and gangs which wind up as I found out running the prison. Fear is promoted in our society through the media in order to get us to purchase things. In a sense the media uses fear as a money maker. Think of all the advertisements that use fear to get us to purchase something such as insurances, medications, etc. We shouldn't resist most fears but simply listen to what they are telling us so we can evaluate them. As inferred the greatest antidote for fear is knowledge. If we are not discriminating fear especially negative fear can dominate our lives. Without any doubt fear is a survival mechanism in telling us what and who to avoid. Thank God the fear emotion is always with us. Most fears are given birth in our imagination. We should always ask ourselves when we experience fear what are we fearing and most of all why should we fear it.

If you don't learn to deal with fear especially while incarcerated, it will diminish your psychological and physical health. Unchecked or imagined fear can and will eventually overtake you and devastate your life as it did with me and my life. Over time uncontrolled imagined fear will hasten your death. It has been proven that stress one of fear's derivatives and their accumulative negative effects on the mind and body will hasten your death. The negative effects of fear can accumulate in the mind to the point where they become intolerable to the mind and body. Think about how we feel with the fear of losing a very close loved one such as a lover or a child. At that point we become very vulnerable to mental and physical breakdowns. I believe that uncontrolled and under rationalized fear is the biggest demon in our lives whether we are incarcerated or not. It can inhibit us from achieving our true potential in our lives. Our Creator implanted the potential for greatness in us, but uncontrolled fear inhibits our ability to manifest that greatness. Fear can and does inhibit us. That is one of the biggest reasons most people don't reach their true potential in their lives. It is also why about five percent of people earn ninety-five percent of the income in our great country full of economic and social opportunity. What I state is worldwide. Even in the most underdeveloped third world countries there are very affluent people who started out in life with nothing. Most of the very rich today didn't emerge from their mother's womb with a silver spoon in their mouths. That is an incredible fact when you realize in spite of some slight differences bodily make up, we are all created the same. Perpetual fear is an unnatural state and is deadly. In my case the accumulative negative effects of fear and overwhelming stress caused me to fall into a vegetative state where I developed kidney disease, cardiovascular disease, type II diabetes, disassociative amnesia, major dehydration, and most of all I lost my mind. I lost my memory and my ability to understand the most basic and simple instructions. I even had to be catharized to urinate. When I was accused of crimes, I was rendered defenseless because I had no memory of the facts and could no longer rationalize. I couldn't relate the facts to the appropriate people for my defense.

There is so much what I will term negative fears in prison especially as you can imagine in the maximum-security section of a maximum-security prison. As stated previously my life was threatened when I said good morning to a black inmate, again when three back men stated they hated white men and again by a cell mate who objected to me shaking a small packet of sugar. One of my cell mates had stabbed someone fifty-one times. Another cell mate killed his three-month old son. I knew another inmate who was nicknamed "Chainsaw." I will leave to you to imagine why he was called that. He was apprehended in a line at the airport with blood seeping out of his baggage. You dare not provoke them even inadvertently if you valued your life. If you are going to endure and recover in prison especially in the most dangerous sections of prison you have to learn how to deal with negative fear and control it. Fear will generate more fear. Fear seeds itself and feeds on itself. Unchallenged negative fears will cause more fears almost like an addiction.

What is the purpose or cause of fear? Fear is meant to warn us but not control us and especially our emotions. Our primal survival instinctual way of dealing with fear is what is the flee or fight response. In prison you are confined to pod which contains about a hundred inmates or a cell usually with another inmate. Fleeing the scene is not usually viable option. You just can't leave your sell or the pod when you feel like it. Fleeing the scene may not be an option in a professional or home environment. If you are over 70 years of age as I am in tenuous health, fighting isn't an option plus it prison rules forbid it. If you are caught fighting even if you are defending yourself, you are automatically thrown in the "Hole" no matter whose fault it is. In the worst case but all too common in prison you risk being stabbed with a shiv or some type of sharp object when fighting. I had one cellmate while I was recovering from a heart attack who was stabbed in both eyes with a pencil. The atmosphere while incarcerated could cause anyone's imagination to run wild. Fighting is not an acceptable response in a civilized society.

Without being able to flee or fight you learn the most feasible option which is to stop get control of your emotional state by hesitating. Before you react, you need to take about ten deep breaths or as many as possible at the moment. An incident or even the negative atmosphere can cause you to become emotionally aroused but that will only cause your cognitive ability to assess the situation to decrease. Any emotion or feeling is preceded by a thought so the first thing you should do when hesitating is discovering the thought the root of the fear. The worst thing that you can do in prison is to display any type of anger which can be fear based if you value your life. I will discuss anger later in this chapter. At least take some breaths and relax so you start to rationalize. The key to triggering emotional responses of fear, stress, anger, aggression and anxiety is an almond shaped portion of the brain called the amygdala which is located in each of the temporal lobes of the brain. When the amygdala is stimulated by a thought it sets of fight of flee response to fight or runaway. It sends stress hormones such as cortisol to the extremities of the body to strengthen them so they can ready the body to fight or flee. It should be noted as the amygdala is strengthened the prefrontal cortex of the brain which is the executive center of the brain is weakened. The prefrontal cortex is the rational thinking center of the brain that separates us from the lower animal life. Too much secretion of cortisol can shrink your brain. Cortisol increases the size and sensitivity of the amygdala and can make us more prone to fear and its derivatives especially anger. Keep in mind that the amygdala is prewired to process more negatives than positives so it prone to a negative reaction and can easily create a fearful negative state. As a consequence, when we are in a fearful state our reasoning and rationality is reduced. Caution should be on the increase as the amygdala is stimulated or set off. When the emotional response of fear is triggered, you want to resist any aggressive response. You want to override any hostile response with a calming response so you can rationalize the fear. Deep breathing is an immediate and good calming response. Just recognizing the fear and determining the thought that caused it can have a calming response. Whenever you label and emotion such as fear you start to diminish its strength. You want to appreciate the fact that you have the ability to positively deal with the fear. Appreciation is a positive response to calm the amygdala. Visualizing a beautiful scene in nature is another calming response. We all have some very beautiful memories that will serve to calm us.

The techniques that I will describe in this writing are also what you should do outside of prison to deal with fear and its derivatives. Even if your fear is instinctual and totally automatic which is a minority you should try not to automatically react but rationalize and think of the consequence of your words or actions. Think about the biblical saying "This too shall pass" because it will especially with your positive actions. By rationalizing you realize that fear like anything else is made up of parts and as you break something down into its parts it loses its strength. The stronger the emotional response to fear the more the reason to break it into its parts. You should also realize that we have a tendency to exaggerate our fears and give them too much power over us. What is almost just as bad is that we underestimate our ability to deal with what we fear which exacerbates the negative effects of fear. We claim all our fears to be instinctual which is a myth. We have the ability to reduce that power of a fear just by challenging it. What is within our minds is more powerful than what is without us. In a fearful state we have a tendency in most cases to jump to fictious conclusions that will probably never occur. At least sixty percent of fears are unfounded and never come to past. Twenty percent of fears are based on our memories past events which will probably never happen again. Ten percent are very petty, and the rest are probably justifiable but not to the extent that we anticipate them. Fear distorts our thinking. We tend not to think rationally when we are consumed by or experiencing fear. We don't want to be fearless because so much of our fear is good in that it steers us away from danger and keeps us on a safe path.

At least ninety percent of our fears are preceded by what I term a noninstinctual thoughts generated by us and our perceptions of a situation. We have about sixty-thousand or more thoughts a day of which most are negative which has its basis in primal instincts in dealing with the untamed wild world, but it is no longer valid way to think in a civilized society. You might say that our minds have not caught up with the realities of our present-day civilization. The threats of the wild in a civilized society are mostly in zoos and prisons. About ninety percent of our thoughts are repetitive which means that one negative thought can grow into many negative thoughts as we repeat a negative thought over and over again for days into the future. The repetitive nature of negative of thoughts makes us very vulnerable to fall victims to fear and its negative effects on our lives. The more we realize the repetitive nature of our thoughts the more the reason that we have to guard the gates of our mind, so we are not bombarded with negative thoughts. Also remember that most negative thoughts have no basis in reality yet they can have a negative effect on our minds, bodies and therefore our lives. You could consider negative thoughts as lies and a lie repeated often enough can become reality to us. You can create your own misery and unnecessary suffering by not controlling negative thoughts. You can cause false negative thoughts to become true to you through repetition. I consider negative thoughts a curse and demonic in nature. The best antidote for a negative thought is positive thoughts which can be repeated over and over again due to the repetitive nature of thoughts. You have the choice of automatically repeating a negative thought or a positive thought. It is all in your control. Keep in mind that you can only have one thought at a time so a negative thought can easily be overridden with a positive thought. This way the repetitive nature of thoughts becomes an asset instead of a liability. Just because a thought may be instinctual does not mean we have react to it especially repetitively. This may seem like a lot of effort to control our negative thinking but keep in mind that the genius of our Creator endowed us with the ability to form habits which will reduce any effort. It only takes three weeks through repetition to establish a good habit or substitute a good habit for a bad one.

There is a lot of things that we don't have control over in our lives, but we absolutely do have control over our thoughts. A word of caution we can also make a habit of thinking negatively without much effort and generating more and more negative thoughts. Also, your body will react to your every thought be them positive or negative. The body does what the mind tells it to do. It is up to you what kind of thoughts you are going to be bombarded with and how they will affect your body. Yes, some negative thoughts are automatic that you can't control but that doesn't mean you have to dwell on them especially over and over again. You have the ability to drown them out with positive thoughts. Make a habit of drowning our negative thoughts with positive thoughts. It is a habit that will serve you well for your entire life both physically and mentally. You exercise physically to protect and develop your body now do it with your mind. It only takes a few weeks minimal effort and repetition to create a good thought habit. Like every coin has two sides so does every thought. Every thought has a negative side and a positive side. Make a mental game of turning negative thoughts into positive thoughts.

It is said by many noted professionals that a man is what he thinks about. It is also said that what you fear most you can bring about. The law of attraction states that what you think about most you will draw to you. If that is true, then if you have a tendency to think negatively that is what you will draw to you. That is true for what you fear most. Keep thinking about what you fear most, and you will draw it to you. You can create a miserable life for yourself by your thinking. Consider what I wrote about drawing negativity into my life in the chapter on law of attraction. The good news is if you think positively, you will draw that to you and create a great life for yourself. A lot of us are afraid of the future because we think we can't control it. I say that we can control our future by what we think about and what we will draw to us. No matter what you perceive in an event look for the good in any event because there is good in every event just like people. Make sure even your fictitious or imaginary events are positive in nature. Einstein described the infinite power of the imagination to shape reality. I was incarcerated with the worst of the worst, but I had to find good in them if I was going to survive. Even in negative events there is a powerful good lesson attached to it which will bring us closer to success and a positive future. The more you have to look for the good in a situation or event, the more powerful of a force it will be and the greater the reward.

We have a tendency to fear or worry about the future, but it can be reasoned that you can design a very positive future with a positive thoughts about it. Let your mind be your positive fortune teller and creator. You may not be able to predict the future, but you can ensure that it will probably be positive by making a habit of thinking positive thoughts or reading positive affirmations, positive articles, positive books and watching positive motivational videos. Your subconscious mind will feed back to you what you feed into it. Dare to become the great designer of your future with very positive thoughts about it. Create a picture of it through your writings. Put it in writing to reinforce your great future in your mind.

Because we are emotional by nature, we have a tendency to react to our feelings instead our rational mind. To avoid thinking with our feelings we have our old friend the habit to support us. Make a habit of thinking about the basis of our feelings which are a positive or negative thoughts. We need to see our mind as a garden and each thought as a seed. Always keep in mind that we will reap whatever we sew. Sew a nutritional plant and that is what you will reap. Sew a poisonous plant and that is what you will reap. You are seeding your future through your thoughts. Don't take your thoughts or feelings for granted analyze your thinking to determine if it is positive or negative. If you are feeling bad discover the thought that created that feeling. Most of all if you are feeling good discover the thought that created that feeling and make a note of it in a journal or in your mind. If it is negative thought change it with a positive one; remember you can only have one thought at a time. You owe it to yourself and to your mind to nourish it with positive thoughts so you can expect positive results and a great future. Feel good by thinking good thoughts and harbor those in your mind. Let me state again human beings like games so make a game of turning negative thoughts into positive thoughts so it won't be a burden. We also need to learn to react to facts not fiction which so many of our thoughts are. Unless we can perceive something through one of our five senses of sight, hearing, taste smell or touch it is not factual and probably fiction. Don't waste your time thinking about what will never be unless that is what you do want it to be.

The lack of confidence in oneself is one of the causes of a lack of courage to overcome fear and to put it into proper perspective. To help us build and gain confidence in ourselves we need to realize that every day that we have lived is an accomplishment. If we survived the past, we are likely to survive and achieve in the future. If we did it yesterday, we most likely will do it today. If we are still alive, we are successful. Life is very challenging so every day that we have lived is a feather in our cap or a badge on our chest. If you have made a lot of mistakes in the past find the positive lesson in them to avoid history repeating the mistake and use that lesson to create a positive future. Yes, history can repeat itself, but it can for the positive or the negative. If you are afraid of your negative past keep in mind that history doesn't have to repeat itself. The longer we have lived the more successful we are. Yes, some days we are more successful than others and some people are people are more successful than others depending how we measure success. We must believe and get used to the fact that if we are still alive we have been successful and will continue to be successful through the force of habit. In a sense we have established a pattern of success and courage to deal with our fears. Also, the more successful people are the ones who tell themselves that they can rather than they can't. They have the courage to take the first step knowing and having faith that more courage will emerge along the journey to success. Taking action to accomplish an honorable and worthwhile goal diminishes fear. It is worth your while to build your self-esteem with positive memories and positive affirmations about yourself because that will determine your level of personal and professional success. Beautiful people do beautiful things and remember God does not make junk and that includes you. Consider the magnificence in God's creations such as all forms of life and the universe. Realize that you are part of that magnificence. God did not start screwing up when God created you. You may say that some people are born with disabilities, but they are also born with offsetting strengths. Most disabilities are man-made and not God made. If there a natural disability, there is an offsetting strength. If the offsetting strength isn't there naturally there it can be developed. Consider athletes with so-called major disabilities and how they develop and offsetting strength. When I couldn't remember I developed the ability to write much better than before. It was a latent ability within me.

We all have some disabilities to overcome and if we focus on them, they will reduce our courage. We also have many offsetting strengths and to deny them is total ignorance. If we focus on our strengths, it more than overshadows our so-called disabilities and drastically increases our courage. One of our nation's longest serving president's Franklin Roosevelt served his terms from a wheelchair. He didn't focus on the fact that his legs were crippled from polio. He focused on his strengths especially his oratory strengths. He realized that he still had had a great mind and lots of determination to overcome the loss of the use of his legs. What is interesting President in one of his speeches said: "The only thing we have to fear is fear itself". The current governor of Texas Greg Abbott governs from a wheelchair. He was crippled while jogging to improve his health when a tree fell on him. That tree didn't stop him from achieving success. Thomas Edison who invented the light bulb which lights up our worlds had just a few months of formal schooling as a little boy. His persistence and genius turned darkness into light. His lack or formal schooling was considered a major disability, but it didn't disable Edison. The same is true for Henry Ford who is credited for putting America on wheels which created the suburbs. Until Ford made the automobile affordable to the average person and household most people in their lifetime never traveled more than ten miles from their home. Ford only had eight years of schooling in a one room schoolhouse. He had the entire automobile association against him, but it didn't stop him from becoming a great industrialist and one of the country's richest men. It appears that those men decided to ignore what the naysayers said about them and their conditions in their lives. Disabilities and disadvantages became opportunities for them to stand out from the crowd and shine brightly like gold. For a while Henry Ford worked for one of Thomas Edison's companies obviously Ford had his own vision for success. By the way he didn't build his first automobile until he was past mid-life. Success can come to all those who sincerely seek it.

Our Creator also endowed us with the ability to have faith in ourselves to deal with most situations and what we can't deal with to have faith in our God. Keep in mind that we don't wish our children with harm and neither does our loving Father, Our God wish His Children harm. As we try to create things with excellence so does our Creator. As stated, where there is a perceived weakness in creation there are many more offsetting strengths. You have to look at yourself and any other of God's creations holistically. That is why people with disabilities accomplish some incredible things. They count their blessing and search for and find all of their strengths. Hearing that they can't only strengthens their resolve. Self-talk can diminish fear or increase it. Without a question the very best antidote for fear is our faith in God the infinite knowledge and power. Consider the vastness and infinity of the universe. When we get to the point where we can't deal with our fears we should remember and say the prayer "God grant me the grace to accept with serenity the things that I cannot change the courage to change the things that I can and the wisdom to know the difference". Share your fears and insecurities with God and see how you feel when you do. Even if you doubt's God's existence say that prayer and see how it makes you feel. When we don't take control of our fears and put them into proper perspective by challenging them, they can become our biggest self-made disability. Uncontrolled and persistent fear becomes terror which is deadly. Controlled and properly rationalized fear remains our friend and guides us from danger in living our lives. Keep in mind it is natural to exaggerate and overreact to our fears. It is just as natural to underestimate our abilities. Some things are bigger than us but not bigger than a Supreme Being. I know without a question that what got me through and to survive what you read about in this book was my belief in God. When we are connected to the Supernatural, we are truly courageous. I should be dead because I endured two strokes and three heart attacks, during one heart attack my heart function dropped to a mere twelve percent, almost nothing. You might say that I kissed death. Something greater than me renewed me.

Let me state again fear is like anything else in the universe; fear an energy which is made up of parts. Those parts are atoms. When you break fear down into its parts with God's guidance it becomes very controllable, and I mean very controllable. It loses its power over our emotional state. Consider anything man made which most of our fears are when we start to take it apart it loses it strength. As an example, consider a piece of rope it is made up of compilation strings. Dissect the piece of rope into its parts which are braided strings. Unbraid and separate those strings and the rope loses its strength. Consider steel is the basis of our cities, its skyscrapers and most parts of our automobiles. Steel is made up of carbon, manganese and chromium. Remove or separate from the whole any amount of those elements and steel loses it strength. Consider a machine take it apart and it loses its power. Dissect your fear by saying what am I afraid of, why am I afraid of that, what is the worst that can happen to me, have I ever dealt with a similar situation, how did I overcome this type of fear in the past? Take your fear apart into its smallest parts and your fear will be diminished in its strength. Ask yourself is it really that big of a deal? When you accept the worst that can happen things get better.

Consider one of biggest fears death one its main parts is the fear of the unknown. People who believe and know that they are going straight to heaven when they die don't fear death as much as those who believe in a hell. Those who believe that death is just an eternal peaceful sleep don't fear death as those who fear an eternal hell. They claim that people who have near death or out of the body experience no longer fear death. It is interesting that people who kiss death or come so close to it no longer fear it, why? That demonstrates how knowledge can diminish fear. It is like they challenged their fear of death and just didn't accept it. When you learn not to longer fear death you also don't fear most things in life that you did before, and you take the chances on things that will enhance your life.

In regard to the fear of death consider another fear that of loss. It is inevitable that upon our death we will lose all of our possessions so resolve to just enjoy our possession while we have them. When you drive through an inner city ghetto, visit a junk yard, or landfill it and see what eventually happens to most of our possession it helps us to establish our priorities. Do what is reasonable and necessary to protect them but know that fearing their loss will diminish the enjoyment of possessing them. You will also lose your loved ones upon your death or their death and that is where your top priorities should be in your life. You can love your house, car, or other possessions that you highly value, but they can't love you back. They can serve you, but they can't love you.

We all crave love and affection. It is completely natural to us. Therefore, we fear and hate rejection, at least I do. That is why I went into sales, just like I joined the U.S. Air Force when I'm afraid of height. Rejection like its father fear is part of life. We reject others and others reject us but when we are rejected our first reaction is to internalize it and personalize it. When we feel rejected, it is our ego that is injured. The bigger our ego the more sensitive it is to rejection and the more intense the pain. Dissect rejection and you must realize that rejection can only have a negative effect on us if we believe what the rejector said about us or did to us. Most of the time the rejector says nothing but we imagine that they said something. We then have to realize that what others say to us, or about us or to us can only matter if we believe it and let it harbor in you. It only matters what we say to ourselves about ourselves. The next time you feel rejected think about how you reject people without knowing a thing about them. You reject telemarketers, you reject other drivers on the road, you reject people who don't act like you, you reject people who may act strange in some way as compared to you, you reject people who don't dress like you or people who don't have the same beliefs as you. I could go on and on, but rejection is just part of life and we are as guilty of it as those we think are rejecting us. We don't reject people for the most part we reject their action, but rarely do we reject the person.

A lack of self-belief in ourselves and our abilities makes us very susceptible to rejection. Sometimes a lack of self-belief stems from our standard of success. When we compare ourselves to people who we believe are more successful than us it can diminish our belief in ourselves. Someone may be more successful than us in a particular area of their life that doesn't mean that they are more successful in all areas of life. Are we any less than them? I suggest you measure your success against yourself and as long as you are progressing in your life even with setbacks you are successful. Please allow me to refer to President Lincoln since he is considered by most Americans as one of the most noted men in history. Lincoln lost eight elections, had a mental breakdown, went bankrupt but won three elections and we built a wonderful monument to him. The lesson that we must learn from Lincoln' life is that we have to be very discerning how we judge people and especially ourselves. Lincoln's fame came from less than ten percent of his life and he is considered one of our greatest presidents.

Rejection can be good if it alerts us to an unacceptable behavior that can socially and professionally inhibit us. Most importantly stop focusing on those who reject you focus on those who accept you. Keep in mind that positive thoughts offset negative thoughts so start thinking about all those who accept you and love you. Feel sorry for those who reject you because they are probably projecting their own inadequacies on to you. You also have to accept rejection as part of life. To expect that everyone you come in contact with is going to accept you is unrealistic. You don't accept everyone that you come in contact with so why should everyone accept you? When you feel rejected, it is time to accept yourself because you probably haven't accepted yourself enough.

Fear of failure is part of life and developing just like other fears. I consider fear of failure the great inhibitor. I also believe that fear of failure is part of success and that we have to fail our way to success. We try like hell to avoid failure because it hurts but we learn the most through our mistakes and failures. Think of all the things you had a desire to do in your life, but fear of failure inhibited you from doing it. We all have a fear of failure starting in our childhood. Every time we tried something new to us, we had a fear of failure but as children our desire to do it was stronger than our fear of failure, so we did it anyway. Consider how we learned to walk. We tried to walk because we wanted to be mobile and be like the other children. We fell down, sometimes we hurt ourselves, but we got up and tried again and we learned to walk. In our childhood our desire to do and learn outweighed our fear of failure. As we age our fear of failure can outweigh our desire and it can inhibit us from achieving our true potential in life. Maybe we need to regress to childhood states in order to succeed. Instead of seeing failing as just part of life we negatively stigmatize it just like we do mental health disorders. We don't realize that in most new things that we try we fail before we succeed. It is part of our progression in life. Success demands failure. Failure is part of learning. Hopefully we don't fear learning, but we fear failing because it is painful to us. We are the ones who label most events in our lives. When you truly see failure as learning it diminishes the fear. And you will never know what your true limits are until you test them by failing. Failing is painful to us because it injures our ego, but we must realize that success demands failure. As inferred earlier as our ego increases in size so does the emotional pain of failing. Our society accepts trial and error, but error is actually failing. Error can be considered synonymous with failing but we don't stigmatize error to the degree as we do failure. With trial and error, we keep trying until we get it right. Being too quick to label and effort as failing demonstrates the limitations of our thinking and labeling. Error teaches us how something can't be done and so does failing. The bigger the failure the bigger and more valuable the lesson. Failing brings us closer to success as long as we keep trying. Failing simply tells that we have to try harder or try another way. Experimenting can lead to failure but we don't negatively stigmatize experimenting. Think about if some of our greatest inventors stigmatized failing as society does, they would have driven themselves to suicide long before their success.

When we examine the lives of some of the most noted people, we find that failure was part of their development and lives. In the present day, Bill Gates one of the world's richest men failed in his first company. Walt Disney failed in his first animation company before he succeeded. As I mentioned earlier, we built a magnificent monument to Abraham Lincoln because he is considered on our greatest presidents but early in his career, he failed more than he succeeded. When Lincoln did succeed he succeeded in a tremendous way. Donald Trump our previous president, he and his companies filed for bankruptcy six times before he ran for president. Our current president Joseph Biden failed twice in his quest for the presidency before he succeeded. Those people failed their way to success. Hopefully with each failure they learned a valuable lesson so they could keep moving forward. We don't fail when we keep moving forward maybe in a different way, but we keep moving forward. Failure can be a tremendous learning experience and one of the best antidotes for fear is knowledge which can come from failing. I wonder how many times the developers of the Covid 19 vaccine failed before they got it right?

When failure starts to inhibit us or frightening us, we should ask ourselves like any other fear why. If we are inhibited because we don't know how to do something, we should ask ourselves can we learn to do what we are fearing. When you fail ask yourself what have you learned from that failure? Remember what I inferred that knowledge overcomes fear. You never truly fear unless you never try, or you give up too easily without a proper effort. You also need to establish what is your standard for success. A quest for perfection can lead to failure because your standard for success may be set too high. Too often we give up when we are about to succeed that is basis of the story of how the turtle winds up winning the race because others gave up. Keep in mind that when you are determined to do your best at any effort you have nothing to fear. When you do fail and have given that endeavor your best efforts you should first congratulate yourself for trying. You never truly fail as long as you keep trying. You have been failing your whole life but you have also been succeeding more because you are still alive. We focus more on our failures than on our successes because we are too critical of ourselves and unrealistically, we never expect to fail. Criticizing yourself causes too much pain. Guilt is synonymous with pain and suffering. Read what I said about the Law of Attraction and guilt. When you enjoy and feel good about what you are doing you are successful.

The point is challenge your fears and dissect them into their parts and fear is diminished. Just realizing what your fears are made up of can diminish them. A frightened mind is not a logical mind. The last point is the more we challenge our fears or are exposed to them the weaker they get. We kind of get used to them and can say to ourselves well that didn't hurt or that wasn't so bad. We can even realize that most of our fears have no factual basis. You can practice challenging and confronting your fears in your mind so they will lose their control over you in an imaginary sense and then in a real-life sense. The more that you are exposed to a fear even in your imagination the less impact it will have on you.

As inferred earlier fear is meant to alert us to a possible danger just like the yellow light in a traffic light. If we are not careful and act cautiously another car could collide with ours. It doesn't mean that another car will collide with yours. Some of us jump to conclusions in our minds that it will collide with you and your car. Most of our fears are learned and are not instinctual which means they can be controlled by us and unlearned.

Negative thoughts are the birthplace and nursery for fears. The nice thing about thoughts even sudden or automatic ones is that our thoughts can be controlled by us not our loved ones and friends but us. Fear is an emotion that is always within us ready to respond to a perceived threat, but it is up to us as to what degree that fear is within us.

Once again fear can be our friend or foe. Some people use fear as a tool to challenge themselves in sports to enhance their self-esteem by challenging their fears. They can raise the bar of what is fearful to increase the challenge and their self-esteem. Some people even become addicted to the adrenaline rush by challenging and conquering a fear. Athletes continual challenge and break old records and set new ones. They learn to deal with fear, so it doesn't hurt or diminish them as much.

To say that being incarcerated in a maximum-security prison is very stressful is an understatement. Stress is a reaction to and a derivative of fear just like panic is but not as threatening as panic. Panic is an uncontrollable and usually irrational and an overreaction to fear. Chronic stress is cause of most of our maladies. Stress is one of the worst things that inhibits the mind and body's ability to heal and rejuvenate itself. Chronic stress inhibits learning and limits your memory. Continual negative thoughts can create chronic stress and can be the cause of major diseases. Most medical professionals now consider stress as the number cause of death. Just as belief can be a healer stress can be a killer. If we want to ensure our longevity, we need to control our stress level by simply controlling our thoughts and our perceptions of circumstances. The more that we believe stressful thoughts the more we suffer and the sicker we get.

Stress is a mental or emotional strain created by adverse circumstances especially fear. One form of stress is a result of fear which is one of the most common adverse circumstance. It is up to us to determine what circumstance we perceive as being stressful and just how stressful the circumstance is to us. Some people who are not happy with their occupation will perceive it as being stressful. Others who love that same profession will probably not see it as stressful. They see their profession as a hobby more than a job. The same can be true for a marriage. A couple who is ready to file to be divorced find their relationship as being extremely stressful as compared to a happily married couple who can't wait to spend time together. The extent to how much a circumstance can be changed should indicate how stressful it is. If we see the circumstance as beyond our ability to control it than it will be very stressful. As we can change a circumstance for the better it will diminish the stress attached to it. If we can't change the circumstance such as our job or marriage, then it is time to change our attitude or perception of it. Your attitude towards something is an indication of how well you will deal with it. It is time to look for the good in it and not focus on the bad. Whatever you focus on you will probably bring about.

Since stress is a derivative of fear it should be treated the same way as fear. As inferred over time uncontrolled fear will hasten your death and so will stress and its accumulative negative effect on the mind and body. Stress ages the body and all its organs well beyond the norm. Without a question uncontrolled fear causes too much stress. My research on mental health taught me that at least three of my major health disorders namely pseudo dementia, disassociative amnesia and acute anxiety were caused by too much or overwhelming stress. The unchecked or suppressed anxiety turned into life devastating depression. As stated earlier those disorders devastated my life and if it wasn't for my loving sister and other loved ones, I would have ended my life. Chronic stress drove me into an animalistic state which lasted almost three years. It caused me to go from being a multimillionaire to lying on a prison floor in solitary confinement soaked in my own human waste. It caused to go from being a multimillionaire to dead broke. Not only did I lose a fortune I lost my mind. Now, that is as low as you can go. The nice thing about that was that I couldn't go any lower and it was time for me to climb back up. Physically I couldn't go any lower without breaking through the concrete floor. Two of society's major psychological disorders anxiety and depression inflict at least a quarter of us. Their resulting behaviors such as excess alcohol consumption and illicit drugs use devastates lives. They affect almost thirty percent of adult Americans and all too many children. Again, it is said, and I believe that the number one cause of death is too much stress. Psychological professionals claim that stress related ailments account for over seventy-five percent of all visits to a physician's office. Hypochondria is a definitely a major health disorder with more than three million cases per year in the U.S. Stress shrinks the brain and inhibits the production and flow of positive neurotransmitters of serotonin and dopamine which are meant to enhance our lives. Many neurological professionals believe that stress is also the cause of eighty percent of all diseases.

I had to learn to control my stress level while incarcerated. If I didn't learn to control my stress level, I would continue to lie on the prison floor physically and mentally. Again, let me emphasize that the number one cause of stress is uncontrolled fear of something or many things. Stress is a reaction to fear just like panic is but not as threatening as panic. Let me state again chronic stress is the cause of most of our maladies. Continual negative thoughts can create chronic stress and can be the cause of major diseases. If we want to ensure our longevity, we need to control our stress level by simply controlling our thoughts and how we perceive the events in our lives. If we are going to fear something we should fear negative thoughts and negative thinking which as inferred is the biggest cause of stress.

If we control our thoughts, it will cause us to live healthy lives and serve a positive role of scaring us when we divert from that healthy path. We have to view pain as a friend although chronic and acute pain isn't. When we discover the source of our pain just like fear it doesn't hurt as much because we have removed one element of the fear the "unknown". As inferred mankind due to a primal instinct when we had to exist in an uncivilized world negative thoughts had their purpose when man had to fight off dangerous animals. In that uncivilized time, we were equipped with as some psychological professional term them automatic as automatic negative thoughts or ANTs. I like to think of them in today's civilized world as red ants which can inject a poisonous venom into your skin just like negative thoughts are poisonous to your mind and therefore your life. The best venom for ANTs is to challenge them and substitute a positive thought. When you are in a negative frame of mind it can take five positive thoughts to overcome the negative state. A positive thought is a great vaccine. Don't count on automatically generating positive thoughts when you are in a negative frame of mind. Prepare a list of ten positive thoughts that you can refer to when in a negative frame of mind. The best list of positive thoughts is a list of ten ways in which you are blessed. Even in the worst cases we are all blessed in many ways. Start your day for reviewing your list of blessing and thanking God for how much you are blessed. You will probably realize that you are being blessed more by focusing on your blessings. Gratitude is a great antidote for fear because it helps calm the amygdala. In our civilized world ANTs are obsolete. Some of you might say they are not obsolete it some our cities. Today we don't fight off wild animals instead we call the police. Start making a habit of generating automatic positive thoughts or what I call APTs. Become a person who is "apt" to think positively.

Worrying a derivative of fear of the future puts in you in a negative frame of mind. Negative thoughts are also the birthplace of our worries. Ninety percent of our worries have no place in reality and never take place. If you doubt what I say, then keep it list of your worries and see how many of them turn out to be valid. Most worries come from our imagination instead of reality. "What If" negative questions are breeding grounds for worrying. "What if this happens" or "what if that happens" and I say "what if nothing happens" especially the way I worried about it? Worries cause us to suffer about things that in most cases will never happen. They also cause us to suffer way ahead of time about the negative things that do happen.

In other words, worrying causes us to suffer too much and too long about the actual event. Worrying never solves a problem and does more harm than good. Planning for the problem if it is based on facts and taking the appropriate action solves the problem. There is a big difference between planning and worrying. Planning is deciding what action to take in case an event takes place. Planning is a positive action. Worrying is a matter of living in and trying or predict the future. If we were good at predicting the future, we could just stay home and invest in the stock or commodities markets to avoid financial worries. If you are living in a hell of worries the worst thing you can do is to stop and wallow in your worries. If you are in a burning hell you don't want to stop and burn to death you want to keep moving forwards not backwards. You want to get out of the destructive place with a few burns to your body as possible. Most of us are afraid of a hell. We should feel the same way about worrying. Thinking ahead is good. Worrying is bad for us just like its father fear. If you are truly and factually worried about something, then plan for it don't worry about it. Take action instead of worrying about it. Take the time to write it out and then dissect it like you would a fear. The only true control you have about your future is to think positively so you will attract a positive outcome to any event. Worrying does not change an outcome, positively planning and positive action does. Spend your energies on doing something positive don't drain your energies by worrying. Worrying is caused by the unknown so make things known through learning and gaining knowledge about the subject. If you worried about heart disease, then learn about it so you can avoid it or minimize its causes and effects. You can watch your diet and exercise more. If you are worried about getting lung cancer do the same and don't do things like smoking. Just like our fear of death if we knew for sure what good came after death, we wouldn't worry about it and fear it. Our Creator knew that if we definitely knew what good and ecstasy would come after death suicide would become an option when we faced high hurdles and challenges in life. Why struggle let me end my life and just go on to ecstasy? We can overcome our fear of the unknown just like we do when visiting places that we haven't been before and are unknown to us. Learn as much as you can about them instead of worrying about it. Maybe it is a foreign country where we don't speak the language or any place that we haven't been before. Make it an adventure by learning not a worry.

A good way to control worrying is to postpone your worrying to a certain time of the day. I like to postpone worrying until I physically exercise to diminish any buildup of anxiety. Postpone your worries to that certain time and see how much you still worry. Those who spend their time in living in the present and doing their best have nothing to fear about the future if something negative happens they will handle to the best of their ability. They made a habit of doing so. If they can't handle it, they can rely on their faith in that past performances and their abilities.

The last thing I would like to address about fear is anger because so much of our anger has its basis in fear especially the fear of loss of something or fear of the loss of control of your life. Maybe your angry over being unjustly hurt. Like fear anger is an emotion. It is triggered by a thought just like fear so we should dissect and analyze the thought that triggers our anger. Angry behaviors are learned especially in childhood. The more angry behaviors are tolerated or accepted the more they are reinforced and the more they will be used. The anger was placed in us so in primitive times we could react quickly to a threat or danger. Anger breeds anger so it can be habitual. Revenge is a reaction to anger after being hurt by someone. Revenge hurts you more than the person who hurt you. As the old Chinese saying infers those who seek revenge need to dig two graves. In today's society anger is an antisocial condition and can create very painful consequences in your life.

Prison life is very difficult because you lose so much control over your life it is easy to get angry over your loss of freedom. You lose your freedom by being incarcerated and you lose freedoms while incarcerated which can increase your anger. The only control you have while incarcerated is to how you react to what happens to you. You need to keep in mind that your anger needs to be acted on and not acted out. I'm sure that any prisoner of the right mind would agree that not to control your anger in prison is suicidal. Temper tantrums don't go over very well in prison and are sure to get you beat up or at a minimum get you thrown in the "Hole".

As stated, before anger is an emotional state and it parallels that of fear, stress anxiety and aggression. Let me state again they are all triggered by the area in the brain called the amygdala. It triggers emotions which releases adrenaline, raises you blood pressure, makes your heart beat faster and also causes the fight or flight syndrome just like fear does. You might say it prepares you to do battle when you perceive a threat to your being. That threat could be the loss of something or loss of control in your life. All this energy and blood being driven to your extremities to do battle also takes it away from your prefrontal cortex the executive center of your brain where you rationalize. It can and usually weakens the functioning or your prefrontal cortex. You might conclude when you get angry you don't rationalize as much, and rationalizing is what you should do in a civilized society. Many of us are of the opinion that anger strengthens us but let me remind you that the mind is greater than the matter. Yes, our muscles gain strength when we are angry but the mind which controls when and how to use those muscles loses strength when we are angry. That is why people do irrational and stupid things when they are angry. Anger has a punishment attached to it since it hurts you much more than who or what caused your anger. Be aware that your ability to rationalize will be diminished when you are angry. Avoid making decisions or taking action when you're angry. Your imagination can trigger your amygdala, but it can also quiet it. I believe that in a civilized society that anger especially violence which is a reaction to anger makes anger an obsolete emotion. I will admit that our society doesn't always act civilized, and our prison and jails are a manifestation of that. Anger should be treated the same way as fear and even more aggressively. As inferred when we sense ourselves getting angry, we have to hesitate and start rationalizing. We also have to keep in mind that when we trigger the amygdala with angry thoughts we are not as likely to rationalize. It is time to take a break, if possible, flee the scene and calm ourselves with rational and very calming thoughts. Keep a list of very happy memories even if they are totally unrelated to whatever angered you. Plan for your angry times by preparing a list of happy memories. Don't count on remembering happy memories when you are in an angry state. The quality of our decisions when we are experiencing anger will diminish it is totally natural. Don't think that it won't. It is all the more reason we should exercise caution when angry and try like hell not to react to our anger. In most cases we need to see it as fear based and we need to analyze what are we so afraid of. When you sense yourself getting angry keep in mind that anger has a punishment attached to it since it hurts you much more than who are what caused your anger. You are punishing yourself more than the person who hurt you.

In summary react to anger by rationalizing and know that if react another way you are likely to make a stupid mistake which your will regret. Try saying a prayer to ease your anger. Try and take a break from what is initiating your anger, if possible, flee the scene. If you are in a business or social setting with others excuse yourself and use the bathroom. Don't tempt your angry feelings by staying put. Be smart and leave the scene. It is not a good time to test yourself. The good news about the amygdala is that meditation calms it so you can control its sensitivity. Meditation increases your rationalization and strengthens the prefrontal cortex so you can make good sound decisions. Let me state again for emphasis that anger needs to be acted on not acted out. Take a moment to make a list of what your gained on a short-term basis, a mid-term basis and especially a long-term basis through your anger. You will find that it won't take hardly any time at all, and you won't need hardly any paper. You might need a piece of paper the size of a postage stamp to list what you gained from anger compared to what you lost. In today's society anger diminishes your power over others and causes them to question your maturity. Anger causes you to lose respect of yourself and by others that you may be trying to manipulate with your anger. Consider how you view others that act out their anger. How does having a temper tantrum make you feel? We admire and respect those who control their emotions and resulting actions. Haven't we heard others say look how calm and controlled he or she is in maddening situations. Let me state again that anger is an obsolete emotion it just doesn't work very well in today's society. This subject makes me think of Mahatma Gandhi and what he accomplished with his cool and calm demeanor. Consider how many great leaders used Gandhi as role model. We fought many very bloody battles to gain our independence from Britain. Gandhi gained independence for India, the second most populated country in the world, without firing a shot. A saying that stands out in my mind is "The person who wins the argument is the person who won't argue". Always keep in mind when you get angry that time can cure most wounds or a at least diminish their hurt.

Please be patient with me so I may discuss more about faith. Faith is the best cure for fear, worrying, stress and anger. I fell into demented and vegetative states of being from trying to go it alone without God as my partner. I got so bad that I acted like an untrained animal. It was one of the main reasons for my downfall. In my life especially in prison I saw many men use God as a last resort as I did instead of having the wisdom to use God as a first resort. As I look back on my life, I realize that had I placed my faith in God and used God as my confidant and mentor I could have reduced my pain and suffering or even avoided them altogether. With God as my mentor my courage to deal with any negative situation would have soared to the heavens and so would have my rationalization. If I learned anything, it is never to try and go it alone without the Supernatural. It was egotistical and arrogant of me to try and go it alone without God's help and guidance. It is said that no mind is complete by itself, and no man is complete by himself without God. Since mankind first walked the face of this earth man has searched the security and comfort by bringing themselves as close as possible to God or gods. Consider the number of shrines and temples are found among the ancient ruins. Were all those generations wrong? Consider how we respect those who act as supernatural intermediaries such as priest, ministers and pastors. I like to go with the odds in favor of my beliefs and 93% percent of the world's population believe in a god or gods.

You never know when you will need God's strength and understanding especially when even your loved ones don't understand you, God will. You can't just leave it up to your loved ones to understand you because they have their own issues to deal with. Some of them don't understand themselves. Also, with many mental health disorders the symptoms come and go which makes it difficult for others to read and possibly diagnose you. This is especially true for the elderly because their lives and actions are dominated by customs, traditions, procedures and habits where they may act normal much of the time. I guarantee you the one thing that others won't fully understand sometimes even partially is mental illness or temporary disorders having to do with life events. Why, because we have yet to fully understand the workings of the brain. Some scientists claim that it is the most complicated thing in the universe and that we will never fully understand it. You have to keep your ego under control and be open to criticism because with some mental health disorders you lose a lot of your ability to be self-conscious. You are also as the old saying says you are too close to the forest to see some of the trees. Plus, no two people think exactly alike. Don't kid yourself that you will never suffer from a mental health disorder. Half the American public will suffer from some type of mental health disorder sometime during their life.

In a worldly sense I learned to honor and respect the family unit no matter how small or large. In my case when I was down and out, when no one else was there family members were there. When I read the cards and letters that I got in prison I realize how much my family was there to comfort me even though at the time I wasn't cognizant to realize it. If I can impart any bit of knowledge on you through my writings it is to always to cherish your God, yourself so you can cherish your family, and honor your fellow humans. A life of service to your fellow human is a great life that leaves a great legacy.

Most worldly goods are not worth the amount of effort that we put into them because they will deteriorate and disappear with time. Goodness, love and kindness will carry through the worst of times and circumstances because when others won't respect you, you can respect yourself. We have spiritual muscles besides physical ones and goodness, love, kindness, and truth are some of them. Keep in mind that through the ages the most noted were the most peaceful and loving. Think of Gautam Buddha and Jesus Christ they weren't millionaires or billionaires when it when by materiel goods or money, but they were when it came to knowledge especially knowledge of the spirit. Mohammed gained his insight when sequestering himself in the desert. Part of Mohammed's teaching was that the rich should give generously to the poor and that the Arab tribes should stop fighting among themselves. Jesus fasted for forty days and nights. I learned to live without most worldly and materialistic goods in prison and I'm very glad that I did. I found out that I could be as happy in a prison cell as I could in a house with thousands of square feet. I found that I could be as happy in a prison bunk bed as a king size bed. The house and the bed may have been more comfortable, but they didn't make me happy. That was a function of a decision on my part, my attitude and my belief in the Supernatural. I simply made a decision to be happy and to count my blessing and I was happy. I challenged myself on a daily basis to find happiness and to be happy because I realized that if I could be happy in a prison cell, I could be happy anywhere. The ultimate lesson that I learned is that when you are down and out love is everything and materialism is worthless.

Now I can go on and place my priorities and efforts where they should be with God and my loved ones. Assets and resources of any type have no true and sacred value until they are put to a sacred, honorable and productive use for the good of mankind. In our society money has power attached to it especially when it is put to a Godlike purpose in serving our fellow man. The quest for money with the proper purpose in mind is not bad. Adjacent to the interstate north of Denver is an automobile salvage yard where they crush cars into a compacted state even the most luxurious and most expensive ones. To most people next to their house a car is their most valuable materialistic possession. When I picture that salvage yard or the dilapidated houses in an inner-city ghetto in my mind, I say to myself that many of us put more effort in maintaining our materiel possessions than our relationships with our loved ones even with the Supernatural. That salvage yard or ghetto is a manifestation of what eventually happens to all materiel possessions even our precious homes. Yet, God's love and strength will transcend all fear, hurt, pain, suffering, time and even death. When we stand before God now and when we transcend to a higher plane of existence, we won't be judged by the size of our estates but by the good we do and did do with those assets. You want to leave a divine and sacred legacy not a worldly one. A casket of coffin can only hold so much besides the body. I've never seen a house, car, a closet full of fancy clothes or the contents of a bank account in a coffin.

I wasn't a bad man, but I made more than my share of mistakes and that is why I woke up and found myself lying on a prison floor. When I woke up, I read and researched every book I could get my hands on in jail, and that is limited, to figure out what happened to me. The books didn't give me the ultimate answer that came from God's voice. The biggest mistake that I made was to sacrifice my physical, mental and spiritual health for the goods and pleasures instead of the ways of the spirit and if I may say the "Holy Spirit." It was my spirit inspired by God that lifted me up from as low as you can go as I have written to live again in more important ways now and in the future.

As a good friend of mine in prison states, nothing can interfere with divine intervention. No man or his institutions can interfere with God's predetermined destiny for us. God didn't create you to fail because to say the least that would be ridiculous. Just like man doesn't create machines to fail and surgeons don't perform operations for patients to die. God created you to succeed and to manifest the greatness that is in you through your thoughts and actions. The potential for greatness is in you as much as any vital organ. God made me see every obstacle, challenge, hurt and even failure as just a lesson on my way to success. It was God's way for me to mature and see the light. If you do the same, you will succeed and manifest through your successes the greatness that was implanted in you. May God bless you, enlighten you and inspire you as you continue to read and comprehend this story. Don't feel sorry for me but envy me for being so enlightened and empowered by God Almighty for finding a key to happiness and contentment in my life. When you run out of fuel ask God for some. See it as just taking your car to the gas station. It works! By the way the fuel is called love. The key to a happy life is service to our fellow man. Goodness, love, understanding and kindness always comes back to you.

Remember that every feeling be it fear or otherwise has it origin in a thought. The more you control your thoughts the more you control your feelings. Now you might say that isn't easy to do in a negative environment such as prison. That is where prayers come into the picture. Prepare a list of very positive spiritual affirmations especially things that you are grateful for or should be grateful for. At the end of the book is a list of thoughts that I would use to lift me out of depressed states. I wrote over 4,000 of them. When you prepare your list refer to the biblical quotation at the beginning of this story. Listen to the spirit within you and be guided by the "Holy Ghost."

Gratefulness and appreciation are great antidote for negative thoughts. If that fails, then transcend from your needs to the needs of others. Whenever I would get depressed while incarcerated, I would leave my cell and do something nice for a fellow prisoner especially the most repulsive ones that were so hard to be around. The ones that everyone else rejected. I once heard that something supernatural happens when we transcend our needs to the needs of others. I found that to be so true. Ask yourself, did God create us that way? God gave us the ability to love so we would love and should love.

Here is a contradiction of behaviors for you to think about. Consider what we spend on alcohol, drugs both legal and illicit, luxury housing, luxury cars, clothing, cosmetics, grooming products, entertainment, vacations, and fine foods. I could go on and on but you but the idea we spend an enormous amount of money on things that make us feel good. Beyond the basics to satisfy human needs for survival almost all of our spending beyond that for that to satisfy our basic human needs for survival is spent to make ourselves feel good. We don't buy anything to make ourselves feel bad or do we? Humans are a product of their environment and what they expose themselves to which can determine what type of thoughts that they will have. A positive environment can lead to positive thoughts and consequently positive feelings. The same is true for a negative environment which can lead to negative thoughts and consequently negative or bad feelings. When it comes to your environment, thoughts, and feelings the idea that opposite attract don't apply.

Keep in mind that humans are more emotional than rational beings. We turn on the TV to entertain ourselves and to keep us informed of the latest happenings in our society and the world. Unfortunately, when we expose ourselves to the media be it newspapers, magazines, radio, TV, or social media we are also exposing ourselves to bad news and negative advertisements. We are exposing ourselves to negative stimuli which can generate negative and fearful thoughts. It is a proven fact that negative news attracts and sells and so does negative advertisements. The news media giants know it and so do the advertisers. There is the contradiction we spend time, money, and effort to make ourselves feel good and then we expose ourselves to negative media which negates a lot of our effort to feel good.

The news media emphasizes the negative aspect of news to draw us in and advertises emphasize the negative consequences on not using the advertised products which can create fearful thoughts. The news and the advertisers exploit the negative for their selfish purposes not ours. All of those negatives can enter if unfiltered into our subconscious minds which can affect and not challenged affects our moods. I'm not purporting that all news is bad and that all advertisements are negative. We should be aware and alert to how news and advertisements are affecting us. When we need to question the basis of our moods as we do our thoughts.

Bad news sells more than good news. Most of the news is negative which causes fear in us. Minimize your exposure to negative media just like you would advise your loved ones to do. You are exposed to enough fearful thoughts on a daily basis just by through living without willfully exposing yourself to unnecessary ones. Most negative news you can't do anything about except to raise you guards and in most cases unjustifiably. See negative news and advertisements like primitive man perceived wild animals. It is media's way of manipulating us but no one likes to be manipulated. Stop negating the good with the bad.

Here are some additional thoughts about fear. Familiarity and knowledge breeds feelings of safety and comfort. Some types of music can stimulate courageous feelings within us. The same is true for our body language. Walk in an upright and straight position. Discipline yourself to keep your mind in the present moment because most fearful thoughts concern the future. Many depressive thoughts concern the past. When you goals in life are clothed in honorable purpose and meaning it eases the effort to overcome fearful thoughts. Irrational fear can be a relentless force in your life if you don't challenge fearful negative thoughts. Imagine how you will feel if you allow yourself to continually succumb to negative thoughts. Focused and meditative breathing can diminish fearful thoughts and feelings. Discipline yourself to have positive thoughts about the future using positive motivational materials. The more you can relax the easier it will be to control and diminish your fears. Don't assume that you can't control negative thoughts and fearful feelings. You are empowered and can be empowered to control the negatives. The more that you exert positive control over negative thoughts and fearful feelings the happier and more successful your life will be. To be crippled by fear is real and true failure because the people who truly fail are those that don't even try to control and overcome their fears. When all else fails help others to overcome their fears. Exerting control over your fears diminishes their intensity and increases your self-esteem. Above all practice mindfulness and be in tune and conscious of your thoughts so you can recognize which ones have a negative and fearful influence on your life. See the good in any fear or it derivatives and you will diminish its effect.

One last thought or idea, the mind thinks in pictures. When we have a thought, the mind creates a picture of that thought in our mind. Use that function of your mind to control your thoughts and generate positive thoughts by going through your picture albums. Look for and find ten pictures that generate good very pleasant thoughts and consequently the same type of feelings that empower you. Transfer those pictures to your phone and look at them when you find yourself in a negative frame of mind and see how it makes you feel. It can have the same effect that music can in empowering us. Look at all ten pictures to for this exercise to have the maximum effect. I wish you happy thoughts, happy feelings, and much enjoyment.

CHAPTER 49

Overcrowded Jails And Prisons

There are 2.3 million people incarcerated in the United States. The United States has a population of 328 million. There are 1.7 million people incarcerated in China. China has a population of one billion 444 million people 4.4 times that of the U.S. If China incarcerated at the same rate as the United States, they would have penal population of 10.1 million people. If the United States incarcerated at the same rate as China, we would have a prison and jail population of 386 thousand prisoners or 1,914,000 less people incarcerated. Very, very conservatively it costs about $35,000.00 per year to incarcerate a prisoner. If we incarcerate at the same rate as China, we would save about 67 billion per year. What is disturbing is that most states spend more on incarcerating than they do on education or health care. What is most interesting is that when education increases crime decreases. The states with higher college enrollment rates experience less violent crime rates than the national average.

We criticize China for incarcerating more than a million Chinese Uighur Muslims in internment camps which is wrong but who are we to criticize the Chinese when we are incarcerating our people at a rate of four times the rate of the Chinese. You may think that the Chinese are not catching as many criminals as we are, but I rather doubt that in their communistic and dictatorial society. Maybe you just don't dare break the law in China.

Our prisons are overflowing with the incarcerated housed in very unhealthy environments which was manifested in the environment they are housed in. How unhealthy? A prisoner has to share a ninety-six square foot cell with another prisoner which amounts to forty-eight square feet per person. The average three-bedroom home in this country is 1,700 square feet which is shared by five people, parents and three children. That amounts to 340 square feet per person seven times that of an incarcerated person. It makes so-called social distancing impossible for the incarcerated. When a prisoner is infected with a contagious disease it is very likely that others will be infected including the staff. This was manifested during the recent Covid 19 pandemic. Almost instinctively since man first appeared on the earth man has sought more space for himself. This what has been the motivation for mankind to venture out and explore new territories. Unfortunately, in many cases mankind has sought another man's territory and the riches it contained. This has been a cause of crime and wars through the ages. When we incarcerate, we go against this instinctual behavior for more space and repress it by housing prisoners in what amounts to a cage. Treat prisoners or anyone like wild animals and they will act that way.

Incarceration causes man to lose his freedom to roam and the loss of the essential contact with loved ones. I found that contact with loved ones was the biggest loss and the worst punishment a person could suffer by being incarcerated. Otherwise, prison isn't that different than a military camp. See how soldiers feel when they are stationed far away from their loved ones and families.

The United States with 4.3% of the world population of people and twenty-five percent of those incarcerated worldwide. The only countries that come close to the U.S. in their incarceration rates are Turkmenistan and El Salvador with populations that of Colorado. Both countries are considered third world countries. Either the rest of the world is wrong in the way they incarcerate, or we are wrong in the way we in the way we incarcerate. Keep in mind that the world outside of the United States encompasses 95.7% of world's minds and maybe world's intellect.

Is high our incarceration rates a function of our economics or our so-called justice system? Are we seeking justice or revenge? Justice is defined are fairness, equitableness, righteousness and moral rightness. Revenge is defined as hurt or harm to someone for an injury or wrong done at their hands. Those who seek revenge hurt themselves more than the perpetrator of crimes. With revenge you are causing more hurt and harm if you believe that whatever we put out that is what will come back to you. Many criminals' memories of their crimes fade almost into oblivion as they age. Time does diminish memories and their intensity. Most prisoners start to commit crimes when they are young when their minds are not full developed. The human minds are not fully developed until they are in their mid-twenties. Some minds are late in developing due to socioeconomic conditions and many minds deteriorate with age or drug use to say the least. No human mind remains stagnate as it ages. The power of most minds diminishes with old age which is manifested with dementia. This is especially true of our memory which starts its decline at fifty years of age. Without forgiving the perpetrator of the crime the victim will continue to suffer more than the perpetrator who will forgive themselves at least partially for their wrongful actions. It is just part of human nature. It is not fair, but it is natural.

In today's American Society I believe that we are seeking revenge more than justice. That revenge is hurting us with the high cost of incarceration and our high recidivism rate. I believe that with many prosecutors who are seeking to establish a reputation for being tough on crime because it is politically popular to do so they are seeking to score a knock-out punch more than justice. This will aid them when seeking further and higher political office. The same is true when it comes to our sentencing laws and practices. We are seeking to quell the masses who are victims of crimes and others through their close association with the actual victims. We do what is politically acceptable instead of what is scientifically and socially right. I believe that we have to look at crime as we do natural disasters such as floods or hurricanes. Crimes are just very unfortunate circumstances caused by dysfunctional cultures and societies. Consider how many crimes have their basis in illicit drug and alcohol use. Many people will rebel at what I just wrote but many studies have shown that roughly half of all criminals have or have suffered from some type of mental health disorder that may have caused them to commit crimes. We know that those mental disorders are exacerbated while incarcerated which makes the problem grow in size. We also know that those mental health disorders are not consciously self-imposed but are caused due to genetics, culture or society. Culture and society also encompass socio economic conditions such as poverty and lack of education. Education solves many social problems, and a lack of education causes them.

Two things can contribute to our overcrowded prison system one is the number of people being convicted the other being the length of their sentences. If people break the law and commit crimes that deserve punishment, so we need to seek other ways to punish besides prison such as probation and restitution where applicable. If we truly believe that a person is a danger to society and need to be incarcerated, we need to consider how long do they need to be incarcerated. Life sentences may be popular with society when the crime is heinous, but it takes away the incentive for the perpetrator to change for the better or rehabilitate themselves. People need incentives to change that has been proven on both sides of the prison walls. For many making an easy buck especially to support drug habit was their incentive to commit larceny of getting something for little or no effort. Making easy big bucks was their incentive to become drug dealers whether it was to support their personal drug habit or not.

What causes people to commit crimes? Without a question one of the biggest reasons mankind commit crimes besides insanity is greed. Illicit drug use becomes a mental health problem through addiction. Greed is considered an intense selfish desire for wealth, power and possessions. Criminals want what the other person has without having to earn it. Greed is not considered a permanent condition within a person especially when they have suffered and are suffering because of it. Suffering does bring about change. The best lessons that I learned in my life was when I was desperate and on my knees on a prison floor. Keep in mind how some people are cured of addictions when faced with death. The War On Drugs which filled our prisons to overflowing conditions was supposed to create enough pain to cure the drug problem, but it didn't. Due to greed with some guards and prisoners' illicit drugs are available in prison.

As previously inferred another major reason if I believe that some of the causes are mental health issues which can be permanent, temporary or momentary in nature. Most mental health disorders don't create a permanent disability. Most of those that are permanent can be properly managed with medications and therapy. That is not likely to happen in prisons. That poses the question how long should people with mental health disorders be incarcerated when it is proven that incarceration exacerbates their disorders. Just like people can have momentary memory loss they can have moments of insanity when confronted with traumatic events in their lives. Momentary disorder is manifested with suicide with death of a loved one or other major loss such as love in a divorce or other very close relationship. Temporary and momentary insanity does not mean that a person is evil or permanently a bad person. With adolescents I believe you have a term that I call momentary immorality. Their brains have not fully developed yet to make good decisions. As inferred some adolescents and so-called adults for many reasons such as family dynamics are just very late in maturing.

We have closed most of the major mental institutions because we perceive many mental health disorders as being temporary in nature and that these people could be better served in their communities. Now we are finding that we were wrong because as we closed the mental hospitals, we had to build more prisons and bigger jails. The American Public is buying more firearms. Unfortunately, an individual who experiences a mental break down are three times as likely to find themselves in a prison instead of an appropriate mental institution. It is the reason why so many county sheriffs and wardens claim they are running a mental hospital instead of a jail or prisons. Where else can we place these people if the proper institutions are not available when we judge that they are a danger to others and themselves. But let me state again most of the time the breakdown is not permanent and don't create a permanent disability, but we treat it as such with our sentencing practices and laws. The penal institutions cause many individuals with mental health disorders become worse and worse. The practice can create permanency in the mental health disorder.

To reduce our high incarceration rate, I believe the answer lies in education, mental health treatment and reevaluation on a timely basis. The human body and its mind is in a constant state of change either for the positive or the negative. The possibility of early release overriding mandatory sentences can incent positive change. The positive change can be initiated through empowering the individual to change through positive motivation instead of repression which prisons are noted for. The positive change can be determined through consistent evaluation just like we do in our educational system. Cause the prisoner to progress through elevation through a grade system like schools do. We know how empowering education can be and positive words can also have a very positive effect. Let the prisoner progress through positive ranks through the prison system just like guards do instead of the criminal ranks of the prison gangs.

There are too many negative words and phrases in prison without them being counteracted with positive words and phrases. Educate the prison staffs and the prisoners as to positive thinking and expression and all will benefit from both sides of the walls. We need to empower prisoners to change through very positive motivational programs. The prisoner must see themselves as a positive contributor to society instead of a criminal. Change through education to enhance their basic beliefs about life. Education can do some of it and positive motivational programs can do some of it. Cause the prisoner think that they can and they will. Some of the most notorious dictators proved that you can change people's thinking for the worse such as Hitler and Stalin. The most successful people proved how you can change people's thinking for the better such as our founding fathers of this country. Consider what Abraham Lincoln did with segregation. We have to stop hoping that the prisoner will change in a very negative and repressive atmosphere. Change the atmosphere by placing more educators and therapist in the penal system. It may cost in the short run, but it will pay huge dividends in the long run. What is the cost of a mass shooting?

CHAPTER 50

Is Loveland, Colorado
Really A Loving Place?

Since 1947 the City of Loveland, Colorado has claimed to be the Sweetheart City very loving place mainly because of how they embrace Valentine's Day. Each year prior to Valentine's Day about 100,000 people from all over the country and 110 countries mail their love one's Valentines Greetings to Loveland so it can be hand stamped with a love cachet and postmarked as being from a Loveland. It is Loveland's way of spreading some love on that special designated love day.

Unfortunately for a 73-year-old woman by the name of Karen Garner who suffers from dementia and sensory aphasia someone forgot to inform some members of the Loveland Police Department and the Walmart Corporation of Loveland's sweetheart philosophy. On June 26, 2020, Ms. Garner a mother of three and grandmother of nine tried to walk out of a Walmart Store with $13.88 worth of merchandise that she supposedly forgot to pay for. As stated earlier in the writing forgetfulness and loss of memory are very common symptoms of dementia. One of the symptoms of sensory aphasia is the inability to understand what is being said which is another symptom of dementia. As I described before when I suffered from diseases which mimicked most of the symptoms of dementia I saw, you I could hear you, but I couldn't understand what you were saying to me. You might as well been speaking a language which was totally foreign to me. I was in a very incognizant and confused state when people tried to communicate with me. I wasn't aware of my surroundings and what was happening to me.

Walmart personnel confronted Ms. Garner about not paying for the merchandise. She offered to pay for the merchandise, but they wouldn't allow her to do that. They insisted on summoning the police in spite of Ms. Garner's obvious confused state and age. Ms. Garner left the store without the merchandise and started walking home. On her way home about two blocks from her house she was stopped by an Officer Hopp of the Loveland Police. She continued to walk and was stating over and over again I'm going home. Her continual saying over and over again "I'm going home" should have been a red flag that something was not right with her. In spite of Ms. Garner's obvious confused state as the videos of the incident indicate Officer Hopp grabbed Ms. Garner by the wrist twisted it behind her back and took her to the ground. That is a standard procedure for police work, but should it be when an elderly person in a confused state is being manifested in a person's words and actions? Common sense dictates that you can't treat an elderly person like you would treat the young or middle age especially one with dementia. As we age our bones and joints deteriorate and lose their strength. Like it or not the older we get the weaker we get. It is the natural law of nature. We lose bone and muscle mass as we age especially women after menopause.

While wrestling her to the ground Ms. Garner's shoulder was dislocated, her arm was broken, and her wrist was sprained. Officer Hopp may not have known that Ms. Garner was suffering from dementia, but common sense tells you that there are very few old women who are thieves. She doesn't look like a "spring chicken". Your life experiences and common sense should tell you that something is wrong with situation and instead of reacting it is time to use your brain. Police procedure may dictate what you should do when you sense that a person might be resisting and is trying to get away but do standard procedures apply to a five-foot tall eighty-pound seventy-three-year-old woman especially in Loveland? We hire police officers with more than adequate IQ's so they will use their brain when circumstances dictate. A five-foot tall eighty-pound old woman who is looking and acting confused dictates that you may deviate from the normal procedures. First of all, you don't handcuff a person of Ms. Garner's stature with her hands in her back. Common sense dictates that you are dealing with a weakling in a childlike state. You put the handcuffs on gently because you can see that their skin is obviously aged and in most cases very thin. The upper layer of skin of the elderly the epidermis shrinks as they age. The skin is very easily bruised. In a civilized society you don't push an old lady to the dirty, gritty ground. You don't take old ladies to the ground no matter their disposition. The video shows a bystander commenting to one of the police officers on how Ms. Garner was being treated. One of the officers told the bystander to mind their own business. The police did try and explain their actions to another bystander because their abusive behavior was very obvious to the man who took the time and effort to leave his car in defense of Ms. Garner. It is the business of any human being in a civilized society to comment when it is obvious that an old lady is being mistreated. At least the bystanders had respect for old age. Why did the bystanders have to comment? What were they witnessing?

Why did it take for over ten months almost a year for the video of the incident to surface in such a sweetheart city? Why did it take filing a Federal lawsuit for the videos to surface? Whose job is it to review officer's conduct especially when it concerns an elderly woman. Is arresting a very elderly woman an everyday occurrence in Loveland? As the Chief of Police Bob Ticer claims he didn't know she was wounded for over ten months. She is still a seventy-three-year-old woman which should have been a huge very glaring red flag to any officer of the law. Why did they have to carry her into the police station?

The video shows that they carried Ms. Garner into the police station and into the cell like a wounded wild animal. Common sense dictates that if she couldn't walk into the station other members of the police staff should have asked why. Is it a common occurrence for old woman to be carried into the Loveland Police Station? Common sense and human decency also dictate that she couldn't walk that she should have been at the very least placed on a gurney or wheelchair. If she was resisting, she could have been strapped to the gurney. As stated, the chief of police stated that he didn't know that Ms. Garner was injured. How often does the Loveland Police Department receive hospital bills for an elderly woman? Does the police department indiscriminately pay hospital bills without the police chief questioning them? Someone of higher authority who supervises the officers and reviews police reports should have known or at least inquired and brought it Chief Ticer's attention. Ms. Garner had to be taken to the hospitals because of her injuries. She also had a bloody nose and bruises to her skin. Those injuries alone should have alerted the police department staff. How many inmates each day have to be taken to a hospital for treatment? Why didn't someone of authority who may have seen a petite and fragile old woman in a cell in so-called civilized and loving Loveland, Colorado asks what is that old woman doing here and why does she have to go to the hospital? Everyone concerned acted like she just didn't matter. They waited six hours before getting her treated for her injuries. She endured the pain and agony of her injuries for six hours. I sure wouldn't want to wait six hours to be treated for six hours for a sprained wrist, a broken arm and a dislocated shoulder. The elderly have much less ability to endure pain than the average person. The elderly feel pain more intensely than the middle aged or young. Karen Garner is an elderly woman, a mother of three and a grandmother of nine and in a civilized society her life does matter very much.

There seems to be little communication in the chain of command in the Loveland Police Department. Why didn't the police chief know of a so-termed very unusual arrest in his department? Please allow me to repeat again the victim is a 73-year-old woman with bruises, a bloody nose, a dislocated shoulder, a sprained wrist, and a broken arm all of which caused her to have to be taken to a hospital and the Chief of Police didn't know what happened to her? We are not talking about the police force of a major metropolitan city but a town of 66,000 people. Chief Ticer's staff must think that he doesn't give a dam, or someone is not being totally truthful about who knew what and when they knew.

I believe that the problem doesn't just involve the three officers involved in the incident but the toxic culture within the Loveland police force. That is probably why no other members of the police department didn't speak up about how badly an elderly lady was treated for over ten months. I also believe the basis on this inhumane incident has it basis in the officers basic beliefs about Ms. Garner. I'm willing to bet that they looked down on Ms. Garner and they viewed Ms. Garner as an old thief and an old "pain in the you know what" who may have been inadvertently resisting them and causing them discomfort. They didn't view her as a mother and grandmother. They didn't see her "as a giver of life" which all mothers are and are God's tool to perpetuate the human race. Why else would they have treated her so inhumanely? I'm sorry to use the phrase "pain in the you know what" but that is how the officers acted like they were dealing with some old street walker in a town's red-light district looking for illicit drugs. What were these officer's beliefs which caused them to act in such an uncivilized manner? If she had held an important political position, I'm sure this incident would never occurred. What position is more important in our world than the Godlike position than "giver of life"? Her children and grandchildren wouldn't be alive without her parental sacrifices. What if it was the officer's mother or grandmother? You could tell from the videos that Officer Hopp's ego was being challenged when Ms. Garner would not comply with his orders. How dare she not comply with an officer of the law as he stated whose police car lights were on and sirens blasting. He sure showed her that he wasn't going to play her game as his words in the video indicates.

After her incarceration there is a video of the arresting officers watching a video of her take down and apprehension. That video showed them laughing at their actions and especially when they heard a popping noise which was probably her arm being broken. When they should have been alarmed at their inhumane actions they were laughing. The female officer seemed to be somewhat alarmed but not the male officers. Would they be willing to show that video to their parents and grandparents? Instead of caring for her like civilized people would demonstrate respect for an elderly lady they laughed at her and their actions. By taking away her dignity they lost their dignity.

Why did this woman's family have to seek the remedies of the Federal courts and wait months for justice? We couldn't admit that we are wrong sooner? We need the so-called justice system to tell us we are wrong? Where are our God given consciences? A mistake admitted quickly demonstrates courage, intelligence, humility and good moral values. A mistake not admitted creates suspicion and increases in size. Maybe the City of Loveland isn't as loving as it purports to be but is starting to be. As of this writing the City of Loveland admitted the huge mistake by settling this case with an award of three million dollars to Ms. Garner without having to subject Ms. Garner the misery of a court trial. Unfortunately, they need to educate their police force in the proper use of force when it comes to the mentally disadvantaged and the elderly. I believe that a lot of the mistreatment has so much do with education and is also fear based. Procedures don't cover every situation education which will heighten the use of common sense can.

What about Walmart the largest and probably richest instore retailer in the world, what did they think of what happened on their premises?

There are about ten million elderly who suffer from some form of dementia in the United States and that population is growing more and more as each year goes by. Do they and should they put up signs that no one with dementia or signs of it are allowed to shop there? Forgetfulness is a common problem with the elderly. Our memories start to decline at fifty years of age. It frightens us to start losing our memories. The employees who confronted Ms. Garner summoned the police because they claim that Ms. Garner reached for an employee's mask. Aggressive behavior is common for someone in the latter stages of dementia. As an example, I used to urinate wherever I pleased no matter where I was or whose company I was in just like an untrained animal. It is uncivilized as to what happened to Ms. Garner and someone from the upper echelon of Walmart should have spoken up and tried to lend assistance no matter whose fault it was. It would have been a lot better than negative publicity. I'm not the only elderly person who wonders about Walmart's lack of appropriate humanistic action. What about Walmart's elderly employees? Positive action in offering assistance by the Walmart Corporation would have made for great human relations instead of doing nothing. It appears that Ms. Garner's pain and suffering meant nothing to Walmart. Her life and wellbeing meant nothing to Walmart. There are fifty-five million elderlies in this county. That is a huge pool of buyers with a lot of buying power. Most of the elderly tend to be frugal and shop at discount stores. If it doesn't make humanitarian sense to the chief executives of Walmart it sure makes good business sense. I'm not the only senior citizen who will consider what happened to Ms. Garner when I need to shop. May I remind the head executive of Walmart that Sam Walton was an elderly man for the last ten years of his life. How would he have felt about how Ms. Garner was treated? It appears the bigger our corporations get the more they insulate themselves from human suffering.

Ms. Garner's daughter state that her mother's dementia has exacerbated since the incident. Any psychological professional will state how trauma will intensify any psychological disorder. Trauma is the worst thing that can happen to a victim of dementia. Ms. Garner's dementia and her suffering will probably get much worse.

The incident in Loveland and those poor souls in New York is an indication of how we view the elderly in the United States. We don't' view the elderly positively because they remind us of what we don't want to look like and be like as we age. Consider what we do to hide the grey hair and cover up the wrinkles. The elderly reminds us of what we will have to deal with and look like as we age. Consider how you feel when you start to forget or can't remember. See how you feel when you can't find your purse, wallet, or care keys. It will remind you of what will happen in your life. We don't see the elderly as the creators of our lives and the perpetuators of the human race. I doubt if what happened to Ms. Garner would have occurred in most Asian countries. When I go on my daily walks, I wear a hat that says I'm a U.S Air Force veteran. People say to me when they walk by thank you for your service. I would rather they say to all the elderly thank you for giving us life and perpetuating our race. We can help make their so-called "Golden Years" as truly golden. Before we blame them for our weaknesses, we can thank them for our man offsetting strengths and our lives. See the grey hair and wrinkles as an indication of wisdom not scars from the years. In the future when we see an elderly person, we can make a habit at least to ourselves of saying "Thank you for our lives and perpetuating our race" we wouldn't be here without your efforts and sacrifices. Always keep in mind that how we treat the elderly is how we will be treated. We are training the younger generations through our words and most of all our actions as to how to treat the elderly. Buddha taught to be compassionate with the aged because someday we hope to be aged. Throughout history we have judged societies and civilizations by how they treated their children and the elderly! Let's start celebrating Mother's Day and Father's Day every day.

CHAPTER 51

How I Endured And Recovered From Demented State

- The number one thing that I did to recover was to have faith in the destiny and mission that my God had established for me. God had brought me back to a normal life so I could be God's messenger and do God's work. My endurance of each assault or abuse only strengthened my faith in the Supernatural. I knew that I wasn't alone in my journey of recovery. Daily prayer and reading positive affirmations helped to keep me on the right track.

- At times I may have not of thought that I could, but I didn't think that I couldn't. As time passed in my recovery, I only thought that I could endure and recover. I took it for granted that I would endure and recover. Endurance reinforced my belief in a very positive future fueled my recovery. Each assault strengthened my belief in myself and manhood.

- I started to read everything that I could get my hands on about the brain, mind, learning and motivation. I saw my incarceration as a learning experience instead of punishment. It was like I was in a seminary to learn and grow in many ways especially spiritually.

- I wrote about what happened to me, what was happening to me and the positive lessons that I was learning and experiencing. Writing helped me clarify what I was learning and reinforcing it in my mind. Writing gave me a feeling of accomplishment. As stated, I wrote over four thousand affirmations about what I was learning. I listed one hundred of them in the last part of this book and will publish the rest in a separate book having to do with Attitude and Motivation.

- I saw any assault or abusive behavior as just another lesson. Endurance made me grow stronger and helped me to emerge from the demented state.

- I realized that I had disappointed and hurt my loved ones, I had to rise again for them. I would help them to have faith in me again.

- I physically exercised as much as I could no matter how painful it was for me because I realized that physical exercise would bring me out of the demented state that I was in. I learned that I had to do everything possible to keep moving forward physically and mentally. I learned to respect the interdependence of the mind and body. What is good for the body is also good for the brain and vice versa.

- When I realized that in many ways that I was almost dead in my demented state I was very appreciative to be recovering and coming back to life in many ways. When you emerge from nothing which is a very demented and animalistic state you learn to appreciate everything, every little ability and every day. Appreciation and gratitude were key in my recovery. I often tell people if you want to be happy go to prison because you will learn to appreciate the most basic things in life.

- After my revelation from God my incarceration took on meaning and purpose. It was like I was in a seminary to learn so I could fulfill God's mission for me. It caused the humiliation of being incarcerated to be an honorable experience in that I was doing God's work by just surviving and coming back to life.

- Helping unfortunates gave immediate meaning and motivation to my life especially during the low times. It caused me to appreciate my ability to help and aid others. The best way to deal with feeling sorry for myself was to help someone else. I transcended from my needs to those of the less fortunate.

- Times in solitary confinement or in isolation gave me the opportunity to reflect on and analyze my life.

- I guarded the gates to my mind not to allow a negative thought to harbor in me a very negative environment. I learned to be appreciative on the most basic things such as walking and just being able to think again rationally and reasonably. I realized that if I could be happy in prison, I could be happy anywhere. I learned the power in a thought be it positive or negative.

- I chose to be a role model to my fellow inmates in that I could recover and grow in spite of age, handicaps, disabilities, abuses or other challenges in a very negative environment. I wanted to be an inspiration to my fellow prisoners and I believe that I was.

- Being incarcerated taught me what was really important in life which is my relationships with God, my loved ones and others. Materialistic goods meant little or nothing to me.

CHAPTER 52

Conclusion

Once again, the people who abused me and committed atrocities on me have and will have their excuses. I have plenty of excuses. Some denied me of the rights that I swore to defend on August 25, 1964, when I voluntarily left my family from a car on Whitehall Street in New York City. Not once did I hesitate to do my duty. I just did my duty, and I did it excellently as my performance reports indicate. I considered it a privilege. I also served my family, communities and country in many ways after my military service. I rarely if ever refused to help my fellow man.

I never once complained, no matter what until my prosecution and incarceration. May I say again two wrongs don't make a right and evil enhances evil. We judge societies by how they treat their populace, consider history. We especially judge them for how they treat their children and the elderly because as we age whether we like it or not, we return to childlike states. We eventually become weaklings if we live long enough. The elderly and the mentally ill are much more vulnerable to pain, suffering and are more defenseless than the average person. Jails and prisons are not designed to house the elderly or the mentally ill. If you doubt that visit a jail and then visit a home for senior citizens.

At what age are we considered elderly? Colorado Law states 70 years of age for this writing elderly was defined at sixty-five plus years. Federal Court Rulings state a person at 70 and has a mental condition is considered "At Risk" and a crime against them is considered a "Hate Crime." Who should do the hating? I know that I'm not going to stoop so low to hate because I will only hurt myself more than any abusers could. Hating will cause me to be the same as the abusers. I ask that the law enforcement personnel that assaulted me stand next to me for the American Public to judge them and me to see who was bullying who. If I wasn't strong enough to undergo surgery, did it also apply to receiving proper and deserved health care because I am an honorably served veteran? Does it also apply to being assaulted? When people say to me, thank you for your service I want to cry out and I say to myself: why was I assaulted and abused so many times? Why were my abusers so misguided and not held accountable for their misdeeds? Many of them were later promoted. Promoting them condones their behaviors. I'm sure John Walshe isn't an isolated or only case of abuse. Some of these individuals have a history of busing prisoners and some of the institutions have a culture that condones abuses. As I write about this it is with tears in my eyes and why wouldn't it? Fourteen assaults and at least ten hostile acts in just a few years that would cause anyone to have tears in their eyes never mind three heart attacks, two strokes and two triple A aorta aneurysms. Worst of all my guts hung out of me so painfully for five years.

I wrote the following to myself when I started to regain my cognitive ability and before I took God as my partner at my revelation: "My death is near, and the penal system is expediting it. In a way I'm glad that I'm close to death because I'm in such chronic and acute pain especially from my hernias. It hurts just to walk. Sometimes I have to crawl like an animal. It is also very painful every time I hear a sudden unexpected loud noise, a very loud voice or someone hollering. It is like being punctured in the heart. Most of all I have little desire to live in a society where there is so little regard for its elderly, fathers, grandfathers and its veterans. Again, how do we criticize other governments like the Syrian, China, North Korean and now populaces such as the Taliban's and their associates for their conduct as stated in my writings when we do the same to an elderly man?

What I have written may sound self-serving and it is, but does that diminish it or make it wrong? The problems that this document illustrates are growing not shrinking in size. They expect the incidence of dementia and Alzheimer's disease to triple in the years ahead. Addiction of all types is growing as manifested in the opioid crisis and now fentanyl. When the public cannot easily get the opioids that they are addicted to then they will switch to illicit drugs which will present greater problems. Pill popping has become a greater problem that the traditional illicit drugs. Now fentanyl usage is becoming a crisis even in the most remote states. As life expectancy increases so will all the associated diseases and the need to move mental health to the forefront without stigmatization.

No one leads a life without mistakes and wrongs some small some large some our fault and some not. When we make them or commit them what degree of understanding and acceptance do we expect? Mistakes admitted voluntarily demonstrate courage, humility, confidence, intelligence and trustworthiness. Mistakes not admitted increase in size and significance. They raise suspicion and put the victim in control. As we study history, we look down on societies that had no or little regard for their elderly but what are we doing in this country as compared to other developed countries? We are the richest country in the world, but we are poor in mind when it comes to treatment of the elderly.

Our knowledge and treatment of mental health disorders must increase to avoid the kind of elderly abuse that I have been subjected to. Now we know the amount of abuse and to the extent that I and others have endured the potential for abuse is there. We are going to have to ask how can people who lead good lives in their retirement years resort to criminality when all their traditions, instincts and habits dictate otherwise? Is it criminality or a mental health breakdown? At that point should we imprison or properly diagnose, treat and if necessary, hospitalize? Recently in the news there was a story of a 95-year-old man a resident of a nursing home in Boulder, Colorado killing a caregiver. He shot the man which to me is so unfortunate akin to a natural disaster. I feel very sorry for the families and loved ones of both men. When I heard that story after experiencing living in a demented state for years, I automatically thought that the man must be suffering from dementia. I didn't automatically think of him as a murderer as so much of society does. We automatically incarcerated the man but now thank God he is confined in a mental institution instead of a jail. I hope that he is appropriately evaluated, analyzed, diagnosed and institutionalized in a proper mental institution if appropriate instead of incarcerated in a penal institution. Unfortunately, many of the elderly lose their positive mental abilities to reason and rationalize as they age. It is not of their volition but as a result of age and deterioration of brain and therefore the mind.

Years ago, you rarely if ever heard of a 70 plus year-old being abused by the institutions that were supposed to protect him and that he swore to protect. If what I have written increases awareness of elderly abuse and mental illness, then it can serve the needs of many good and unfortunate people in the present or the future. Let us remember that "Elderly Lives Matter Too" no matter what their condition. The older they are the more we should seek to understand. There are no insignificant lives and a long as we remember that and respect that the human race will mature and endure.

Don't be overconfident as I was and say it can never happen to me especially if you have been very successful and affluent. Most of all when the stressors of life try to bring you down don't try and go it alone without your fellow man and especially your God. When you need divine intuition and strength to endure as I did it can come from God just for the asking. As the Gideon Holy Bible quote Mathew 7:7:8 &12 states: "Ask and it will be given to you; seek, and you will find; knock and it will be opened to you. For everyone who asks receives, and he who seeks finds, and to him who knocks it will be opened. Therefore, whatever you want men to do to you, do to them, for this is the Law and the Prophets."

Please know that anyone who did abuse me I wish you well because to endure and tolerate I had to and did grow stronger. I don't seek revenge which can only hurt me more than the perpetrators. I'm recovering more and more as each day goes by. I became a better man in prison although it took me almost three years to recover from that ordeal. Growing can be painful. I don't wish you any harm or punishment but hope that you will be better educated about the elderly, their needs and how to better treat your fellow man. I wish all those who abused me enlightenment. Terminating or firing doesn't solve the problem that only transfers the problem to another area. Education and strong desire to grow solves problems!

I pray for forgiveness from all those who were hurt by my mental incapacity. All I can say is that I didn't mean to hurt you. I also pray for anyone who suffers from any form of dementia and other mental illnesses. I pray that for understanding by their loved ones in knowing that abnormal behavior is a result of the disease not them or personality flaw. After recovering from a demented state, the most that I can say about it is that I wouldn't wish it upon my worst enemy if I had one.

May I say again, two wrongs don't make a right and evil enhances evil. Let me close this story with a quote from the Bible. Mathew 25:40: "Truly I tell whatever you did for one of the least of these brothers and sisters of mine you did for me." I may have been abused and beaten by the system, but I wasn't defeated. Look at me and examine me I'm almost normal again whatever that is! Lastly, I would like to think that "My Elderly Life Matters Too" no matter my age and condition. One final and very important thought "The way we treat the elderly is the way we will be treated when we are elderly which will happen sooner than later".

Whether we aware of it or not we are becoming closer to being elderly as each day passes.

Lastly, let me state if you want to be happy imagine being a prisoner because it will teach you to better appreciate some of the most basic things in life. You will truly learn the value in gratefulness and appreciation. May God Bless You And Yours!

CHAPTER 53

Some Affirmations And A Prayer I Wrote to Lift My Spirits While Incarcerated

- Recognize the power in "Thy will be done."
- In living your life, you either progress or regress but you don't stand still.
- Have a sense of purpose in what you do. See the ultimate good in it even if it is cleaning sewers. There is higher good and purpose in everything.
- Change your thinking and you will change your life.
- You are in control of your thoughts and God is in control of the rest.
- True freedom comes from overcoming fear especially the fear of death.
- If you love what you are doing because you see the higher purpose in it and good in it you will have the motivation to be highly successful.
- Love more than you think and think loving thoughts.

- Over ninety percent of our habitual thoughts are negative. Guard the gates of your mind and just don't let anything in. Make sure that a thought deserves entrance to your precious mind just like nourishment to your body.
- Instinctively we pay more attention to the negative. Make a habit of the opposite.
- We all crave love and acceptance, and it is a very rare person that doesn't, so why don't you admit it and use it with those you interact with?
- It is not possible for us to break the law especially the natural ones without hurting ourselves.
- A true test of a person's character is their ability to subordinate their impulses to good and loving values and principles.
- Don't be so quick to react to a thought, especially a negative or immoral one.
- Happiness starts with finding goodness in your life and you.
- Always, always, always avoid being critical of the other person's behavior.
- Courage is yours for the asking. It is called faith in your Creator.
- You were created to and meant to be happy.
- There is an amazing and incredible intelligence, and it is yours for the asking and taking. It is called the Supernatural and you open the door to it through silence.
- Let the Holy Spirit enter your life to energize you, guide you and assist you. Make it a key component of your life. It is yours for the asking if you listen for it and to it.
- You can't hurt another without hurting yourself more and this is so true for you because you have such a large conscience John.
- Pleasure is just a temporary feeling or sensation. Don't pay too much for it.

- What does pleasure actually do for you? You can gain as much happiness and contentment which is longer lasting by avoiding the bad, doing what is right.
- Do we have as much respect for God's creations as we do for human creations?
- Prejudice decreases with education and knowledge.
- "The difference between hindsight and foresight is fact" which demonstrates the value of knowledge.
- The past doesn't dictate the future. You and God dictate the future through your thoughts. Control your thoughts and your thinking.
- You can only consistently depend on God. Everyone has their own limitations.
- Meditation increases our ability to learn.
- How you look spiritually is more important than how you look physically.
- Visualize what you would like to learn and remember. Learn like a professional actor and act out and picture every detail in your mind.
- Before you pass up an activity that you would like to do but don't know how, ask yourself: can I learn to do that because learning stimulates the brain and its growth?
- Throughout history the most admired are the most loving and peaceful such Jesus and Buddha.
- When you are reborn the negative past doesn't matter except for the positive lesson learned.
- The more that you focus on what you have done right in life the more it will strengthen you.
- Columbus could have looked at the land mass that he sailed into as an obstacle not a discovery. How do you look at challenges in your life?
- Positive movement forward can break depression.

- Determine what you don't like about yourself and then find the good in it because it is there.
- What you say to yourself and about yourself is more important than what anyone says about you.
- Doing what is necessary to accomplish a goal can be as rewarding as accomplishing the goal and even more so.
- Sometimes wanting something and visualizing it is just as rewarding as achieving it.
- Great dreams are the initiators of great things.
- The more you appreciate what you already have the more you will gain.
- Happiness is fertile ground for success.
- Positive thoughts are a great antidote for negative thoughts.
- Our attitudes can lift us or limit us.
- You create positive energy by doing positive things.
- You may have to look hard for it but there is goodness in every misfortune or problem.
- Love goes beyond the physical and material world into the spiritual realm.
- One of a person's strongest muscles is their attitude.
- Pain becomes meaningful when there is a purpose in it. An honorable purpose eases the pain.
- Acting normal in an abnormal and very stressful situation makes a person stand out from the crowd.
- The more meaning in a life the greater the life.
- Purpose and meaning fuels a life.
- Victor Frankl said: "Forces beyond your control can take away everything you possess except your will and freedom to choose how you will react to it."
- The more faith you have in good the easier it becomes to do good.
- Conflict can initiate agreement when approached in a positive way.

- When you lost it all and still stand tall you can climb any wall.
- When you are witty you cast off self-pity.
- There is plenty for all when people give their all.
- Laughter is a great antidote for stress and stimulates the mind.
- Life is not a bitch but a great opportunity to raise yourself up by meeting challenges and to solve problems.
- Attitude is much more important than aptitude.
- A true failure is one who hasn't tried and will not try.
- When you fail admire your courage for trying.
- Failure and mistakes are rungs on the ladder to success. Abraham Lincoln lost eight elections and won two elections.
- Purity of thought increases power and determination.
- The true you isn't your biological body but your spirit. When your body dies your spirit lives on.
- Treat negative thoughts as telephone calls that you choose not to answer.
- Revenge only causes you to mimic the behavior of the perpetrator.
- Turn losing to wins in your mind by extracting the lesson.
- You change your life by changing your attitude towards life.
- Happiness starts with appreciation of what you already possess such as your life.
- Idleness is for the disabled or dying.
- Once you have established what you should have done differently in the past it is time to put it behind you and plan for the future.
- Learn from the past; don't suffer from it or because of it.
- Enthusiasm can enrich lives and cure many ills. It can be like a magnet in pulling success and goodness to you.
- Enthusiastic and happy people are like a bright shining star in the sky. Society can always use more of them.

- Don't postpone happiness because if you can find happiness in this time you can find happiness anytime. It just takes a positive decision and determination on your part.
- To be creative it only takes a thought.
- Be as quick to think of the positive as you are the negative and you will succeed.
- Reality starts in the mind by imagining what you want to create in your life then focus on that imaginary picture to draw it to you. If you can find an actual picture of it, look at it as often as possible.
- You have nothing to lose by believing in your success and prosperity. Imagine the positive result of what you want to happen and it will eventually happen.
- The more you focus on the good things in your life the more they will increase.
- Don't focus on what you don't have; focus on what you have and would like to have.
- Those who believe in their success will succeed.
- There is a power within you to create whatever you want; it is called desire.
- You are a lot more than your physical body: you are your mind and spirit.
- Gratitude and appreciation create a power within you. They fuel you.
- Count your blessings if you want to be blessed.
- The more sense of meaning and purpose in what you do will decrease the effort in doing it.
- The more love you put into an effort the less effort it takes.
- Those who love their work can't find work only satisfaction.
- Happiness is the key to success not the opposite.
- The more honorable the purpose the greater the satisfaction.
- There is good in everything, find it!

- We need to realize that we take into our minds everything that we see and are exposed to. We have to be very discriminating in what we expose ourselves to if we expect to keep our minds and
- thoughts pure. Remember humans are a product of their environment.
- If someone treats you like dirt it teaches you or reminds you how not to treat others; so thank them for the lesson.
- Don't wait for the motivation to start. Just take the first step and then the next one and the motivation will emerge if you keep the end result in mind. Just keep putting one foot in front of the other. It's just like gas stations on a road trip.
- Anger is the force of death.
- Make a list of what positives you gained with anger and you won't need much paper.
- You don't gain power through anger you lose it.
- Don't start any effort by looking at your weaknesses, start by looking at your strengths.
- When you are happy for what the other person has you will have.
- In establishing your priorities in life keep in mind what we own today someone else will own tomorrow or it will simply fade away.
- In most cases what you resists persists.
- If you want to increase a quality in in person praise it.
- You mind is the true governing power in your life.
- Forgiveness increases your energy and freedom.
- A bad temper leads to few associates.
- God created you to succeed as God did when God created all of your body's vital organs. Society creates failure not God.
- God works where there is an attitude of faith.
- If God is for you who can be against you.

- God is akin to our minds in that we can't see God directly, touch God, smell God or taste God but in silence we can hear God and always know that God is near.
- When confronted with a negative situation or temptation remember the quote "This too shall pass."

MY LORD'S PRAYER

My dear God I honor you and hold you the highest esteem, you, and your magnificent creations. You are the creator and ruler of this infinite beautiful and unbelievable universe. My words cannot do it justice in trying to describe it. It is so vast, wonderful, and inconceivable to the human mind that we can hardly understand it and its purpose meaning and magnificence. May Your will be done in it by me and all your beings.

God my life is nothing and useless without you and so meaningful with you in it. It is like the best part of me is missing when you are not in my life. My intellect and mind are diminished without you. I am a half a man without you and a whole man with you in my life. You energize me and make me pure in mind and spirit. I am like a vehicle with a weak engine when you are not in my life. When I try to be independent and exist without you it only increases my burden and my stress level. God my life just not go well without you. I truly stress too much without you. Glory to you my God, Your Holy Spirit and all your creations. Lord you bring peace, contentment, and joy to my life.

My God I know and believe that you stand for love, kindness, goodness, humility, honesty, and integrity plus equality for all. That is what you expect of me and what I will strive to achieve through my thoughts words and actions. Please guide me in my thoughts and actions so I may be ever compliant with your wishes and desires.

Let me be your gentle and courageous servant expressing love and understanding for all. I know that I exist is such a small part of your world like a drop of water in a vast ocean or like a blade of grass in huge fields of grass. I commit to make my part of it a manifestation of your love and care for all. Lead and guide me to please you in every way that I can and even in ways that I presently cannot. Let me strive to make every thought and action of mine be pure and pleasing to you and cause you to smile. Let them be a reflection of your goodness and powerful embracing love.

May I be accepting and stop questioning that which I cannot understand and is beyond my intellect and understanding. Your actions and desires for me may not make sense to my human mind and perspective but it does to the spiritual mind. May I may be ever obedient and trust in your wisdom and loving nature. May I radiate love and kindness to all even those who have hurt or harmed me. May my doubts be diminished with your guidance and divine knowledge. Let me appreciate on a daily basis of what you have done for me throughout my life. Thank you so much for renewing my mind and my life. May my gratefulness grow and my greed dissipate.

God, I am so much happier, contented, and stronger when you are in my life then when you are not. May I bath in your love and peace. Help me to be calm and stable in spite of my challenges and disorders. Please help me to stay on your righteous path and alert me when I drift from it. If I start to doubt let me focus on the wonderful forces in the powers of love, kindness, and goodness. Let me always understand that you are within me and make you the true and wonderful partner in my life and all that it compasses. God I am never weak or lonely when you are in my life. Thank you Lord!

Printed in the United States
by Baker & Taylor Publisher Services